EUROSPI

A USER'S GUIDE

EUROSPEAK

A USER'S GUIDE

The Dictionary of the Single Market

François Gondrand

translated by
Peter Bowen

NICHOLAS BREALEY
PUBLISHING
LONDON

First published in the English language by Nicholas Brealey
Publishing Limited in 1992
156 Cloudesley Road
London N1 0EA

Translated by Peter Bowen

Originally published in France, 1991, by Les Éditions d'Organisation as *Parlez-vouz Eurocrate?* by François Gondrand

British Library Cataloguing-in-Publication Data
A catalogue record for this book is available from the British Library

ISBN 1 85788 004 8

Typeset by The Midlands Book Typesetting Company, Loughborough
Printed and bound in Great Britain by Billings Book Plan Ltd., Worcester.

CONTENTS

1 INTRODUCTION

A conversation overheard on the train between Paris and Brussels

07.07 The Eurocity slips out of the Gare du Nord in Paris. Breakfast is about to be served. I listen to the conversation between two passengers whose table I am sharing. Judging from what they are saying, they must be engineers:

'I'm finding the work on the CEN committees very hard going. Still, someone has to do it if we want to have our say in fixing the standards. Otherwise the technical barriers won't be removed early enough for goods in our sector.'

'I don't understand why we don't favour mutual recognition of standards over harmonization.'

'You're right. All the more so because the new approach has now been supplemented by the overall approach which relies on criteria which make the competence and objectivity of certification and testing bodies objectively verifiable . . .'

'Whatever happens, if we're not careful essential requirements will be imposed which we don't want because, in this field, other Member States will be able to make us a minority at the Council. Don't forget that the harmonization of legislation with regard to the Single Market comes under Article 100a, in other words a qualified majority.'

The waiter arrived at our table with his strange thermos flasks.

'Incidentally, since you make a large proportion of your turnover on European public contracts, aren't you concerned by the opening up of excluded sectors?'

'Yes, but at least we get an exemption for parts.'

'Besides, it's fortunate that the general business Council has kept the idea of Community preference, even if the divergence rate which has been retained seems low. Having said that, we still have to obtain true reciprocity with non-member countries.'

I think it was at this point that the man opposite me, who had followed their conversation with obvious interest, decided to join in by asking a question:

'Excuse me, but I heard you talking about mutual recognition. Did you know that in my sector, banking, which is very different from yours, we base our activities in the European sphere on the same principle with a single licence? It works very well for us, but is not without its disadvantages, especially with regard to competition from non-member countries. It's not for nothing that the big American and Japanese banking groups have established branches within the Community over the last few years.'

One of the engineers pretended to show an interest in the banker's problems:

'I see that your business also takes you to Brussels. Is your bank directly affected by developments within the Community?'

'Yes. We work with travel agencies which are involved with a certain number of Community programmes: AMADEUS, GALILEO, HERMES . . . we are also affected by AQUARIUS, and by POSEIDOM, which, as you will know, concerns overseas territories. My bank does a lot of business in this area.'

Breakfast was over. I had just paid my bill. I closed my eyes. Amadeus, Poseidom . . . I saw beaches and coconut palms, their leaves gently swaying in the breeze. The music of Mozart flooded my head. I saw Neptune rising from the sea carrying his trident.

The driver's voice over the intercom, announcing our arrival at Brussels South, wrenched me from my torpor. My travelling companions were already standing, bags in hand. I was just able to hear one of them ask his neighbour:

'Are you going to the Berlaymont building? Can I give you a lift? There's a car waiting for me at the station.'

'Thank you very much. My first meeting is at DG IV, if you would be so kind as to drop me there.'

I was in a thoughtful mood as I left the station. There was no question that the conversation I had just overheard had covered important subjects which would have increasing repercussions on our daily life: the single market serving 337 million consumers, which would affect all our lives in one way or another; the ability of our businesses to adapt to the new climate of competition; economic competition with the other large industrialized countries; uncertainty over inclusion of eastern European countries in the Single Market; would the Single Market exist at the price of even greater third world poverty?

But what language were they speaking? Was this what '1992' meant? However hard I had tried, I had been unable to understand most of what they had been saying and I had not been able to join in because I lacked any kind of basic knowledge of how the common market actually functions and, in the final instance, I did not know the vocabulary the men had been using.

I decided to do something about this as soon as possible and not allow a single word of European jargon to get by me without at least trying to understand it. The book you have in your hands now is intended to complement the excellent popular interpretations of Europe which are currently available with a collection of definitions of the terms and acronyms most commonly used by Eurocrats or by others when referring to the European Community. I wanted to save others the time and effort it took me to understand the exact meaning of every aspect of European vocabulary.

Most of the terms in this book belong to the administrative and legal language of the Community: they refer to very specific realities which are relatively simple to understand when they are broken down into their basic elements. As with all technical language it is the accumulation of new words which poses problems for novices and which may discourage them from attempting to learn the language.

At the same time you will discover that this language, which is, it must be said, a little disconcerting for the layman, contains only a few words of actual Community slang. You will come across the odd Kangaroo (describing a group of people who have played a role in the progress of European construction), two Blue Angels (I'll leave it to you to look them up in the fourth part of this book) and a few items of vocabulary, understood by the initiated few, such as 'comitology' or 'convergence' – no more than a dozen in total. Community specialists need their own private language too!

Using the dictionary

In the dictionary pages of this book you will find the terms listed which are most often employed by those who deal with Europe. They are mostly common nouns (covering institutions, procedures, Community policy and the vocabulary of external trade) and proper nouns of towns or people which have played a significant role in European construction.

You will also find a large number of abbreviations. Most of the time they refer to Community programmes and databases, or to the names of European bodies or international organizations with whom the main players on the European stage enjoy relations. In some cases, however, it is the abbreviations themselves which precede the definition. These are for bodies which are known mainly by their initials, for example, GATT, EURATOM or COMECON. The Community uses abbreviations a lot. Many of these are acronyms which conjure up a whole array of images: COMETT, DRIVE, BRIDGE, DELTA, ECLAIR, ERASMUS, ESPRIT, ICONE, MITHRA, PROMETHEUS, TELEMAN. Our Eurocrats have truly fertile imaginations! Yet this makes it all the more easy to remember the acronyms.

Each term or abbreviation included is followed by:

- the full name (in the case of abbreviations)
- a brief definition
- in some cases one or two examples to explain the meaning(s) of the word concerned
- references to the most recent Community documents, as they appear in the various editions of the Official Journal of the European Communities (OJ)
- cross-references to other terms defined elsewhere in the book (these cross-references appear either as asterisks after a word or a group of words or as key words in capitals at the end of a definition); readers can, therefore, gain further knowledge of a subject if they wish, or jump from term to term, much as if they were using a database.

You may think that this all sounds a bit serious, but this book has no other pretensions than to be a reference work; this makes it, by definition, a little austere. So, to add some colour (and, at the same time, to enable the reader to become familiar with Community language) the author has added some exercises to give you a chance to see how much you know already. These come before the dictionary itself and are in the form of exercises and translations from English into Eurospeak and from Eurospeak into English. They are followed by a brief guide to enable you to assess your knowledge. Then it is up to you to decide whether you need to perfect your knowledge of the Common Market by referring to specialist or popular works on the subject (in your areas of interest) or if this book will suffice to answer whatever queries you may have.

Most of the definitions are derived from official documents, in particular from treaties or from the first articles of Directives or Regulations which are specifically devoted to defining terms which are to be used in the document. Other articles take more liberties with the subject concerned in order to make it as comprehensible as possible. Having said that, a work such as this, even if it does not claim to be absolutely comprehensive, could not be produced without help from experts as the Community is a very complex and diverse entity.

I would like to thank Emmanuelle Butaud, Florence Nicolas, Thierry Allix, Pierre Baudin, Aurelio Finetti, Robert Fries, Gérard Imbert, Emmanuel Julien, Bertrand de Maigret, Philippe de Montgolfier, Emile Noël, Daniel Paris, Jean-Claude Séché and Bruno Vever for checking the definitions in their fields of expertise. I would like them to know that, if the following pages attain a certain level of accuracy, this is due to their efforts, and that any errors which may have crept in are entirely the fault of the author. I would like to thank in advance any readers who would be so kind as to point these out to me in order that they may be corrected in the next edition.

Good luck, then, on your voyage of discovery!

2 EXERCISES AND TRANSLATIONS

English–Eurospeak

It is always more difficult to express yourself in a foreign language than to understand a foreign language. For this reason, in the following exercise, English sentences are followed by their equivalent in Eurospeak to give you an idea of how the Community language works and to prepare you for the translation exercises from Eurospeak to English

The asterisks refer to words defined in the dictionary section of this book.

English	**Eurospeak**
I want to export some peanuts to another country in the Common Market.	I want to market (1) some nuts (2) in another Member State* (3). *(1) With the establishment of the single or 'internal' market, 'export' is no longer strictly speaking the correct term.* *(2) The generic administrative term for this type of product.* *(3) The expression used for the signatories of the Treaty of Rome*.*
England opposes the Delors plan, especially concerning the creation of a European bank.	The United Kingdom (1) has indicated its refusal to accept the proposal made by Jacques Delors to establish the equivalent of a European central bank. *(1) Beware! In international relations, England, Wales, Scotland and Northern Ireland are known as the United Kingdom.*

Germany does not agree with the proposal from Brussels concerning differences in the rates of value added tax.

Germany has disassociated itself from the proposal by the Commission* of the European Communities* (1) concerning VAT* rate bands.

(1) It is wrong to say 'the Commission in Brussels'. 'Brussels' is even worse, a vulgarization which appals the officials concerned! Learn to say 'the Commission of the European Communities' or just 'the Commission'. This will show that you know at least something about Community life . . .

How do I send my products across the borders with other countries in the Common Market?

How do I transport my goods across the internal frontiers (1) of the Community*?

(1) Since 1968 the borders between the countries in the Common Market have become less and less important. They are called 'internal frontiers'; the term 'frontier' is used for the external frontiers of the Community, i.e. those which separate Member States from the rest of the world (called non-member countries*).*

European citizens working for firms in Common Market countries other than their own should continue to enjoy the same tax and welfare benefits as in their own country.

It seems judicious to arrange for Community* nationals who work on a contractual basis in another Member State* to be covered by agreements which guarantee workers'* rights within the framework of the Regulation* on freedom of movement*.

Collaboration between the groupings of companies from different European countries is an important element in setting up a true Common Market between these countries.

Trans-border cooperation within the Community* is essential for the creation of the Single Market (1).

(1) Since the Single European Act, the terms 'Single Market' and 'internal market' are used increasingly more often than the term 'Common Market'.

The Treaty of Rome does not allow limits to be fixed on the quantities of products imported or exported from one Common Market country to another, nor does it allow any other barriers to the movement of products from one country to another to be imposed.

One of the principles of the EEC* Treaty is the prohibition of quantitative restrictions* on imports* and exports*, and of measures having equivalent effect*.

There should be a European Act to prevent governments opposing the introduction of certain products on their market by adopting new technical specifications which allow them to refuse entry to goods or machines which do not conform.

There should be a Community Directive*(1) to prevent the formation of new technical barriers* to the free movement of goods which could result from a Member State* adopting regulatory or legislative measures.

(1) European law is expressed in the form of Directives, Regulations and Decisions.

The Commission in Brussels must lift the obstacles standing in the way of setting up one large market which result from differences in the conditions under which our firms and those of our neighbours work.

The Commission* of the European Communities* shall take the necessary measures to remedy distortions of competition* arising from trade agreements which lead to the compartmentalization of markets.

It would be of advantage to European businesses to be able to choose legal forms allowing them to cooperate across their borders.

The creation of a form of optional legal partnership within the Community would be of considerable benefit as an instrument to encourage industrial cooperation within a unified market.

Now that you know what you are up against, try some 'Eurospeak' translations.

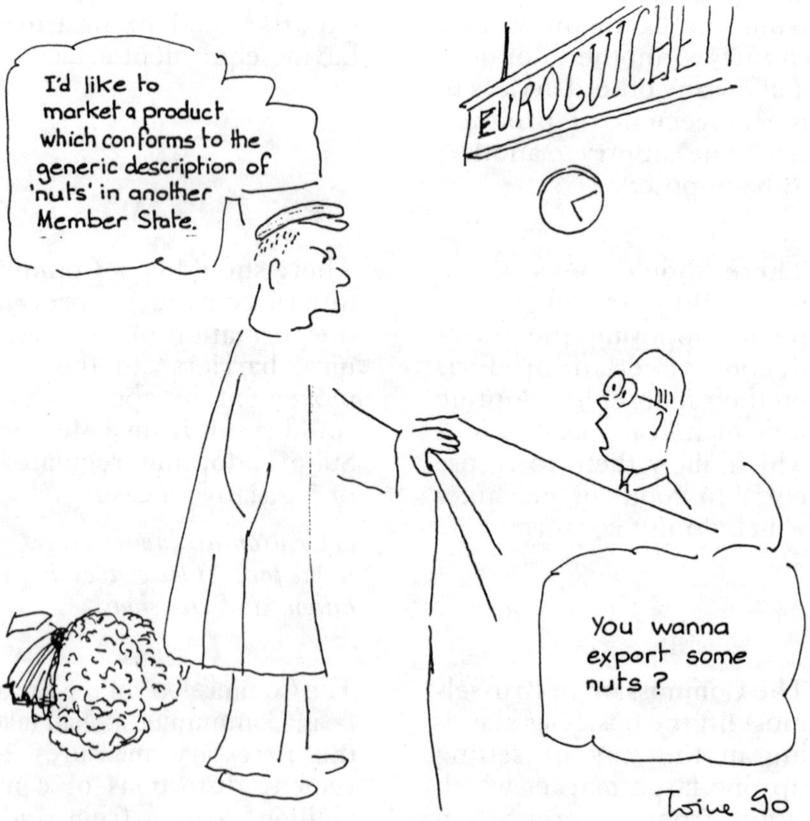

Eurospeak–English

Try to translate the following sentences into standard English. Generally speaking, they are arranged in ascending order of difficulty. Having said that, you may not agree if you are familiar with one or more of the areas covered.

After a series of short sentences, there are two 'longer passages'; these assume a good knowledge of Community law and the machinery of the EC.

This time there is no translation provided. The dictionary in the fourth part of this book will help you understand the words marked with an asterisk. Make a note of the number of times you had to look up a word or acronym in the box at the end of each translation.

Add up the number of words and acronyms you have had to look up (even if you were only checking) and write it in the box at the bottom of the page. Carry the number over to the next page and fill in the final total on page 19. Then consult page 20 for an initial evaluation of how fluent you are in Eurospeak.

Short Translations

Number of words looked up

CEN* and CENELEC* are working towards the standardization* of technical rules* with GATT* rules. ☐

Standardization of taxation of savings income should be completed before the free movement of capital* is introduced. ☐

The Commission* has just elaborated a proposal for a Directive* intended to cover conditions for the export* of foodstuffs* to all non-member countries*. ☐

The Food Aid Committee will administer the open credit accounts for LDCs*. ☐

We will need to be vigilant regarding the Community* approach to the agri-foodstuffs* sector; it seems to be more than a little backward-looking, still based on the single rurality, while important decisions are left to the CJEC*. ☐

Total ☐

Number of Words consulted

Carried forward [ ]

The Commission* has started to modify the method for calculating refunds* for processed products. [ ]

The praesidia of COPA* and COGECA* categorically reject any further weakening of the CMO* relating to cereals. [ ]

The principles of mutual balance of advantage and of reciprocity* are accepted within the framework of GATT* or the OECD*. [ ]

At the last COREPER* meeting the three countries which had expressed reservations about STABEX* during the 'general business' Council* sided with the majority*, thus opening the way towards renewing Lomé III* by way of the ACP*/EEC* conference*. [ ]

Total [ ]

Number of Words consulted

Carried forward [ ]

The opening up of public contracts* (with the exception of excluded sectors*) will contribute, as a result of the links with European standardization*, to the abolition of technical barriers* in the trade* of industrial products, in conformity with the programme of action in the Commission's* White Paper* on establishing the internal market*. [ ]

The package deal* price from the Commission*, whose budgetary quasi-neutrality should be emphasized, sanctions the progressive abolition of monetary gaps*, which will lead to the abolition of all MCA* for currencies subject to the rules of the EMS*. [ ]

Administrations are obliged to assume that products manufactured in conformity with harmonized* standards* (or, provisionally, with national standards*) conform to the 'essential requirements'* established by the Directive*. [ ]

Contracting authorities* may award public supply contracts* by using the negotiated procedure*, where irregular tenders have been submitted in response to an open or restricted procedure* or where tenders are unacceptable in accordance with national provisions. [ ]

Each contracting party within the Harmonized System* Committee has the right to one vote. Following customs union* or economic union* where one or more Member States* are contracting parties, these parties will together express only one vote. [ ]

LDCs* will be able to incorporate products of Community origin* in the goods that they manufacture without losing the GSP* origin for processed products which are then exported to the EC*. [ ]

Total [ ]

Number of Words consulted

Carried forward

Transparency in the procedures* and practices for awarding contracts is a prerequisite for achieving freedom of establishment* and freedom to provide services* with regard to public works contracts*.

Those affected by a national measure in the Member States* have the right to ask national courts to invoke the principle that the measure, which has not been notified under Directive* 83/189, may not be used to their detriment; this is an essential aspect of the new approach*.

Products originating in one Member State* or which are in free circulation* there and which have been exported to another Member State* shall be allowed to be reimported to the first State without being subject to any customs duty*, quantitative restriction* or measures having equivalent effect*.

Taking into account the low efficiency of supervisory and protective measures the NCPI* should be able to finalize the anti-dumping* procedure expediently.

The requested authority must communicate to the applicant authority the provisions relating to the application of customs duty* and of charges having equivalent effect*, as well as of agricultural levies* and other forms of taxation laid down in the CAP*.

The introduction of the concepts of identical national treatment and of reciprocity* in the second banking Directive* ought to allow the Community* to settle the problem of its relations with non-member countries*.

Total

Number of Words consulted

Carried forward ☐

The draft Directive* on Public Limited Liability Companies in European Law* ought to make it possible to avoid systematic recourse to PPO* and PEO* and to reduce the urgency of the policy for the harmonization* of company law*. ☐

There are still a number of quantitative restrictions* on national quotas* within the MFA* and the GSP*. ☐

If the branches of credit institutions* in non-member countries* do not benefit from the freedom to provide services* or from freedom of establishment* in Member States* other than the one where they are established, applications for approval* may be submitted in so far as these credit institutions* benefit from reciprocity* arrangements in the non-member countries* in question. ☐

The compensatory levy* for these goods represents all of the deferred or refunded variable component and a percentage of the fixed component of the levy for the import* of these same goods from non-member countries* into the Community* of Twelve*. ☐

It would be interesting to speculate on the effects of the transition from the unanimity* rule (confirmed by the Luxembourg* compromise) to the qualified majority* rule in a large number of areas. ☐

Decisions of the Court* are coming to cover more irregularity proceedings, but also more and more cases of preliminary referral* in the interpretation of Community* Acts*, laid down in article 177 of the EEC* treaty. ☐

Total ☐

Number of Words consulted

Carried forward

The present regulation* determines the particular provisions which are applicable to inward processing* arrangements relating to Community* goods and to outward processing* arrangements relating to goods which are traded within the Community* and to the system of processing under customs control* relating to Community* goods.

Products subject to a Common Market Organisation* and imported from non-member countries* may, under certain conditions, be placed under customs warehousing* or free zone procedure while collection of import* duties is suspended.

A Member State* whose central rate* or market rate* indicates an Ecu* currency value higher than the agricultural conversion rate* receives MCA* on imports* and grants them on exports*.

Total

Longer Passages

Number of Words consulted

Carried forward ☐

A

In order to maintain a true system of common prices* between Member States* which implies that the value of prices expressed in Ecus* is equivalent to that of prices* expressed in the national currencies of the Member States*, green exchange rates* ought to follow the fluctuations of the central exchange rate* and the market rate*. However, since the first modification of monetary parities following the implementation of common prices*, Member States* are not prepared to accept the consequences for official prices and subsidies* expressed in national currencies. If the currency of a Member State* has been revalued, the value of these prices and subsidies* is reduced according to the new rate of exchange although its Ecu* value remains unchanged.

The Member States* have tried to attenuate the effect of currency movements on agriculture by changing the adjustment of green rates to the new actual parities, while maintaining the value of official prices expressed in national currencies at their former level. As a result, monetary gaps* have appeared between green exchange rates* and the market rate*. Therefore, green rates must be progressively realigned to actual rates.

To maintain the appearance of a system of common prices*, agri-monetary regulations* allow the application of MCA* when the green exchange rate and the market rate differ. This just about eliminates the gap. For those Member States* whose green rates are lower than the market rate*, the MCA* is applied as an import* levy* and an export* subsidy. It is thus called a 'positive' MCA*. For those Member States* whose green rates are higher than the market rate*, the MCA* is applied as an import* subsidy and an export* levy*. It is thus called a 'negative' MCA*. ☐

As far as real monetary gaps* are concerned it is important to note that, within the framework of the switchover* mechanism, the RMG for a country with a weak currency consists of two parts: the artificial RMG

Total ☐

Number of Words consulted

Carried forward

(or that part of a positive RMG which would arise from a change in the central rate* of the strongest currency and would become a negative RMG by implementing the corrective factor*) and the negative RMG arising from a modification of the central rate* of the strongest currency.

B

A Member State* may, after the Council* has adopted a harmonization* measure by qualified majority*, decide to take derogations unilaterally, having failed to obtain the inclusion of safeguard clauses*, by invoking the essential requirements* listed in article 36 of the EEC* treaty*.

It seems that we are faced, in this case, with an exception to the procedure laid down in article 100a, which was introduced by the Single Act*; it seems like a return to the spirit, if not the content, of the 'Luxembourg* compromise'.

However, in spite of appearances, such practices do not call primary Community law* into question, and secondary Community law* even less.

Should we fear, in spite of everything, that certain States plead article 36 to avoid certain Community regulations* which do not suit them?

The reply to this might be:

1. That the Council* has instructed the Commission* to limit this kind of abuse.

2. That the most important matter is that the Council* should be in a position to continue its harmonization* work towards achieving the Single Market*, taking into account the general approach defined by the troika* of the European Council*.

Total

Number of Words consulted

Carried forward ☐

Besides, a Member State* which wanted to exclude itself in this way from a Community* regulation* would not be entitled to adopt specific national provisions derogating from the Community* regulation* adopted by qualified majority* without invoking article 36 to justify its position. Failing this the Commission* and, if necessary, the CJEC* – after referral for irregularity proceedings – would be entitled to consider the merits of the case. In this case invoking the principle of subsidiarity* would be no more than a pretence, just as the broad balance* principle constitutes a perversion of the unified economic area system. If the idea of abandoning sovereignty had not been accepted, neither the Community of Six*, nor the Community of Nine* and certainly not the Community of Twelve* would have seen the light of day. ☐

On the other hand, comitology*, COREPER* meetings, the different shuttle possibilities provided for in the cooperation procedure* and, to a certain extent, the Opinions* of the EP* committees and the own-initiative Opinions* of the ESC* constitute as many barriers designed to draw attention to the essential requirements* as certain Member States* would be liable to be able to invoke even before the Council* could adopt a joint position*.

Total ☐

Hello, is that Neptune?
No, sorry, it's Poseidom
Toni 90

How fluent are you?

Over 80
If you had to consult the dictionary more than 80 times (or if, despite doing this, you have still not completely understood the meaning of some sentences), you need to do some serious reading on the workings of the Community.

50–80
If you had to consult the dictionary between 50 and 80 times you need to examine in some detail a few Community documents or to familiarize yourself further with the institutions and procedures of the European Economic Community and Eurospeak in general.

20–49
If you had to consult the dictionary between 20 and 50 times you have an adequate knowledge of the Community. Use the dictionary to confirm what you already know or to obtain greater insight into certain words or abbreviations.

Less than 20
If you had to consult the dictionary less than 20 times you have a good knowledge of the Community.

0
If you understood everything, well done! If you know two Community languages well you can apply for a position as a Community official. Advertisements are published in the Official Journal of the European Communities. In any case, it's worth confirming the meaning of a few of the terms you think you understand – you can never be too careful!

3 EUROGLOSSARY

This section contains a few of the more common terms used in Eurospeak, for some of the institutions of the Community. It is intended for quick reference. Most of these are described more fully in the dictionary section.

1992 The Single European Act* foresees a single market* established between Member States* by 31 December 1992.

Commission of the European Communities Community* institution conceived to uphold the treaties*, to be the Community's* executive body to initiate Community* policy and to represent the Community* in the Council*. Formed on 1 July 1967; based in Brussels. Representatives from each Member State – two Commissioners for larger, one for smaller – hold office for a renewable term of four years. Twenty-three Directorates cover specialist areas. Its President is elected by heads of government for a renewable term of four years.

Common Agricultural Policy (CAP) Community* policy to increase agricultural productivity, ensure farmers a reasonable standard of living, stabilize agricultural markets, guarantee supply and ensure consumers reasonable prices for agricultural products. Works using Common Market Organizations* (CMO), price guarantees, Monetary Compensatory Amounts* (MCA), Community preference* and other instruments of policy.

Council of Ministers of the European Communities (usually called the Council) Foremost legislative body of the European Communities* on matters relating to the EEC* and EURATOM*. Comprises Government ministers from Member States – those present are determined by the agenda. The Presidency changes every six months in alphabetical order.

Court of Auditors Community institution* established by the 2nd Treaty of Brussels* on 22 July 1975 to examine the accounts of all Community* bodies and of EDF* operations.

Court of Justice Community institution* set up to ensure that Community law* is observed in the interpretation and application of the treaties* and to review Community* regulations*. Its thirteen judges are appointed by agreement between Member States, and its President elected from the thirteen for a renewable term of three years.

Economic and Social Committee (ESC) 189 member consultative assembly mainly representing employers and trade unions of the Member States.

Ecu (European Currency Unit) European unit of account defined by a rate on the exchange market, calculated from the exchange rates of the currencies which make it up (the currencies of the Member States*).

EURATOM (European Atomic Energy Community) One of the three European Communities*, established by the Treaty of Rome* on 25 March 1957 to create a common energy* market and to raise the standard of living in the Community* via safe, peaceful use of nuclear power.

European Coal and Steel Community (ECSC) One of the three European Communities*, established by the Treaty of Paris* on 18 April 1951 to reduce customs barriers*, progressively abolish quota* restrictions and to coordinate the policy of Member States* in the field of coal* and steel*.

European Council Meeting of the heads of state and of government of the Member States* and the President of the Commission*. The supreme Community* body of political cooperation, stimulating and coordinating Community* activities.

European Economic Community (EEC) One of the three European Communities*, established by the Treaty of Rome* on 25 March 1957. Its main objective is to establish a generalized common market* within the Community.

European Monetary System (EMS) System set up to create an area of internal and external monetary stability in Europe. Exchange rate mechanism to control the fluctuation of currencies of participating countries.

European Parliament One of the four main Community institutions*. Main Community* debating body. Has the power to reject the Community* budget* and works in cooperation with the Council* and the Commission* to draw up the budget*. It has 518 members from the Member States*, elected every five years by universal suffrage.

Federal Europe Possible outcome of the Community* policy towards European Union* (political union), where national governments cede more power to the Community institutions* than at present – United States of Europe. Federalism (*Shorter Oxford Dictionary*): where 'two or more states constitute a political unity while remaining independent as to their internal affairs'.

Freedom of Movement Overriding principle behind the Single Market*: of persons, goods, services and capital between Member States*.

Member States Term used to describe the twelve* signatories of the Treaty of Paris* and the Treaties of Rome* and the Single European Act*.

Monetary Union Economic and monetary union is an objective of the Single European Act*. The three-stage Delors* plan involves the creation of a European System of Central Banks* (EUROFED) and eventual fixed parities between the currencies of the Member States* leading to the creation of a common currency.

Single European Act (SEA) Document which amends and supplements the EEC* treaty* (and the ECSC* and EURATOM* treaties* for the Court of Justice*), signed by the Member States* on 17 February 1986. Its main objective is to create a single market* within the Community* by 31 December 1992.

Single Market Aim of the Single European Act* and the Commission's White Paper*: freedom of movement* of goods, persons, services and capital within the Community*.

Transparency Term used more and more frequently in conjunction with markets or prices: denotes 'above boardness', nothing hidden.

The Institutions of the Community

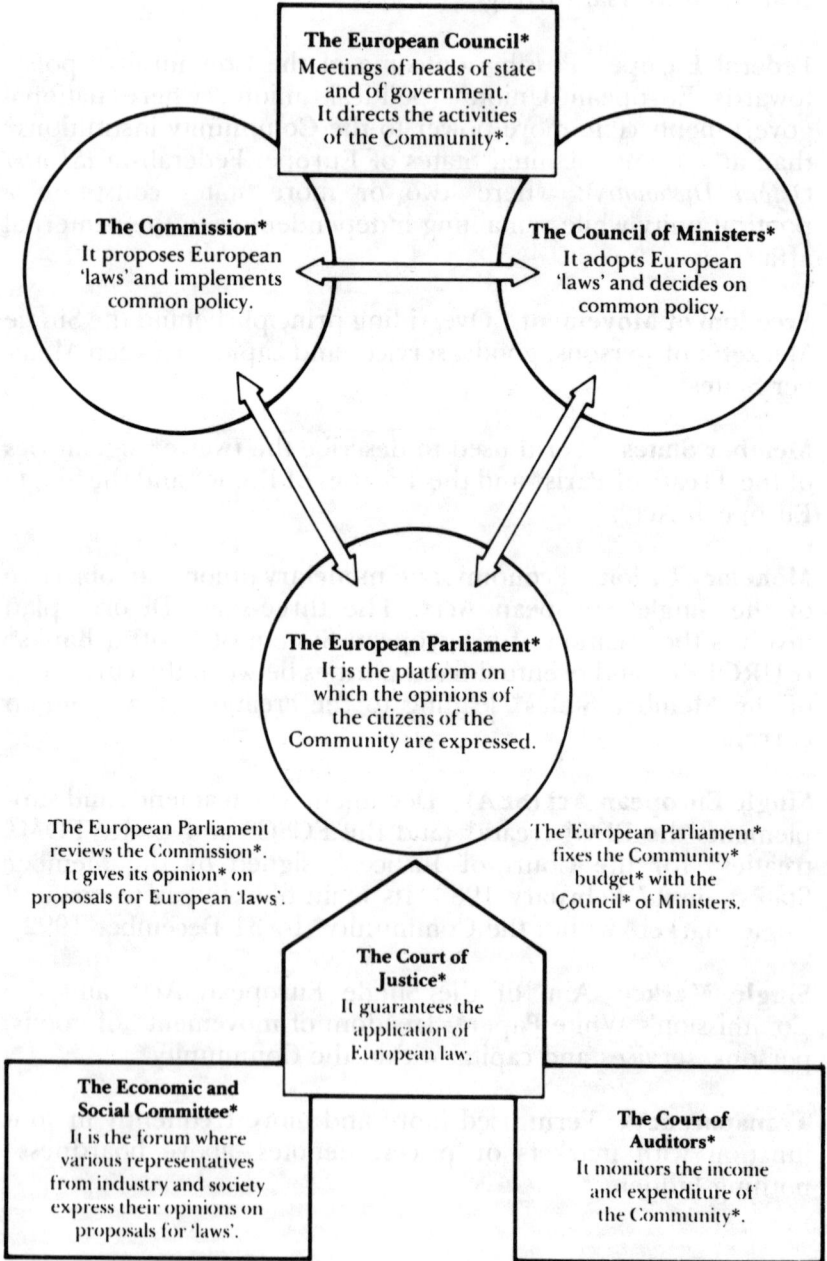

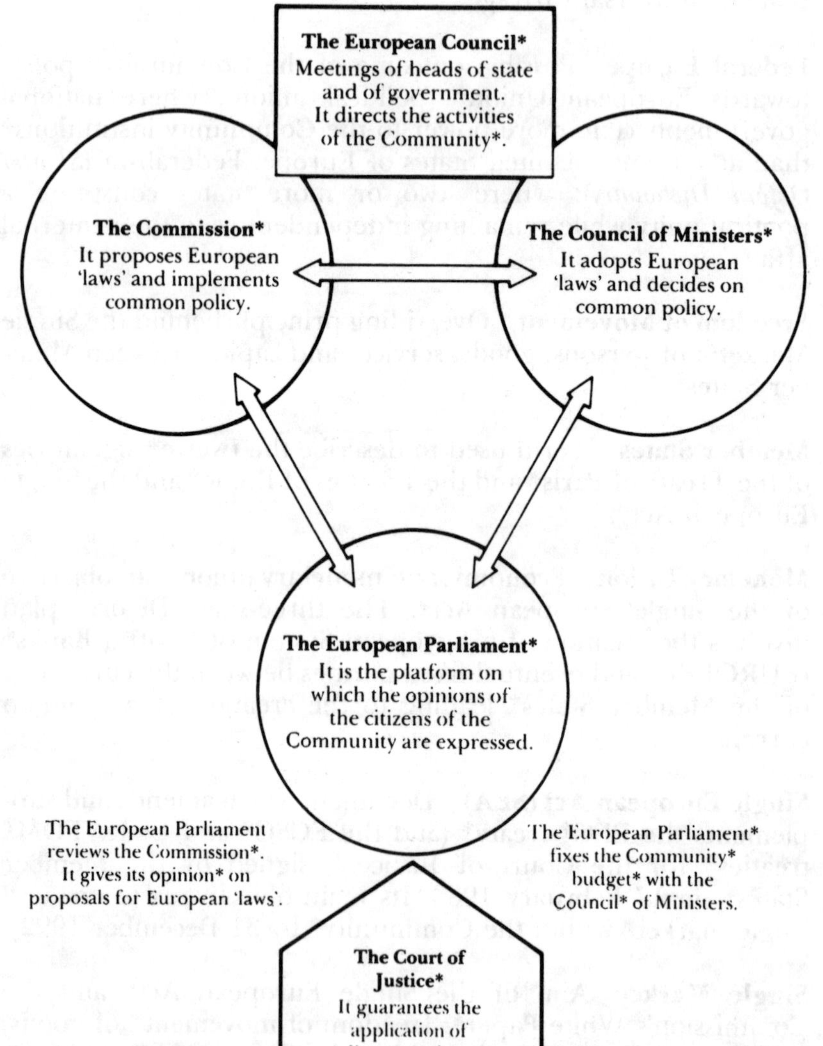

The European Council*
Meetings of heads of state and of government.
It directs the activities of the Community*.
The Commission*
It proposes European 'laws' and implements common policy.
The Council of Ministers*
It adopts European 'laws' and decides on common policy.
The European Parliament*
It is the platform on which the opinions of the citizens of the Community are expressed.
The European Parliament reviews the Commission*. It gives its opinion* on proposals for European 'laws'.
The European Parliament* fixes the Community* budget* with the Council* of Ministers.
The Court of Justice*
It guarantees the application of European law.
The Economic and Social Committee*
It is the forum where various representatives from industry and society express their opinions on proposals for 'laws'.
The Court of Auditors*
It monitors the income and expenditure of the Community*.

Source: European Parliament.

Community decision-making processes

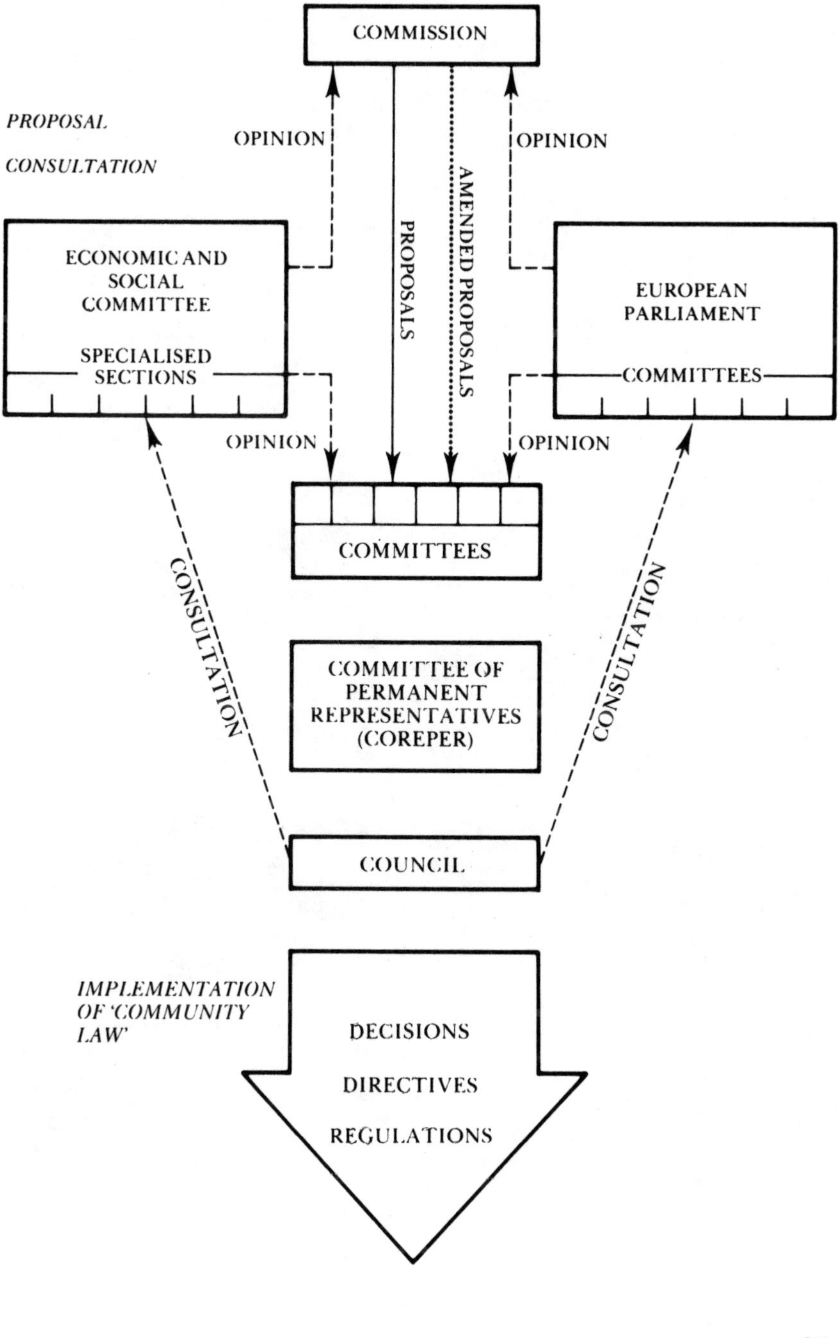
COMMISSION
PROPOSAL
CONSULTATION
OPINION
OPINION
PROPOSALS
AMENDED PROPOSALS
ECONOMIC AND SOCIAL COMMITTEE
SPECIALISED SECTIONS
EUROPEAN PARLIAMENT
COMMITTEES
OPINION
OPINION
COMMITTEES
CONSULTATION
CONSULTATION
COMMITTEE OF PERMANENT REPRESENTATIVES (COREPER)
COUNCIL
IMPLEMENTATION OF 'COMMUNITY LAW'
DECISIONS
DIRECTIVES
REGULATIONS

A DICTIONARY OF THE EC AND THE SINGLE MARKET

A

Abuse of Dominant Position
SEE MERGER, DOMINANT POSITION, (ABUSE OF).

Accreditation (or Recognition) Technical approval granted by a laboratory or by any inspection and certification body*.
SEE EUROPEAN TECHNICAL APPROVAL.

ACE (Action by the Community relating to the Environment) Community programme* to improve the environment* (REG.* 3/84, 28/6/1984, OJ* L 716, 3/7/1984); 3/87, 23/7/1987, OJ* L 207, 29/7/1987). DG XI of the Commission*.

ACJRC (Advisory Committee of the Joint Research Centre)
SEE JOINT RESEARCH CENTRE.

ACP (African, Caribbean and Pacific States) *7/1973*: negotiations between the EEC*, the countries of the Yaoundé* Convention* and 27 other African and Caribbean countries. *28/2/1975*: Lomé* I Convention* with 66 of these countries (development cooperation*). *31/10/1979*: Lomé II. 1984: Lomé III. 1989: Lomé IV.
SEE ERDF, EUROPEAN INVESTMENT BANK, GENERALIZED SYSTEM OF PREFERENCES, ACP-EEC JOINT ASSEMBLY, LESS DEVELOPED COUNTRIES, NON-MEMBER COUNTRIES, STABEX, SYSMIN, YAOUNDÉ.

ACP-EEC Joint Assembly Advisory body replacing the ACP-EEC Consultative Assembly following the Lomé III* convention*.
Members: 66 Members of the European Parliament* and 66 representatives of the ACP* states.
Bureau: 2 Presidents, 18 Vice-presidents who may be re-elected each year. The ACP* Council of Ministers, the ACP* Council of Ambassadors, and representatives of the Council* and the Commission* may attend the two annual meetings. *Resolutions* are submitted to the two Councils. Questions to the Council of Ministers. *Reports* on activities and *proposals for resolutions*.

ACPM Advisory Committee on Programme Management (also CCMGP).

Acquisition of Holdings (in a company) Since 1/1/1991 any natural person or legal entity who or which acquires or disposes of significant holdings in a company quoted on a stock exchange* must inform the company concerned as the change passes different thresholds (10%, 20%, etc.); the company then informs its national supervisory authority (DIR.* 88/627/EEC, 12/12/1988, OJ* L 348/62, 17/12/1988).
SEE PROSPECTUS, PUBLIC PURCHASE OFFER.

Act Written document establishing an agreement. Legal act of the Community* for applying treaties* and harmonizing* laws.
SEE COMMUNITY LAW, DECISION, DIRECTIVE, OPINION, RECOMMENDATION, REGULATION.
Community acts: legal acts of the Community institutions* (SEE DECISION, DIRECTIVE, JUDGEMENT, OPINION, ORDER, RECOMMENDATION, REGULATION, RESOLUTION) compiled in the OJ*.

Administrative Commission on Social Security for Migrant Workers (CASSTM) Community* institution responsible for decisions relating to the interpretation and implementation of Regulations* applicable to migrant workers*. One representative from each Member State* and one representative from the Commission* (in an advisory capacity).
SEE FREEDOM OF MOVEMENT, EUROPEAN SOCIAL AREA.

Administrative Letter Positive written response by the Community* administration to requests for exemption* or negative clearance* with regard to agreements* or practices which have been made known to it under competition* regulations. It has declaratory value. The substance of the agreement may be published in order that third parties affected by it can learn of its contents (communication* from the Commission*, 2/11/1983). The letter itself may be followed by a press release.

Admission to a Stock Exchange Admission, by fixed procedure, of stocks and other financial instruments to the (officially or unofficially) regulated trading conditions of an officially recognized stock exchange. Directive* 79/279/EEC of 5/3/1979 (OJ* L 66, 1979) on coordinating the conditions for admission to official listing.
SEE CIUTS, EUROPEAN FINANCIAL AREA, FREEDOM TO PROVIDE SERVICES, MOVEMENTS OF CAPITAL, PROSPECTUS.

Adonnino (Pietro) Member of the European Parliament*

(from Italy), author of a report on 'Europe and its citizens' submitted to the Milan European Council* (29/6/1985).
SEE FREEDOM OF ESTABLISHMENT, FREEDOM OF MOVEMENT, SINGLE EUROPEAN ACT.

Advertising Any provision which prohibits or limits advertising for imported products or which fixes criteria or conditions which, while they are applicable to both national and imported products, nevertheless tend to favour national products or discriminate against imported products, may be considered to be a measure having equivalent effect*, contrary to the principle of freedom of movement of goods (DIR.* 70/50/EEC); Judgement* 152/78, 10/7/1980; art. 30 and 36 of the EEC* treaty*).
A Member State* does not have the right to prohibit a business-person from advertising on its territory. See also Judgement* of 7/3/1990.
Broadcasting: where television advertising is concerned, any discrimination against broadcasts from another Member State* is prohibited, except for reasons relating to public order (art. 56 of the EEC* treaty*). See Judgements* 155/173, 52/79. Joint position* on minimum standards* for programming. Directive* 84/450/EEC concerns *misleading and unfair advertising* (10/9/1984, OJ* L 250, 19/7/1984).
Comparative advertising: authorized from 1/1/1993 under certain conditions and controlled by individual Member States* (Commission* proposal of 22/5/1991).
SEE ALSO AGREEMENTS BETWEEN UNDERTAKINGS.

AECMA (Association Européenne des Constructeurs de Matériel Aérospatial)
SEE EUROPEAN ASSOCIATION OF AEROSPACE MANUFACTURERS.

Aeronautics
SEE AERONAUTICS (PROGRAMME), EUROPEAN CIVIL AVIATION CONFERENCE, EUROCONTROL, GALILEO.

Aeronautics (Programme) Part of the BRITE*-EURAM* Community research* programme* aimed at acquiring technology* in the field of aeronautics*: aerodynamics, structures, materials, accoustics. Budget: 60m Ecus* (1989-1992). DG XII of the Commission*.

AEROPA Association of international and regional airlines, consumers * associations, European local administrations and chambers of commerce and industry.

AFNOR (Association Française de NORmalisation) *(French standards association)*: Public utility association responsible for planning and approving standards* in France, for coordinating the sectorial standards* offices and for the promotion and availability to industry of all French, European, national and international standards*. 1926. Tour Europe – 92049 Paris, La Défense Cedex 7, France.

Agreements between Undertakings Formal or tacit agreement between undertakings operating at the same stage of commercial activity (horizontal agreements) or between manufacturers and the distributors of their products (vertical agreements), which have the effect of limiting other undertakings' access to the market or their freedom to compete, or which prevents prices being fixed freely according to the market situation by artificially forcing them up or down; which limits or controls production (quota* agreement), markets, investment or technological progress; which allocates markets or supply sources. This type of agreement, as well as any abuse of a dominant position* on the internal market or a substantial part of it, and a situation whereby a client or supplier is economically dependent on one undertaking and has no alternative, is prohibited by the EEC* treaty* (art. 85 and 86). The Commission* has indicated by way of general communications* that it considers certain agreements to be not subject to the prohibition in art. 85: in particular, and under certain conditions, exclusive representation contracts, cooperation in certain areas (statistics, research* and development, after-sales service, advertising*, labelling*) or sub-contracting, 'minimum importance' agreements, ie those which are considered to have a negligible effect on competition* or on intra-Community trade because of the size of market share and of the turnover of the undertakings involved ('de minimis' rule). These communications* are not prejudicial of the decisions of national courts or of the Court of Justice* of the EC*.
Courts do not need to await the decision of the Commission* in a specific case; 'any agreements or decisions prohibited pursuant to this article shall be automatically void' (art. 85.2). The Commission* may impose fines* on undertakings which contravene these provisions; the fines* are paid to the Community*.
SEE CARTEL, SOLE DISTRIBUTION, TAX-FREE SHOP.

AGREP Community* data base*: publicly financed agricultural research projects. CEC*, Brussels.

Agricultural and Agro-Industrial Research Community programme* to promote quality and diversity in agricultural products, to increase the competitiveness of businesses in the agricultural and agri-foodstuffs* sector, to improve the management of rural areas and to protect the environment: primary production, farm and forestry inputs, treatment of biological raw materials and end use of these products. Budget: 55m Ecus* (1990-1994). OJ* C 146, 1985. DG IV of the Commission*.

Agricultural and Forestry Tractors Directive* of 3/5/1988 (OJ* L 126, 1988).

Agricultural Machinery Harmonization* Directive*.
SEE NEW APPROACH.

Agricultural Prices The single agricultural market presupposes uniform prices and a common pricing policy (see below). The Common Market Organizations* and the annual fixing of prices (by the Council* following proposals by the Commission*) for the marketing year are the instruments of this policy. Public expenditure for common market and pricing policy is financed by the EAGGF* guarantee section.
Target price: price which the Common Market Organization* aims to guarantee the producer for certain products (cereals, rice, sugar, milk, olive oil, colza and sunflower seed).
Guide price: target price for beef and wine, soya, linseed, dehydrated lucerne and raw cotton.
Norm price: target price for tobacco.
Threshold price (cereals, sugar, rice, dairy products, olive oil): price fixed by the Community* in order that the selling price of an imported product, taking into account transport costs, is at the level of the target price for that product. The difference between the world selling price and the threshold price is made up by a levy*.
Sluice-gate price: price equivalent to the cost price of pork, eggs and poultry produced in the most technically efficient non-member countries*. An extra amount is added to the levies* on products sold below cost price in order not to let products enter the Community* at prices which would be lower than the sum of the sluice-gate price and the levy* (protection level).
Reference price: price fixed according to the Community* producer price for certain fruits and vegetables, wine and some fisheries* products. It represents the minimum price at which

a product may be imported from a non-member country*. A charge is levied if the reference price is not adhered to.
Intervention price: price at which intervention bodies are obliged to buy the products offered to them (sugar, butter, powdered milk, some Italian cheeses, olive oil, colza, sunflower seed, beef or sheepmeat) or at which they may buy products (pork); the price is lower for cereals, rice, colza, sunflower seed and, in some cases, tobacco*.
Basic price: stabilizing price for the pork market; it is used to fix the threshold for intervention measures on the market (purchases or aid for private storage).
Common prices: prices adopted each year by the Council*, following proposals by the Commission*; they are applicable uniformly throughout the Community*.
Official prices: agricultural support prices (intervention prices, export* refunds, import* levies*, aid for production and consumption) fixed by the Council* or the Commission*, part of the agricultural Common Market Organizations (CMO*).
SEE CMO, COMMON AGRICULTURAL POLICY, COMMUNITY PREFERENCE, GUIDELINES, MECHANISMS FOR STABILIZING BUDGETARY EXPENDITURE.

Agricultural Regulations All the provisions adopted under the Common Agricultural Policy* and specific regulations adopted under art. 235 of the EEC* treaty* relating to goods resulting from the processing of agricultural products. Eg Reg.* 1468/81/EEC.

Agricultural Research Programme Community research* programme* (1989-1993): to counter surplus production; to encourage structural change; to improve the state of agriculture* in under-developed regions. Budget: 55m Ecus*. DG VI and DG XII of the Commission*.
SEE AGRICULTURAL AND AGRO-INDUSTRIAL RESEARCH, AGRICULTURE, COMMON AGRICULTURAL POLICY, RESEARCH POLICY, RESEARCH AND TECHNOLOGICAL DEVELOPMENT FRAMEWORK PROGRAMME.

Agricultural Structure Policy Part of the Common Agricultural Policy* (CAP), it consists especially in increasing the productivity of farms by rationalizing and modernizing their structures, in expressing Community* solidarity in favour of farms and regions which have the most need of this, and in helping to manage the agricultural markets.
SEE EAGGF, EUROPEAN REGIONAL DEVELOPMENT FUND, STRUCTURAL POLICY.

Agricultural Unit of Account Common monetary unit used until 1979 (SEE EMS) to fix common agricultural prices*. The unit was then converted into the currencies of the Member States*.

Agriculture (programme) Community* programme*.
SEE AGRICULTURAL RESEARCH.

Agriculture
SEE AGRICULTURAL RESEARCH PROGRAMME, AGRICULTURE (PROGRAMME), CADDIA, CEJA, COMMON AGRICULTURAL POLICY, COPA, ECLAIR, EUROPEAN CONFEDERATION OF AGRICULTURE, FFSRS, FOODSTUFFS, IARC, RURALNET, SPECIAL COMMITTEE ON AGRICULTURE, STANDING COMMITTEE ON AGRICULTURAL RESEARCH.

Agri-Foodstuffs
SEE CONFEDERATION OF AGRI-FOODSTUFFS INDUSTRIES, CONSUMPTION, FOODSTUFFS.

Aid State aid which distorts competition* within the EC* and the EFTA* convention* (art. 3) is prohibited. The Commission* must be informed in due time of any projects to provide or modify aid and must check their compatibility with art. 93.3 of the EEC* treaty. If necessary it will set up a monitoring procedure and may demand that the aid be paid back to the State which granted it without its authorization.
SEE AUTOMOTIVE INDUSTRY, IRON AND STEEL POLICY, PUBLIC UNDERTAKING.

AIM (Advanced Informatics in Medicine) Community* research programme* on advanced informatics* in medicine* to improve health care and reduce costs by promoting cooperation between specialists in management, research* and teaching, in universities and hospitals, and in the medical equipment, communications, pharmaceutical and biotechnology* industries. Budget: 20m Ecus* (1988-1990). Decision* 88/57EEC (OJ* L 314, 22/11/1988). DG XIII/F of the Commission*.

ALPES (Advanced Logical Programming Environments) Project in the ESPRIT* programme (France, Italy, Portugal, Germany).

AMADEUS EUREKA* project to set up a computerized European travel reservation system (Air France, Iberia, Lufthansa, SAS). Companies for software development (Nice, France), marketing (Madrid, Spain) and data processing (Munich, Germany).
SEE GALILEO.

Amendment Alteration by the European Parliament* to a document which has been submitted to it. The cooperation procedure* lays down that amendments made by the Parliament* which have not been accepted by the Commission* may only be adopted by the Council* by unanimity*. At a second reading, the Parliament, with a three fifths majority, may approve proposals for non compulsory* expenditure which the Council* has not accepted.
SEE BUDGET.

AMUE
SEE ASSOCIATION FOR THE MONETARY UNION OF EUROPE.

Annual Accounts, Consolidated Accounts Draft Directive* on simplifying them for SME* (SEE ALSO DIR.* 78/660, 83/349; COM (89) 561).
SEE COMPANY LAW.

Annual Effective Global Rate Rate which, on an annual basis, makes the actual values of all existing and future commitments (loans, repayments and charges) entered into by the lender and the consumer equal. 1987 Directive* on approximation of legislation on consumer credit. *22/2/1990*: transparency of offers.

Anti-Dumping Anti-dumping duties may be levied when the imported product in its finished form is subject to duty and when the assembled parts originating from the country in question exceed a certain percentage of the whole.
SEE DUMPING.

Appeal Action brought before the Court of Justice* of the European Communities* to annul a Decision* made by a Community institution* or to record an infringement of the treaties* by the government of a Member State*.
Appeals for preliminary ruling are introduced via a national court (interpretation of the treaties* and institutional acts, validity of these acts), or directly if the applicant appeals directly to the Court of Justice*.
Direct appeals: *in cases of irregularity* (by the Commission* or a Member State* against a Member State* accused of not having conformed to Community law*); *for annulment* (against compulsory Community* acts*: conformity to the treaties* and Community law*, disputes between institutions); *against inaction*

(to penalize silence or inaction on the part of the Council* or the Commission*); *for liability* (to claim for damages caused by the Community institutions* or their agents in the performance of their duties).
A *petition for review (appeal)* is possible in the Court of Justice* where new evidence is found which was not available at the time a Judgement* was made and which could have produced a different outcome.
Awarding public supply and public works contracts**: an appeal Directive* of 22/12/1989 (OJ* L 395, 30/12/1989) lays down various measures to assist undertakings which consider themselves to be injured by contracting authorities* not respecting Community* regulations.

Application First part of appeal* proceedings in the Court of Justice* of the European Communities*.
The application must be sent, by registered post, to the registry of the Court within two months of the publication of the act* concerned, or of its notification to the applicant, or, failing this, of the day on which the applicant first gained knowledge of the act* concerned.

Applied Monetary Gap (AMG) Real monetary gap* minus the neutral margin. The percentage applied in calculating MCA*.

Aquarius Community* operation to safeguard the sea*.
SEE ENVIRONMENT.

Arbitration Procedure whereby two parties turn to the judgement of a third to solve a dispute between them. An *arbitration clause* may be included in a contract. The Court of Justice* of the EC* is entitled to arbitrate in cases falling under the ECSC* treaty.
An *award* is made by the Court of Justice* of the EC* to solve a dispute between Member States* on matters relating to treaties*.
Arbitration procedure: draft Directive* to abolish double taxation in the case of adjustments to combined profits (group taxation*) COM (76) 611).

Arbitration Procedure
SEE ARBITRATION, GROUP TAXATION.

Architects Mutual recognition* of diplomas within the Community* (DIR.* 85/384 (OJ* L 223, 21/8/1985).
SEE FREEDOM TO PROVIDE SERVICES, LIAISON COMMITTEE OF THE ARCHITECTS OF UNITED EUROPE, RIGHT OF ESTABLISHMENT.

ARCOME Community* data base* of organizations, researchers and publications in the information and communications fields. ECHO* on-line data service.

Area Without Frontiers
SEE COMMON MARKET, SINGLE EUROPEAN ACT, SINGLE MARKET.

ARION (Actieprogramme Reizen met een Instructif Karacter voor Onderwijsspecialisten) Community programme* for educational study visits. 1988.

ARP
SEE AGRICULTURAL RESEARCH PROGRAMME.

Arusha Tanzania. Association agreement* between the EEC* and the East African Community (Tanzania, Kenya and Uganda) (1968-1969).
SEE ACP, LDCs.

ASDEX (Axi Symmetrical Divertor EXperiment)

ASEAN (Association of South-East Asian Nations) Association created on 8/8/1967 by Brunei, Indonesia, Malaysia, the Philippines, Singapore and Thailand. Headquarters in Jakarta. 5 year cooperation agreement with the EC* in 1980. Regional group in the Generalized System of Preferences*.

Assent
SEE OPINION.

Association
SEE SINGLE EUROPEAN ACT.

Association Agreement Agreement between the Community* and a non-member country*, a union of States or an international organization, to create an association characterized by mutual rights and obligations, joint measures and particular procedures (art. 238 EEC* treaty). Unanimity* of the Council* after the assent* of the European Parliament*.
SEE ACP, ARUSHA, LDC, CONVENTION (LOMÉ), YAOUNDÉ.

Association For the Monetary Union of Europe Group of more than one hundred European companies and professional organizations affected by monetary stability, the increasing role of the Ecu* in commercial and financial transactions and by the European monetary structure within the EC*. 26 rue de la Pépinière, 75008 Paris, France.
SEE COMMITTEE FOR THE MONETARY UNION OF EUROPE, ECU BANK ASSOCIATION.

Association Nationale de la Recherche Technique (ANRT) (*National association for technical research*): French association, member of the BC-Net* network: cooperation between undertakings wanting to collaborate on Community programmes*; relay of information on programmes; some members have a 'contact' role: training in computer accessing. 16, avenue Bugeaud, 75116 Paris, France.

Asylum (Right of) Convention between the Twelve*, currently under amendment (to respect the human rights of economic refugees).
SEE FREEDOM OF MOVEMENT, FRONTIER CONTROL, SCHENGEN, SIS, VISAS.

Atmospheric Pollution Regulation* for a programme to regularly survey damage to forests. Directive* of 1991 (OJ* 242, 30/8/1991) on standards* for exhaust emissions from all motor vehicles, applicable on 1/7/1992 or 31/12/1992, depending on the type of vehicle concerned. Budget: 10m Ecus* (1987-1991).
SEE ENVIRONMENT, HEAVY GOODS VEHICLES.

Atypical Work Draft Directives* on harmonization* of legislation on social security, the rights, training*, working conditions* and minimum requirements on health* and safety* of part-time and temporary workers* (fixed-term contracts, temporary contracts) to prevent distortions of competition*.

Authorized Representative Undertaking which is established in the Community* and is treated in the same way as the manufacturer regarding obligations imposed by Directives* and responsibility for the products it markets.

Automatic Public Tendering Community tendering provided for by the regulation of *public contracts**, with the exception of sectors provisionally excluded* from the opening up of these contracts.

Agricultural products: the Commission* may decide to put up for sale goods detained by intervention agencies* by means of this procedure, which also fixes the amount of refund* for sugar and cereals.
SEE COMMON AGRICULTURAL POLICY.

Automotive Industry This industrial sector is affected by draft Directives* on pollution (SEE ENVIRONMENT), by the harmonization of technical regulations* and by competition* law (EXEMPTION* REG.* 123/85/EEC, OJ* L 15, 18/1/1985, ON DISTRIBUTION AGREEMENTS).
Under certain conditions the Commission* may authorize official aid. Since 1/1/1989 authorization has been compulsory for all subsidies over 12m Ecus*.
Import* quotas* are negotiated with non-member countries*. Directive* concerning third-party insurance*.
SEE CARMAT 2000, LOCAL CONTENT.

B

BABEL (Broadcasting Across the Barriers of European Languages) Community programme* (1988) designed to promote multilingualism in European satellite programmes. Financial support for dubbing, sub-titling, multilingual productions and professional training* and technological research*.

Bank An institution whose everyday business involves receiving money from the public, by way of deposit or otherwise, which it uses for its own benefit in discount, credit or other financial operations (definition in French law, act of 13/6/1941).
18/12/1989: Directives* on the liberalization of banking services: freedom to provide services* in the Community* for any bank with a licence in a Member State*; standardization* of the regulations governing equity capital* (DIR.* OF 7/4/1989, OJ* 1124, 1989) and on solvency ratios* (fixed at 8%) (DIR.* OF 18/12/1989, OJ* L 386, 1989); reciprocity* for non-Community banks if the governments of their countries grant EC* banks the same treatment in the applicant country (comes into force 1/1/1993).
SEE EUROPEAN INVESTMENT BANK, EUROPEAN BANK FOR RECONSTRUCTION AND DEVELOPMENT, PAYMENT CARD, SINGLE LICENCE.

Bank for International Settlements Club of central banks, established in 1930; manages the EMCF* and the financial operations connected with the administration of the EMS*. Headquarters in Basel, Switzerland; the governors of the banks meet there every month to settle matters concerning monetary strategy.

Banking Federation of the EEC European organization of the professional organizations of Belgium, France, Germany, Italy, Luxembourg and the Netherlands (1960). Relations with the Community* and with non-member countries*.

BAP (Biotechnology Action Programme) Community research* programme* in biotechnology* (bio-computing, biotic materials, biological research* for application in industry and agriculture*). Budget: 75m Ecus* (1985-1989). Decision* 88/240/EEC (OJ* L 206,

30/7/1988). DG XII of the Commission*. For 1990-1994 SEE BRIDGE. DG XIII of the Commission*.
SEE BIOLOGY, BIOTECHNOLOGY, EBCG, RESEARCH AND TECHNOLOGICAL DEVELOPMENT FRAMEWORK PROGRAMME.

Barriers The treaties* establishing the European Communities* and the Single European Act* aim to establish a Common Market*, an area without internal frontiers*: this entails removing the *physical barriers* (customs controls of goods and persons, national quota* restrictions for non-member countries*), *technical barriers* (different national specifications – standards* and regulations; compartmentalization of public contracts*; barriers to the freedom of movement* of persons, to the freedom to provide services*, to the freedom of movement of capital*, to competition*; legal and fiscal barriers to cooperation between businesses and regarding patent rights) and *fiscal barriers* (VAT*, excise* duties, taxes on savings).
SEE CUSTOMS CLEARANCE, FRONTIER CONTROL.

Basel-Nyborg Agreements These agreements came out of an informal meeting of the Economics and Finance Ministers of the Twelve* on 12/9/1987. They strengthen monetary cooperation within the EMS* by creating a more flexible and better balanced system whilst maintaining the initial objective of greater internal and external stability (prices and exchange rates) in Europe.
Measures designed to increase alignment of monetary policy: bi-annual monitoring by the Monetary Committee* of possible inconsistencies and developments incompatible with those in non-member countries* and monthly study of the progress of exchange rates and interest rates; monitoring by the Committee of Governors of intervention policy and of exchange rates and interest rates in order to facilitate suitable responses from the countries within the EMS* and from non-member countries* regarding their currencies. Aims: to defend the stability of the EMS* parity structures, to discourage speculation, to limit monetary realignment, and to take into account disruptions which might be caused by developments in currencies of non-member countries*.
Measures designed to improve the intervention mechanism of the EMS:* the possibility of very short term financing (90 days, renewable) was extended to European central banks for intervention when currencies do not keep within the margins permitted them; the Ecu* to take on a liberalizing role as a completely separate currency in relations between European central banks. *Aim*: to

make 'intramarginal' operations official; they are not explicitly provided for in the documents establishing the EMS*.
SEE EUROPEAN FINANCIAL AREA.

Basket of Currencies Currencies whose fluctuations on the exchange market are used to determine the value of the Ecu* (or of any other currency).
SEE EMS.

BCC
SEE BUSINESS COOPERATION CENTRE.

BCNET (Business Cooperation NETwork) Decentralized network of business advisers completed in 1988 by the Business Cooperation Centre (BCC*) in the Commission*: coordination of offers of and requests for transnational cooperation on a financial, commercial or technical level. DG XXIII of the Commission* (BCC) 80, rue d'Arlon, 1040 Bruxelles, Belgium.
SEE EURO INFO CENTRES.

BCR (Community Bureau of Reference) Community programme* to improve the reliability of chemical analyses and physical measurements (applied meteorology and reference material) in order to produce equivalent results in all Member States*. Budget: 59.2m Ecus* (1988-1992). Decision* 88/418/EEC (OJ* L 206, 30/7/1988). DG XII of the Commission*.
SEE CHEMISTRY.

Benelux Abbreviation of the Economic Union of Belgium (BE), the Netherlands (NE) and Luxembourg (LUX), established by the treaty of The Hague on 3/2/1958 (came into force 1/12/1960). Intergovernmental cooperation in economic, monetary, fiscal, customs and foreign policy matters. Headquarters in Brussels*, Belgium.
SEE CUSTOMS UNION, FREE TRADE, TAXATION.

BEP (Biomolecular Engineering Programme) Community programme*. DG XIII of the Commission*.

BEUC (Bureau Européen des Unions de Consommateurs)
SEE EUROPEAN BUREAU OF CONSUMERS' UNIONS.

BIAC (Business and Industry Advisory Committee to the OECD*) 13/15, Chaussée de la Muette, 75016 Paris, France.

BIC
SEE BUSINESS INNOVATION CENTRES.

Biology
SEE BAP, BEP, BIOTECHNOLOGY, BRIDGE, EBCG, ECLAIR, EMBL.

Biomedical Research and Health Community programme* to ensure better research coordination and to pool available resources: standardization* of the methods and protocols in epidemiology, biology* and clinical research, socio-economic effects on illness and analysis of the human genome. Budget: 133m Ecus* (1990-1994).
SEE GMO.

Biotechnology The White Paper* provides for legal protection in this sector (SEE COM (88) 396) for protecting the environment* and people against the risks arising from the use and dissemination of GMO* (Genetically Modified Organisms): pesticides, chemical products etc.
SEE BAP, BIOTECHNOLOGY (PROGRAMME), BRIDGE, EBCG, ECLAIR.

Biotechnology (Programme) Community programme* designed to strengthen basic biological knowledge and to design technology for application in agriculture*, industry*, medicine*, foodstuffs* etc. Budget: 164m Ecus* (1990-1994).
SEE BIOTECHNOLOGY, ENVIRONMENT.

Blue Angel Internal compilation of the CAP* documents by the Commission* departments. Programme of eco-labelling adopted by Germany to reduce waste* and pollution caused by 3000 products.
SEE ENVIRONMENT, LABEL.

Bonds Negotiable securities with a life span of two or more years from date of issue, whose interest rate and the methods for repaying the principal and for paying interest are fixed at issue.
SEE EUROPEAN FINANCIAL AREA, FREEDOM TO PROVIDE SERVICES, MOVEMENTS OF CAPITAL.

Bonn Federal Republic of Germany.
10/2/1961: Summit (Fouchet* plan).
16-17/7/1978: Summit of Western heads of state and government (economic and monetary affairs).

3/12/1976: convention on protecting the Rhine against chemical pollution.

Boomerang Clause Clause in the EEC* treaty (art. 91.2) and the EFTA* convention (art. 17.2) requiring every Member State* to accept the return of goods exported to another Member State* free of customs duty*, tax, quantitative restrictions* or measures having equivalent effect* in order to protect them against dumping* and subsidy.

BRAIN (Basic Research in Adaptive Intelligence and Neurocomputing) Community programme*. Sub-programme of SCIENCE*. DG XII of the Commission*.

Branch For the advertising of branches established in a Member State* by certain forms of company which come under the law of another Member State*, see Dir.* 68/151/EEC, 21/12/1989 (OJ* L 395, 30/12/1989).
SEE COMPANY LAW, FREEDOM OF ESTABLISHMENT, GROUP TAXATION, SUBSIDIARY.

BRIDGE (Biotechnology Research for Innovation, Development and Growth in Europe) Community programme* to stimulate transborder research* for more rapid production of the biological data, materials and processes necessary for the optimum use of natural organisms: infrastructures, information, adaptive technology, cellular biology and standards* research*. Budget: 100m Ecus* (1990-1994).
SEE OJ* L 360, 9/12/1989. DG XII of the Commission*. This programme is an extension of the BAP* programme.

BRITE (Basic Research in Industrial Technologies for Europe) Community programme* to stimulate modernization of production methods with advanced technology*: manufacturing, chemical*, textile* and metal construction industries. BRITE 2: Budget of 185m Ecus* (1987-1992). Decision* 88/108/EEC (OJ* L 59, 4/3/1988). Merged with EURAM*. See OJ* L 98, 11/4/1988 (includes the Aeronautics* programme): Budget of 499.5m Ecus*. DG XII of the Commission*.

Broad Balance Principle invoked by the United Kingdom in 1974 to justify an adjustment to the contribution of a Member State* to the Community* budget*, where an unacceptable situation results from the fact that payment of own resources*

exceeds what the Member State* would have had to pay if its own resources* had been calculated as its share of the sum of GNPs of all Member States*.
SEE EUROPEAN COUNCIL.

Broadcasting The White Paper* provides for the establishment of a common market* for broadcasting: harmonization* of technical standards*, abolition of legal obstacles (SEE COPYRIGHT).
2-3/12/1988 (European Council* of Rhodes): France proposed a EUREKA* for broadcasting to promote European standards* and the European high-definition TV system (HDTV*) in non-member countries*; the establishment of a EEIG*; meeting on broadcasting in Europe (9/1989); nomination of a EUREKA* officer for broadcasting.
3/10/1989: Directive* on television broadcasting. Any discrimination against broadcasts from another Member State* is proscribed within the Community* (SEE FREEDOM TO PROVIDE SERVICES).
3/1990: Commission* programme of action for 1991-1995 (250m Ecus*) to replace the MEDIA* programme (1986): establishment of a 'European broadcasting area' (training; revival of the programme-making industry in the EC*; new technology; distribution and promotion of sales; finance; multilingualism).
SEE ADVERTISING, BABEL, CERISE, TELEVISION WITHOUT FRONTIERS.

Brokerage
SEE INVESTMENT SERVICES.

Brokersguide Annual register (data base*) of information brokers, compiled by EIMAG (European Information Market Development Group). DG XII of the Commission*.

Brussels Capital of the Kingdom of Belgium. Offices of some of the departments of the Commission* of the European Communities*, of the Council* and of the European Parliament*.
12/1985: European Council*.
8/4/1965: treaty (came into force 1/7/1967): single Commission, single Council*.
22/1/1972: treaty (came into force 1/1/1973): accession of Denmark*, the Republic of Ireland* and the United Kingdom* to the EEC* and to EURATOM*.
10/7/1975: treaty (came into force 1/10/1977) amending the statute of the EIB*.
22/7/1975: treaty (came into force 1/6/1977) establishing the

Court of Auditors* of the European Communities* and increasing the budgetary powers of the European Parliament* (SEE DISCHARGE, TREATY OF LUXEMBOURG).
20/7/1976: treaty (came into force 1/7/1978): signing of the Act* concerning the election of representatives of the European Parliament* by direct universal suffrage; approved by the Council* 20/9/1976; came into force 1/7/1978 after ratification by the national parliaments.
12/1978: agreement on the EMS*.
2/6/1988: agreement on the fourth resource* (SEE BUDGET).

BSI (British Standards Institution)
SEE EOTC, STANDARDS, TECHNICAL SPECIFICATIONS.

BT Technical bureau of CEN*/CENELEC*.

Budget of the Community*: administrative appropriations of the Community* institutions plus operational appropriations to finance interventions*. *Resources* come from contributions from the Member States* (proportional to GNP; SEE FOURTH RESOURCE) and from own resources* (ab initio for the ECSC* and since 1971 for the EEC* and EURATOM*). The latter consist of levies* on imports* of agricultural products from non-member countries*, of customs duties collected at the external frontiers of the Community, of taxes introduced under the Common Agricultural Policy* (CAP) and by a fraction of the VAT* levied in Member States*, up to 1.4% of the amount in each state. The European Parliament* has the last word on non-compulsory expenditure*. *Budgetary procedure* (see figure): the Commission* proposes a preliminary draft budget to the Council* based on the forward projects of the various institutions* (DG XIX). The Council* proposes a draft budget to the Parliament* which examines it in committee* and in plenary sitting. The budget is adopted if the Council* adopts the amendments* to the proposals on non-compulsory expenditure* voted in by the European Parliament* at the first reading. If it amends or rejects these amendments* the draft is remitted (by a two thirds majority*) to the Parliament* for a second reading. The Parliament* has fifteen days to act by a two thirds majority* of the votes cast. The 'Trialogue'*, a conciliation procedure between the Council*, the Parliament* and the Commission* may be used to overcome difficulties. If the President of the Parliament approves the draft, the budget is adopted and he gives a 'discharge'* to the Commission* for its implementation. If

BUDGETARY PROCEDURE

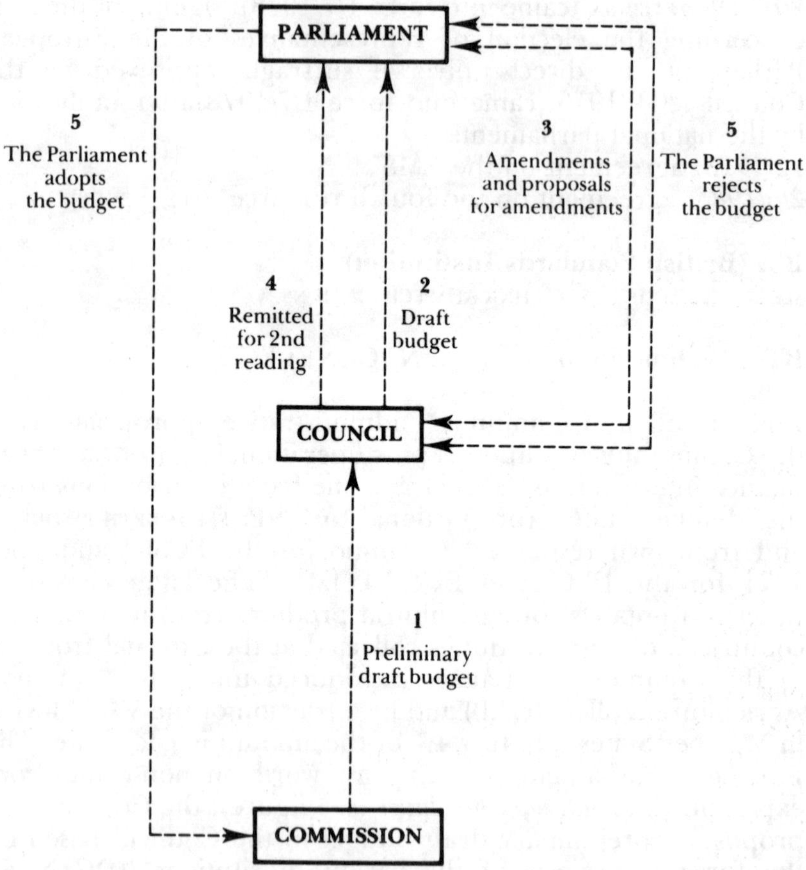

Source : P. Pelou, *L'Europe de l'information* (EME).

he does not adopt the draft the Community operates according to the provisional twelfth system.
The Parliament* may propose amendments* to compulsory expenditure* if they do not increase the total volume of the budget. The Council* may reject them by a qualified majority*. The Parliament totally rejected the budget in 1979 and in 1984. It rejected a supplementary budget in 1982. In 1986 the Court of Justice* of the EC* rescinded a decision made by the President of the Parliament* on the budget. This

judgement set the limits for this prerogative and clarified the interpretation of certain of the rules regarding the budget. The Court of Auditors* monitors the general Community* budget and the ECSC* operating budget for conformity to rules and good external management. The financial controller of each institution controls its internal affairs.
SEE SINGLE EUROPEAN ACT.

Budgetary Compensation Principle invoked by the United Kingdom in 1980 and 1982 to obtain the rebate of a part of its contribution to the Community* budget* arguing that it was the primary 'net debtor' in the Community*. The principle was made official at the European Council* of Fontainebleau (1984) in the form of reduced VAT* payments; it has been used by the United Kingdom, Germany, Spain and Portugal.
SEE BROAD BALANCE.

Building Contractors of the European Community 3, rue de Berri, 75008 Paris, France.

Bureau Managing body of a Community institution*, elected by the members of the institution.
Bureau of the European Parliament:* the President and the 14 Vice-presidents (responsibilities: financial and organizational matters, preliminary estimates, internal financial regulation, general secretariat, membership of committees* and committees of inquiry*, reports for the Council of Europe* etc.).
Enlarged bureau: the bureau plus the group chairmen.
Responsibilities: internal organization, relations with other institutions*, preliminary estimates, parliamentary agenda, oral questions and their debate, written or oral questions for 'question time', legislative programme, speaking time for the non-attached, seating allocation in the Parliament*, extra-ordinary sittings of Parliament*, preliminary authorization for own-initiative reports*, appointment of sub-committees*, hearing* experts etc.
Bureau of committees: a Chairman plus between one and three Vice-chairmen.

Bureau de Rapprochement des Entreprises (BRE) The Bureau is represented by 290 correspondents spread throughout 43 countries. It is directly accessible to businesses for information on opportunities for collaboration that are not confidential in nature.

Business Cooperation Centre (BCC) Established by the Commission* in 1973 to facilitate cooperation between Member State* businesses (Europartenariat*). Set up the BC-Net* network within the SME* task-force (now part of DG XXIII of the Commission*).

Business Economy *22/12/1989*: a Council* communication* on the business economy, defining its sectors and outlining the perspectives offered to businesses by 1992 and their part in Community* policy; objective of equal treatment for businesses in the single market*.

Business Innovation Centres Bring together local authorities, banks and businesses; possibly supported by the Commission* in priority regions (under-development, industrial reconversion, depressed agricultural regions). Set up along lines proposed by the EC*, they are primarily concerned with people wanting to implement technological and industrial projects. *Aims*: to seek out possible business innovators; enable them to receive training; help with setting up the business; follow the development of the project (organizational assistance, advice); help with financing; provide technological information. Exchanges with other centres via the European Business Innovation Centre Network (EBN). DG XVI of the Commission*.
SEE ECSC FUNDS, EUROPEAN REGIONAL DEVELOPMENT FUND, REGIONAL POLICY.

C

C Abbreviation used by the OJ* to denote Information and Notices publications.
SEE OOPEC.

Cabotage Operation by a carrier of one Member State* of transport services in another Member State*, provided for in art. 75, 1b of the EEC* treaty. Also applicable for road transport*, within certain limits (REG.* 4059/89, 21/12/1989, OJ* L 390/3, 30/12/1989). Under the terms of art. 84, 2 of the EEC* treaty, the principle should also apply to shipping (REG.* 4055/86) and air transport* from 1/1/1993 (a company permitted to transport passengers between two towns in the same foreign country).
SEE QUOTA.

CACM
SEE CENTRAL AMERICAN COMMON MARKET.

CADDIA (Cooperation in Automation of Data and Documentation for Imports/exports and the management of financial control of the Agricultural market) Community programme* to prepare an efficient computer data exchange system ('project CD'):
1. To automate information in the administration of European customs union*, the agricultural market organizations (see CMO) and the collection and dissemination of statistical data on Community* trade*.
2. To coordinate the activities of national governments.
3. To prepare standardization* within the Community.
Budget: 22.75m Ecus* (1987-1992). Council Decisions*: 85/214/EEC, 26/3/1985 (OJ* L96, 3/4/1985), 86/23/EEC, art. 2; 8/288/EEC (OJ* L145, 5/6/1987). DG XIII of the Commission*.
SEE AGRICULTURE, COMMON AGRICULTURAL POLICY, CUSTOMS (ALL ENTRIES).

CADOS (CAtalogue DOcumentaire de la Statistique) *(Documentary Catalogues for Statistics)*: Chronological series of statistics for the Community*.

CAEM (Conseil d'Assistance Économique Mutuelle)
SEE COMECON.

CAF (Coût, Assurance, Fret)
SEE CIF

CALL Data base* of invitations to tender from DG XIII/B (industry, and information market) of the Commission*.

CAP
SEE COMMON AGRICULTURAL POLICY.

Capital
SEE MOVEMENTS OF CAPITAL.

Capital and Reserves
SEE EQUITY CAPITAL.

CARMAT 2000 Project in the EUREKA* programme ('EU 13'): to build vehicle bodies based on new materials (France, Netherlands, Germany, United Kingdom . . .). Budget: 600m Ecus*(1987-1991).

Carnet Document issued by the responsible authority in the Member State* of departure so that goods may move throughout the Community* in accordance with the regulations on intra-community movements of goods*. It allows the responsible authorities in the Member States* through which the goods move to monitor the shipment, its re-export and re-import into the Member State* of departure. It must contain a signed commitment by the person(s) responsible for the shipment to pay any duties which might become due following any irregularity or infringement of regulations. Reg.* 8 3/84, 19/3/1983 (OJ* L 151, 7/6/1984).
SEE INTRACOMMUNITY MOVEMENT OF GOODS.

Cartel Horizontal agreement* whose parties operate in the same sphere of production or distribution and who coordinate their operations to limit competition* between each other.

Cassis de Dijon Name given to a judgement* of the CJEC* of 20/2/79 and to the *jurisprudence* resulting from it, whereby any product legally manufactured and marketed in one Member State* must be permitted to be made freely available for consumption in another Member State* without opposition from any particular national regulations, unless these are justified by reasons of general interest ('legitimate reasons').
SEE MUTUAL RECOGNITION, NEW APPROACH, STANDARDS, STANDARDIZATION.

CASSTM
SEE ADMINISTRATIVE COMMISSION ON SOCIAL SECURITY FOR MIGRANT WORKERS.

CBI
SEE CONFEDERATION OF BRITISH INDUSTRY.

CCA (CENELEC Certification Agreement) Certification agreement concerning low voltage electrical equipment for public consumption, signed in 1968 by the members of CENELEC*. An amendment (3/1987) allows the use, under certain conditions, of test results carried out in manufacturers' laboratories to obtain national marks* of conformity to standards*.
SEE CE, COMMUNITY SUPPORT FRAMEWORK, ETSI, ITSTC, MUTUAL RECOGNITION, NEW APPROACH, STANDARDS, TECHNICAL BARRIERS.

CCC
SEE CUSTOMS COOPERATION COUNCIL.

CCCN (Customs Cooperation Council Nomenclature)
SEE CUSTOMS COOPERATION COUNCIL.

CCIR (Comité Consultatif International des Radiocommunications)
SEE INTERNATIONAL RADIO CONSULTATIVE COMMITTEE.

CCL-TRAIN Community data base*: summaries of scientific and technical publications from the Commission* (DG XIII of the Commission*).

CCMGP
SEE ACPM.

CD Project (Coordinated Development of computerized administrative procedures) Project in the CADDIA* programme to establish the infrastructure and data processing services necessary to allow the Commission* and Member States* to obtain and process rapidly and efficiently the information required for the operation of customs union* and the Community's* commercial policies. Decision* 86/23/EEC, 4/2/1986, OJ* L 33, 8/2/1986.

CE
SEE COUNCIL OF EUROPE. Also the French abbreviation for European Community* (Communauté Européenne).

CE (Certificat Européen) The European standard* mark which indicates that the product meets the essential requirements* of the relevant 'new approach'* Directives* and can be marketed in all Member States* without retesting.
SEE CEN, CENELEC.

CEA
SEE EUROPEAN CONFEDERATION OF AGRICULTURE.

CEC
SEE COMMISSION OF THE EUROPEAN COMMUNITIES, COUNCIL OF MINISTERS OF THE EUROPEAN COMMUNITIES.

CECA (Communauté Européene du Charbon et de l'Acier) French name for the European Coal and Steel Community*.

CECC (CENELEC* Electronic Components Committee) Works out standards* and technical specifications*.

Cecchini (Paolo) Senior European official, author of a report entitled 'The European Challenge – 1992: The Benefits of a Single Market' (2/1988) resulting from a survey of 11000 businesses: it evaluates the cost of keeping the market divided and the advantages of a Single Market*.
SEE NON EUROPE.

CECODE (Centre Européen du COmmerce de DÉtail)
SEE EUROPEAN CENTRE OF RETAIL TRADE.

CEDEFOP (Centre Européen pour le DÉveloppement de la FOrmation Professionnelle)
SEE EUROPEAN CENTRE FOR THE DEVELOPMENT OF VOCATIONAL TRAINING.

CEE (Communauté Économique Européenne) French name for the European Economic Community*.

CEEA (Communité Européenne de l'Énergie Atomique) French name for the European Atomic Energy Community.
SEE EURATOM.

CEEP (Centre Européen de l'Entreprise Publique)
SEE EUROPEAN CENTRE OF PUBLIC ENTERPRISES.

CEFIC (Conseil Européen des Fédérations de l'Industrie Chimique)
SEE EUROPEAN COUNCIL OF CHEMICAL MANUFACTURERS' FEDERATIONS.

CEI-BOIS (Confédération Européenne des Industries du BOIS) *(European Confederation of Woodworking Industries)*: 109-111, rue Royale, 1000 Bruxelles, Belgium.

CEJA (Comité d'Entente des Jeunes Agriculteurs de la CEE) COPA* working party for young farmers.

CELEX Data base* of Community law* since 1951 (treaties*, agreements* with non-member countries*, secondary and supplementary Community law*, OJ*, decisions of the Court of Justice*, Community* and national legislation, etc.). Established in 1970. German, English, French, Italian, Dutch. DG IX of the Commission*. On-line data service via EURIS*.
SEE EUROBASES.

CEN (Comité Européen de Normalisation) *(European Committee for Standardization)*: French acronym used universally. Made up of the standards* institutes of the EC* and EFTA* countries; their job is to work out European standards* and to receive notification* of proposed national standards* from national standards* bodies. 2, rue Brederode, 1000 Bruxelles, Belgium.
SEE BARRIERS, BEUC, CE, CENCER, CENELEC, CONSUMPTION, NEW APPROACH.

CENCER (CEN-CERtification) CEN* certification committee (CENCER mark* or mutual recognition*).
SEE TECHNICAL BARRIERS, STANDARDS.

CENELEC (Comité Européen de Normalisation ÉLECtrotechnique) *(European Committee for Electrotechnical Standardization)*: French acronym used universally. Operates in Brussels in coordination with CEN* (same address).
SEE CCA, STANDARDS, TECHNICAL REGULATION.

CENELEC Certification Agreement
SEE CCA.

CENELEC Electronic Components Committee
SEE CECC.

Central American Common Market (CACM) Regional group in the Generalized System of Preferences* (GSP).

Central Bureau For Nuclear Measurements (CBNM) Part of the Joint Research Centre* (JRC) set up under the terms of the EURATOM* treaty (art. 8). Geel, Belgium.

Central Rate Conversion rate (national currency and Ecus*) fixed by agreement between the finance ministers of the Member States* in the EMS* exchange rate mechanism.

Centre For Industrial Development (CID) International body set up in 1977 (art. 36 of the Lomé* convention*) to help establish and support SME* in the ACP* countries. It has no equity capital (except for 40m Ecus* allocated by Lomé* III) and works in close liaison with credit institutions*. It encourages industrial projects with information, studies, financial assistance, training* and investment advice. One director and one assistant director nominated by the ACP*-EEC* Committee on Industrial Cooperation. 28, rue de l'Industrie, 1040 Bruxelles, Belgium.
SEE ACP, EUROPEAN DEVELOPMENT FUND, EUROPEAN INVESTMENT BANK, LDCs.

CEPAC (Confédération Européenne de l'industrie des pâtes, PApiers et Cartons)
SEE EUROPEAN CONFEDERATION OF PULP, PAPER, AND BOARD INDUSTRIES.

CEPFAR (Centre Européen pour la Promotion et la Formation en milieu Agricole et Rural)
SEE EUROPEAN TRAINING AND PROMOTION CENTRE FOR FARMING AND RURAL LIFE.

CEPT (Conférence Européenne des administrations des Postes et Télécommunications)
SEE EUROPEAN CONFERENCE OF POSTAL AND TELECOMMUNICATIONS ADMINISTRATIONS.

Cérame Unie
SEE LIAISON OFFICE OF CERAMIC INDUSTRIES OF THE COMMON MARKET.

CERD (Comité Européen de Recherche et Développement)
SEE EUROPEAN RESEARCH AND DEVELOPMENT COMMITTEE.

CERISE (Centre Européen de Recherche d'Images de Synthèse) *(European Centre for Image Synthesis Research)*: Project in the EUREKA* programme ('EU 15'): two- and three-dimensional images for audiovisual graphics (France, Netherlands, Germany, United Kingdom). Budget: 600m Ecus* over 5 years.

CERN (Organisation Européenne pour la Recherche Nucleaire) (Formerly: *European Centre for Nuclear Research. Now: European Organization for Nuclear Research* (same acronym)): Established in 1954 by 14 European countries (Austria, Belgium, Denmark, France, Germany, Greece, Italy, Netherlands, Norway, Portugal, Spain, Sweden, Switzerland, United Kingdom): pure and scientific nuclear research (non-military). Administers the European Particle Physics Laboratory (particle acceleration: synchrotron etc.). 1211 Genève 23, Switzerland. Prévessin, 01631 CERN Cédex, France.

CERTIFICAT Proposed Community data base* on certification.

Certificat Européen
SEE CE.

Certificate of Conformity Mark of conformity, result of tests carried out by a third party, statement of conformity and other means allowing a product to be declared in conformity with harmonized* standards* or, failing this, with national standards* (COUNCIL* RESOLUTION* OF 7/5/1985, OJ* 85/C 136/01).
SEE EVALUATION OF CONFORMITY, NEW APPROACH, OVERALL APPROACH.

Certificate of Designation of Region Certificate issued by the appointed authority or body, stating that the goods concerned fulfil the conditions laid down to qualify for designation of a particular fixed region (wines from Champagne, Oporto (Port), cheese from Parma (Parmesan) etc.). See also annex D2 of the Kyoto Convention on simplifying and harmonizing customs procedures, 18/5/1973.

Certificate of Origin Document proving that goods for import* are of Community* (or Member State*) origin*; issued following a written request. Reg.* 802/68/EEC, 27/6/1968 (OJ* L 148/1, 28/6/1968).
SEE COMMITTEE ON ORIGIN, PRODUCT ORIGINATING IN THE EC.

Certification of Conformity Act by which a third party attests

that it is reasonable to assume that a product, process or service is in conformity with a standard* or a certified standards* document.
SEE BARRIERS, STANDARDS.

Certification of Quality Control Systems To evaluate and confirm the conformity of quality control systems in a business to one of the models relating to these systems.

Certified Declaration of Origin Declaration of origin* certified by an authorized authority or body.
SEE CUSTOMS ENTRY, DECLARATION OF ORIGIN, ORIGIN.

CG (Coalition des Gauches) Left Unity group in the European Parliament*.

Charge Having Equivalent Effect
SEE MEASURE HAVING EQUIVALENT EFFECT.

Chemistry Council* Directives* to protect workers* against the dangers of exposure to chemical agents (16/12/1988 (OJ* L 356, 1988)); on testing control (87/18/EEC); Regulations* on exports and imports of certain products (88/1734/EEC; 89/428/EEC).
SEE BCR, ECDIN, EINECS, ENVIRONMENT, EUROPEAN COUNCIL OF CHEMICAL MANUFACTURERS' FEDERATIONS, HEALTH, PRECURSORS.

CIAA-UNICE
SEE COMMISSION OF THE AGRICULTURE AND FOOD INDUSTRIES OF THE UNION OF INDUSTRIES OF THE EUROPEAN COMMUNITY.

CID
SEE CENTRE FOR INDUSTRIAL DEVELOPMENT.

CIF (Cost, Insurance, Freight) This label on goods means that the price covers freight and insurance to the port of destination. For export* prices the label is followed by the name of the port of destination.

CIUTS (Collective Investment Undertaking for Transferable Securities) Investment company with variable capital and unit trusts, specializing in collective investment of capital in securities or other assets, subject to the spread of risk principle.
1/10/1989: any undertaking authorized in its own Member State* may market its shares in all other Member States* (DIR.*

85/611/EEC, 20/12/1985, OJ* L 3/5, 31/12/1985; DIR.* 88/320/EEC, 22/3/1988, OJ* L 300, 19/4/1988).
SEE FREEDOM TO PROVIDE SERVICES, MOVEMENTS OF CAPITAL, MUTUAL RECOGNITION, SINGLE LICENCE, TAXATION.

CJCE (Cour de Justice des Communautés Européennes)
SEE COURT OF JUSTICE.

CJEC
SEE COURT OF JUSTICE.

Clearing System for clearing and regulating securities transactions. Harmonization* of national systems has been proposed.

Climatology Community programme* for studying climate and its effects. Budget: 17m Ecus* (1986-1990). OJ* L 159, 14/6/1986; C 301, 25/11/1986. DG XII of the Commission*.

Clothing
SEE EUROPEAN ASSOCIATION OF CLOTHING INDUSTRIES, EUROPEAN TRADE UNION COMMITTEE FOR THE TEXTILE, CLOTHING AND LEATHER INDUSTRIES.

CMO (Common Market Organizations) General rules fixed at Community* level to organize the agricultural markets. In particular: *1. State intervention bodies* which may buy produce (cereals, sugar, milk, beef and sheepmeat – and certain varieties of fruits and vegetables) from producers who wish to sell, at a minimum fixed price (intervention price) for resale in the Community* or in non-member countries*. *2. Protective mechanisms* against foreign trade* for other products: wines other than table wines (whether they are stored or distilled), certain varieties of fruits and vegetables, flowers, eggs and poultry, by means of levies* and customs duties. *3.* Direct additional *aid** for products such as durum wheat, olive oil, certain oilseeds, cotton and tobacco* to compensate for weak or non-existent protection from foreign trade, or lump-sum aid* (per hectare or by quantity of produce) for producers of flax, hemp, hops, silkworms and seeds.
SEE AGRICULTURAL PRICES, COMMON AGRICULTURAL POLICY.

CN
SEE COMBINED NOMENCLATURE.

CNPF (Conseil National du Patronat Français)
SEE FRENCH NATIONAL COUNCIL OF EMPLOYERS

Coal
SEE COAL (PROGRAMME), ENERGY, EUROPEAN COAL AND STEEL COMMUNITY, NON-NUCLEAR ENERGY, RECHAR.

Coal (Programme) Community programme*: mining technology and product beneficiation. DG XII of the Commission*.

Coal Technology Research Community* technological research* programme (separate from RTD FRAMEWORK*): mining technology; product beneficiation. 1990-1994. DG XII of the Commission*.
SEE COAL.

COCCEE (Comité des Organisations Commerciales des pays de la CEE)
SEE COMMITTEE OF COMMERCIAL ORGANIZATIONS IN THE EEC COUNTRIES.

COCOS ESPRIT* project: Components for future Computing Systems (France, Italy, Germany).

CODEST (COmmittee for the European DEvelopment of Science and Technology). Committee consisting of 21 prominent people from the fields of science, technology and industry, nominated by the Commission* to advise it on its policy for stimulating scientific and technological potential in the Community*.
SEE FRAMEWORK PROGRAMME RESEARCH, RESEARCH AND TECHNOLOGICAL DEVELOPMENT.

COFACE (Comité des Organisations Familiales Auprès des Communautés Européennes)
SEE COMMITTEE OF FAMILY ORGANIZATIONS IN THE EUROPEAN COMMUNITIES.

COGECA General Committee of Agricultural Cooperatives in the EEC. Rue de la Science 23–25, Boîte 3, B–1040 Brussels, Belgium.

COLIPA (COmité de LIaison des associations européennes de l'industrie de la PArfumerie, des produits cosmétiques et de toilette)
SEE LIAISON COMMITTEE OF THE EUROPEAN FEDERATIONS OF THE PERFUME, COSMETICS AND TOILETRIES INDUSTRY.

College of Europe Postgraduate training institute. Diplomas in Community law* and economics. 1949. Dijver 11, 8000 Bruges, Belgium.

Combined Deal National provision which makes the import* of a product conditional upon either the export* or the purchase or the sale of a nationally produced product. This kind of 'barter' agreement is prohibited by art. 7 of the EEC* treaty*.

Combined Nomenclature Nomenclature which includes the Harmonized Commodity Description and Coding System*, the Community* subdivisions of this nomenclature ('CN subheadings' where rates of duty are specified under the nomenclature), preliminary provisions, supplementary notes to sections and chapters, and footnotes referring to Community* subheadings. See also Reg.* 2658/87/2658/EEC, 23/7/1987 (OJ* L 256, 7/8/1987).

Combined Tariff and Statistical Nomenclature Combined nomenclature, including the tariff nomenclature* and the statistical nomenclatures*, legally prescribed by the Contracting Party for declarations of goods for import*. Decision* 87/369/EEC.
SEE CUSTOMS (ALL ENTRIES).

COMECON (COuncil for Mutual ECONomic Aid) An intergovernmental organization (members: the Eastern Bloc countries, Cuba and Vietnam) to establish economic cooperation between its members (1949). Headquarters in Moscow. Relations with the EC (trade negotiations).

COMETT (COMmunity action programme in Education and Training for Technology) Community programme* of transnational education and training for industrial and technological development, to stimulate and strengthen cooperation between businesses and all post-secondary education training establishments. Regional or sectoral cooperation between universities and businesses; transnational exchanges of students and graduates. COMETT I: Budget of 45m Ecus* (1986-1989). OJ* L 222, 8/8/1986. COMETT II: Budget of 200m Ecus* (1990-1994). OJ* L 13, 1/11/1989. COMETT technical assistance unit, avenue Cortenberg 71, 1040 Bruxelles, Belgium.
SEE ERASMUS, EURYDICE, REGIONAL POLICY, YES.

COMEXT Statistical data base* of the current economic and social situation in the Community* and the monthly external trade statistics between Member States* and 200 countries (administered by EUROSTAT*).

Comité de Liaison Européen des Associations Hotelières des Six *(European Liaison Committee of Hotel Associations of the Six):* Committee without actual decision-making powers; reports to the Community*.

Comitextil Coordinating committee for the professional organizations of the European textile industries. Rue Montoyer 24, 1040 Bruxelles, Belgium.

Comitology A Council* Decision* of 13 July 1987 (87/3/3/EEC) lays down that committees are responsible for assisting the Commission* in implementing its Decisions*. There are four procedures: for advisory committees, management committees, regulatory committees and for common commercial policy* and safeguard clauses* (following receipt of the Opinion* of the advisory committee, the Commission* makes decisions for direct implementation which the Council* must confirm within three months). The Commission* proposes one of these procedures to the Council*. The European Parliament* has brought an action before the Court of Justice* of the EC* against this Council* Decision*.

Commercial Monopoly Trading monopoly of one commercial product which could be the object of competition* and trade* between Member States* and which could be a significant element in such trade*. All discrimination is prohibited: exclusive import*, export* or marketing rights (art. 37 of the EEC* treaty*). The alcohol monopolies in France and Germany, and the monopolies for tobacco manufactured in France and Italy are authorized in an adjusted form. Otherwise, public undertakings must be treated by the state in the same way as private undertakings (art. 90).
SEE AID.

Commission of the European Communities Community* institution conceived to uphold the treaties*, to be the Community's* executive body to initiate Community* policy and to represent the interests of the Community* in the Council*. *1/7/1967*: merger of the High Authority* of the ECSC* and the Com-

missions of the EEC* and of EURATOM* (treaty of 8/4/1965). The new Commission to continue to act in accordance with the provisions of the treaties* establishing each Community*. *17/2/1986*: the Single Act* strengthened its administrative powers.
17 Commissioners* are nominated by common agreement of the Member State* governments for four years (two for France, Germany, Italy, Spain, the United Kingdom, one for each of the seven other Member States*). One President and 6 Vice-presidents are appointed by the same procedure for two years (renewable).
Each Commissioner* has powers of authority over one or more departments (General Secretariat, Community spokesman, Joint Research Centre*, law, interpretation, conferences, Office of Official Publications*) and the twenty-three Directorates-General:
I External relations
II Economic and financial Affairs
III Internal market* and industrial affairs
IV Competition*
V Employment*, social affairs and education
VI Agriculture*
VII Transport*
VIII Development
IX Personnel and administration
X Information, communication and culture
XI Environment*, consumer* protection and nuclear safety
XII Science and research* and development
XIII Telecommunications*, information industries* and innovation
XIV Fisheries*
XV Financial institutions and company law*
XVI Regional policy*
XVII Energy*
XVIII Credit and investments
XIX Budgets*
XX Financial control
XXI Customs union* and indirect taxation*
XXII Coordination of structural instruments
XXIII SME*, tourism and social economics.
They take part in Council* meetings and attend the European Parliament*.
The Commission* adopts, by majority* voting, communications*, memorandums*, reports*, Regulations* or draft Regulations*

(Directives*, Decisions*, Recommendations*) which only it may submit to the Council*.

It has its own, independent powers in specific areas (ECSC*, EURATOM*, competition*) or as authorized by the Council*, whose Decisions* it implements. Recommendations* allow the Commission* to draw attention to the interests of the Community*.

It publishes an annual general report on the activities of the Communities*.

It monitors adherence to Community* legislation, with regard to both the implementation of the treaties* and of Community regulations* (safeguard clauses*, businesses, fines*, infringement procedures, reasoned Opinions*, referral* to the Court of Justice*). In particular it has significant responsibilities with regard to harmonization* to achieve the objectives of the ECSC* treaty* and to establish customs union* as laid down in the EEC* treaty*. It applies the rules of the treaties* in individual cases concerning governments and businesses (ECSC*, EURATOM*, competition*, Common Agricultural Policy* and establishing the internal market* as per the EEC* treaty*). It administers the Community* budget*, common policy, and Community funds*.

It represents the Community* at trade negotiations (SEE GATT) with the governments of important countries and with international organizations.

Its Decisions* are often prepared by technical committees (SEE COMITOLOGY). It also takes into account the Opinions* of the European Parliament* and of the Economic and Social Committee*, as well as suggestions from other bodies or persons.

Final Community* Decisions* are taken by the Council* after they have been debated by the European Parliament*. However, the Council* may only amend a proposal from the Commission* by a unanimous vote, while it only acts by a majority* if its decision corresponds to the Commission's proposal (cooperation procedure*).

The Commission* takes part in the budgetary procedure (SEE BUDGET, TRIALOGUE).

Each year it publishes a progress report* on the single market* programme (1985-1992) for the Parliament* and the Council* (SEE WHITE PAPER).

Bâtiment Berlaymont, 200 rue de la Loi, 1049 Bruxelles, Belgium.

Bâtiment Jean Monnet, Centre Européen, rue Alcide de Gasperi,

2920 Luxembourg (Statistical office, DG XIII, XVII, XVIII, 2 rue Mercier, 2985 Luxembourg (OOPEC*)).

Commission of the Agriculture and Food Industries of the Union of Industries of the European Community (CIAA-UNICE) Rue de la Loi 70, 1040 Bruxelles, Belgium.

Commissioner One of the 17 members of the Commission* of the European Communities, nominated for four years by his/her government, but independent of it and of the Council*. The Commissioners divide the responsibility for the files handled by the Commission* between them. One President and 6 Vice-presidents nominated by the national governments for 2 years (renewable).

Committee for the Monetary Union of Europe 19 member committee established in 1986: co-presidents: Valéry Giscard d'Estaing and Helmut Schmidt. Secretariat du Président Giscard d'Estaing, 18 rue François Ier, 75008 Paris, France – Büro H. Schmidt, Bundeshaus, 53000 Bonn 1, Germany.
SEE ASSOCIATION FOR THE MONETARY UNION OF EUROPE.

Committee of Agricultural Organizations in the European Community (COPA) Represented at the Commission* (1958). 23/25, rue de la Science, 1040 Bruxelles, Belgium.

Committee of Commercial Organizations in the EEC Countries (COCCEE) Body representing national commercial organizations at Community* level (1957). The Six* have active members. Secretariat in Brussels, Belgium.
SEE EUROPEAN CENTRE OF RETAIL TRADE, INTERNATIONAL WHOLESALE AND FOREIGN TRADE CENTRE, TRADE.

Committee of the Cotton and Allied Textile Industries of the EEC (EUROCOTON) Rue Montoyer 24, 1040 Bruxelles, Belgium.

Committee for the European Development of Science and Technology
SEE CODEST.

Committee of Family Organizations in the European Communities (COFACE) Association grouping together the main national family and professional organizations and the European

Community of Consumer Cooperatives (EUROCOOP). Rue de Londres 17, 1050 Bruxelles, Belgium.
SEE CONSUMPTION.

Committee of Ministers Highest decision-making body of the Council of Europe*, consisting of the foreign ministers of Member States. Meets twice a year. Permanent representatives meet twice a month.

Committee of Permanent Representatives (COREPER) Made official in 1965. It is responsible for preparing Council* decisions, coordinating the work of the various Council* study groups and for assisting and following through the work of the ministers. Its members are the ambassadors to the Community* of the Member States* (COREPER 2 – permanent representatives; COREPER 1 – assistant permanent representatives). They meet representatives of the Commission* every week. A proposal which has been agreed by COREPER becomes item A on the Council's* agenda and is adopted without debate. Otherwise it becomes item B and is debated. There are separate committees for agriculture (SEE SPECIAL COMMITTEE ON AGRICULTURE) and for monetary matters (SEE MONETARY COMMITTEE).

Committee of Small and Medium-sized Commercial Enterprises of the EEC Countries Specialist body of the International Federation of Small and Medium-sized Commercial Enterprises. Affiliated to the COCCEE.
SEE SME, TRADE.

Committee of Transport Workers' Unions in the European Community Representative body in Europe of national transport workers unions (1962).

Committee of Winegrowing Organizations in the European Community Representative body at Community* level (separate from COPA*).

Committee on Origin Committee consisting of representatives of the Member States* of the EC* and one representative of the Commission*, set up in 1968 to consider all matters relating to the application of regulations* on origin*. See also Reg.* 802/68/EEC, 27/6/1968 (OJ* L 148/1, 28/6/1968).
SEE CERTIFICATE OF ORIGIN, PRODUCT ORIGINATING IN THE EC.

Common Agricultural Policy (CAP) Policy broadly defined by art. 38 to 43 of the EEC* treaty* and supplemented by Council* Decisions*.
Objectives: to increase agricultural productivity by optimizing production factors; to ensure a fair standard of living for farmers and agricultural workers; to stabilize the markets; to guarantee supply; to ensure reasonable prices for consumers.
Administration: by the relevant Common Market Organization (CMO*) for each product or group of products (art. 40, 43 of the EEC* treaty*; main Decisions* in 1962, 1963, 1966 and 1968); the CAP operates on the following principles: *freedom of movement of products* within a single market*; *price maintenance*; *Community preference** (import levies* and export* subsidies for the most important products); co-responsibility* systems for producers for certain products; financial solidarity (EAGGF* guarantee section, 1962).
Since 1969 *Monetary Compensatory Amounts (MCA)** compensate for the effects of changes in monetary parity between Member States* where the latter have special parities relating to the effects of the CAP.
Since 1985 the Community* has given the CAP a new direction: expenditure by the guarantee section of the EAGGF* has been limited to 74% of the growth in GDP by volume; *guaranteed maximum quantity*; *mechanisms for stabilizing budgetary expenditure** for cereals, oleaginous products and protein products; set aside* of agricultural land (financial incentives); income aids (PAIA*) and encouragement for early retirement. The fourth resource* guarantees financing for the CAP until 1992. Where the Common Agricultural Policy is concerned, the rules are laid down by the Council* and methods for implementing it are adopted by the Commission*.
SEE ACP, BUDGET, CORESPONSIBILITY, EFTA, FINANCIAL AID, GATT, GUIDELINES, MECHANISMS FOR STABILIZING BUDGETARY EXPENDITURE, NON-MEMBER COUNTRIES, OWN RESOURCES, QUOTA, REGIONAL POLICY, SINGLE EUROPEAN ACT, STRUCTURAL POLICY,

Common Assembly The ECSC* treaty created a debating body, the *European Parliamentary Assembly*. When it became common to the EEC* and EURATOM*, under the name of Common Assembly, this body unilaterally adopted the name of European Parliament*. The Single European Act* made this change of name official.

Common Commercial Policy
SEE COMMON CUSTOMS TARIFF, NON-MEMBER COUNTRIES, SECONDARY COMMUNITY LAW.

Common Currency
SEE MONETARY UNION.

Common Customs Tariff (CCT) Tariff applicable at the external frontiers of the Community* by Member States* on imports* from non-member countries*. Common Commercial Policy* has been part of the objectives of the common market* – distinguishing it from a simple customs union* – since the treaties* of Rome* were signed and this tariff was introduced between 1959 and 1/7/1968 to prevent displacements in the patterns of trade which would have occurred if there had been large disparities between external customs duties*. Since 1968 the Council* has negotiated with non-member countries*, either directly or via GATT*.
1/1/1973: duties abolished for trade with the EFTA* countries. Revenue from the Common Customs Tariff contributes to the Community* budget*.

Common Foreign and Security Policy New name given to European Political Cooperation* following the 1991 intergovernmental conference* which prepared reform of the treaties* from the point of view of political union; particular stress is placed on *security* policy.

Common Market Popular name for customs union* as laid down in the EEC* treaty* of 25/3/1957, the aims of which are free movement of goods, persons, services and capital, as well as the establishment of common policies and a common foreign trade policy, all of which is to be implemented by the Community institutions*.
SEE COMMUNITY, EEC, FREEDOM OF MOVEMENT, OBJECTIVE 92, SINGLE MARKET, WHITE PAPER.
Name also of the sectors of the common market: agricultural common market, transport common market, energy* common market.

Common Market Organizations
SEE CMO

Common Purchase Agreement Not permitted between small

undertakings except to the extent where the purchasing capacity it creates does not go so far as to allow the partners to abuse their purchasing power to the detriment of suppliers.
SEE COMPETITION.

Communauté Européenne (CE) French term for European Community* (EC).

Communauté Européenne de l'Énergie Atomique (CEEA) French term for European Atomic Energy Community.
SEE EURATOM.

Communauté Européenne du Charbon et de l'Acier (CECA) French term for the European Coal and Steel Community* (ECSC).

Communication The name given to the form used by the Commission* for giving out information.
SEE COMPETITION.

Communications
SEE BROADCASTING, HDTV, RACE, TELECOMMUNICATIONS POLICY, TELEVISION WITHOUT FRONTIERS.

Communities The three European Communities (ECSC*, EEC* and EURATOM*), also called the European Community* or the Community*.

Community (or European Community, or EC) Used to describe the three Communities established by the treaties* of Paris (ECSC*) and of Rome (EEC* and EURATOM*).

Community Acceptance Member States* are obliged, subject to certain conditions (acceptance standards*) to accept products from other Member States* onto their territory.

Community Bureau of References
SEE BCR.

Community Data Banks
SEE AGREP, ARCOME, BROKERSGUIDE, CALL, CCL-TRAIN, CELEX, COMEXT, CRONOS, DIANEGUIDE, DOMIS, DUNDIS, EABS, ECDIN, ECHO, ECLAS, ELISE, ENDOC, ENREP, EUREKA, EURISTOTE, EURODICAUTOM, FFSRS, HTM-DB, ICONE, IES-DCI-3, INFO 92, IR-SOFT, MEDREP, MISEP, PABLI, RAPID, REGIO, REM, RURALNET, SABINE, SCAD, SESAME, SIGLE, TED, THESAURUS GUIDE.

Community Funds Funds established by the treaties* establishing the Communities* or set up by the Community* since as instruments for its intervention policies in social, regional, research*, development, energy* and environment* matters, etc.

Community Goods 1: produced or obtained entirely on the customs territory* of the Community*, without additions of goods from non-member countries*; 2: from non-member countries*, but which are in free circulation* in a Member State*; 3: produced on the customs territory* of the Community*, either from goods as in 2 or from goods as in 1 and 2. Reg.* 2144/87/EEC, 13/7/1987 (OJ* L 201, 22/7/1987). Where Community transit* is concerned: goods regularly entering the territory of a fixed Member State* via an internal frontier, unless an external Community transit* document accompanies them. Reg.* 222/77/EEC, 13/12/1976 (OJ* L 38, 9/2/1977).
SEE CUSTOMS (ALL ENTRIES), NON-COMMUNITY GOODS.

Community Institutions Name given to the four main institutions of the European Communities: the Council*, Commission*, European Parliament* and Court of Justice*. See diagram: The Community Institutions (page 24).
SEE SINGLE EUROPEAN ACT.

Community Law Law based on the treaties* (primary Community law*), acts* adopted to apply the treaties* (secondary Community law*) and supplementary Community law (Council* Decisions*, international agreements concluded between Member States* in application of the provisions of the treaties*, etc). Community law takes precedence over national law and is directly applicable.
SEE CELEX, COURT OF JUSTICE, DECISION, DIRECTIVE, EURIS, JUDGEMENT, PRIMARY COMMUNITY LAW, REGULATION, SECONDARY COMMUNITY LAW.

Community Legal System Autonomous legal system consisting of provisions arising out of the treaties* and from the Community institutions*, distinct from both the international and national legal systems; integration with these occurs via agreement* or convention* for international law and directly for national law.

Community Patent Proposal for a single patent (a single, unilateral title which would have the same significance as national

patents in all Member States*) introduced by the Luxembourg convention (15/12/1975), not yet ratified by Ireland and Portugal. *15/12/1989*: an intergovernmental conference in Luxembourg decided that the convention should come into force, following ratification, at the latest by 31/12/1995 or otherwise following a second intergovernmental conference. The European Patent Office (EPO) would keep central records of the patents it awarded, thus avoiding the necessity of translating them and sending them to national patent bodies.
Infringement actions would be possible before national courts of first and second instance (appeal*). Recognition of the validity and the effects of patents by a 'Common Appeal Court'.
SEE EUROPEAN PATENT, PATENT FOR INVENTION, RESEARCH POLICY, WHITE PAPER.

Community Policy
SEE COMMON AGRICULTURAL POLICY, COMMON COMMERCIAL POLICY, COMMON MARKET, COMMUNITY, COMPETITION, CONSUMPTION, CONVERGENCE, SINGLE EUROPEAN ACT, TELECOMMUNICATIONS POLICY, TRANSPORT POLICY.

Community Preference *Agriculture*: Community preference is granted by Member States* for agricultural foodstuffs* produced in the Community* (SEE COMMON AGRICULTURAL POLICY).
*Public contracts**: the Directive* on opening up excluded sectors* specifies that where similar offers are made by an EC* undertaking and a competitor in a non-member country*, preference must be given to the former where its offer varies by no more than 3% (DIR.* of 22/2/1990).

Community Programme Action programme co-financed by the Community* to promote development, research*, technology* transfer, cultural exchanges etc.

Community Quota For international trade, SEE QUOTA. *Transport*: aggregate amount of authorizations for international transport, fixed by means of various regulations at Community* level and shared between the Member States*.

Community Support Framework (CSF) Guidelines fixed by the Commission for the use of structural funds* over five years (1989-1993) for a State, a region* or part of a region affected by the objectives of the reform of the structural funds* (COUNCIL* REG.* 2054/88). A Member State* submits its request stating

the relevant form of intervention (operational programme, individual project, overall subsidy).
SEE BUDGET, STRUCTURAL FUNDS.

Community Trade Mark Commission* proposal to create a single trade mark*. Every trade mark would become applicable throughout the Community*. This would remove the necessity, currently in force, of having to submit separate applications for trade marks in each of the Member States* and would enable protection of trade marks throughout the Community* to be guaranteed (monopoly on the use of a trade mark with regard to third parties, excepting additional elements of quality) (COM (89) 209, 15/6/1989, OJ* C 26/, 19/10/1989). To be issued by a Community* trade mark office (OJ* C 230, 31/8/1984) and COM (86)/42 (OJ* C 67, 1987).

Community Transit Customs procedure whereby goods are transported, without customs control, from a customs office* in one country to a customs office* in the same or another country, crossing at least one frontier. It allows goods to be transported within the EC* or the EFTA* countries (Luxembourg* declaration of 15/6/1987) without undergoing a succession of internal customs procedures. See also Reg.* 222/77/EEC, 13/12/1977 (OJ* L 38, 9/12/1977), 1811/88/EEC, 23/6/1988 (OJ* C 162, 29/6/1988).
External Community transit: procedure for goods which do not satisfy the conditions in art. 9 and 10 of the EEC* treaty*; or for goods which do satisfy these conditions, but which are subject to customs formalities for refunds* on exports* to non-member countries* under the Common Agricultural Policy* (CAP); or for goods which come under the ECSC* treaty* and are thus not in free circulation* in the EC* 'T 1' declaration.
Internal Community transit: procedure for goods which satisfy the conditions in art. 9 and 10 of the EEC* treaty* (except in the case of refunds* on goods for export*); or for goods which come under the ECSC* treaty* and are put into circulation as Community goods* – 'T 2' declaration.
These procedures do not apply to the movement of goods under the temporary import* or temporary admission* procedures: each Member State* may apply its national procedure in such cases.
SEE CUSTOMS (ALL ENTRIES).

Companies
SEE COMPANY LAW, PUBLIC LIMITED LIABILITY COMPANY.

Company Law Art. 54.3 (g) of the EEC* treaty* provides for coordination of the safeguards required of companies to protect the interests of members and others.
This has been given concrete expression by Directives* on harmonizing* the conditions and obligations relating to publishing documents, setting up registers, validating shares and bonds, defining cases of nullity (1ST DIR.*, OJ* L 65, 14/3/1968), build-up and management of capital (2ND DIR.*, OJ* L 26, 1977), the interests of shareholders, creditors and employees in mergers (3RD DIR.* OJ* L 295, 1978) and divisions (6TH DIR.* OJ* L 378, 1982), the annual publication of accounts (4TH DIR.* OJ* L 222, 1978), the consolidation of accounts in cases of legal power of control of a parent company over its subsidiary (7TH DIR.* OJ* L 193, 193), auditors (8TH DIR.* OJ* L 12, 1984), the quotation of the same stock on several Community* stock exchanges* (OJ* L 66 1979, L 100 1980, L 48 1982, L 185 1987).
22/12/1989 (OJ* 395, 1989): 11th Directive* (harmonizing* the publication of particulars of branches established in a Member State* by members subject to the law of another Member State*; publication of separate accounts); and the 12th Directive*: PLCs with one member (single-member companies*).
Draft Directives* on the structure of PLCs (COM (83) 185, OJ* C 240, 1983), on transborder mergers* (COM (84) 727, OJ* C 23, 1985), on public purchase offers* (COM (88) 823, OJ* C 64, 1989).
Draft Regulations* on the European Public Limited Company* (COM (89) 268, OJ* C 263, 1989); on annual accounts and consolidated accounts (COM (89) 561, OJ* C 318, 1989). Regulation* on the control of concentrations* (21/12/1989, OJ* L 395, 1989). DG III and DG XV of the Commission*.
SEE EEIG, EUROPEAN FINANCIAL AREA, INSIDER INFORMATION, MERGER, PUBLIC PURCHASE OFFER, TAXATION.

Compensating Product Any product resulting from inward or outward processing*. See also Reg.* 85/1999/EEC; 86/2473/EEC.
SEE CUSTOMS (ALL ENTRIES), SECONDARY COMPENSATING PRODUCT.

Compensatory Levy Levy collected in the Member State* of manufacture to compensate for the effects of suspension or drawback of customs duties* or of other import* taxes in trade between Spain and Portugal and the other Member States*. Reg.* 526/86/EEC, 28/2/1986 (OJ* L 52, 28/2/1986).
SEE CUSTOMS (ALL ENTRIES).

Competition Competition policy is based on primary Com-

munity law* (art. 85 and 86 of the EEC* treaty* among others). The EEC* treaty* (art. 89 to 91 and 93) gives the Commission* important powers of control and sanction.
SEE AGREEMENT BETWEEN UNDERTAKINGS, CARTEL, CONCENTRATION, DOMINANT POSITION, FINE, MEASURE HAVING EQUIVALENT EFFECT, NATIONALIZATION, NOTIFICATION, AID, PENALTY PAYMENT, PUBLIC UNDERTAKING, TAX-FREE SHOP, TRANSPORT POLICY.

Compulsory Expenditure For the implementation of the Community's* commitments, particularly under international agreements with regard to common policy: operating the CAP* market organizations (SEE EAGGF) and financing a part of the structural funds*. This currently represents 75% of the Community* budget*, tending to be slightly reduced to the benefit of non-compulsory expenditure*.
The European Parliament* may propose amendments* to the compulsory expenditure at the first reading of the budget* if they do not increase its total. These amendments* are adopted if the Council* does not reject them by qualified majority*.

Computer Programs
SEE INFORMATICS, SOFTWARE.

Concentration The result of any act of any kind which involves the transfer of ownership or control of all or part of the rights, assets or bonds belonging to a business or which allows a business or a group of businesses to exert, either directly or indirectly, a decisive influence on one or more other businesses (French law).
In the Community: merger of two or more businesses, or direct or indirect takeover of one business by another, whether it be by purchase of shares or assets, by contract or any other means. Concentrations can affect intra-Community* trade; this justifies the control exerted over them by the Commission under art. 85 (prohibition of agreements between undertakings) and art. 86 (abuse of a dominant position*) of the EEC* treaty*. *21/12/1989*: Reg.* 4064/89, OJ* 1 395, 30/12/1989; 1 73, 20/3/1990 (Applicable on 21/8/1990) giving the Commission* the power to authorize concentrations in the Community*, if the total world turnover* of the undertakings concerned (or one tenth of total results for banks*, or the gross value of premiums issued for insurance* companies) exceeds 5000m Ecus* and if the individual turnover within the Community* of at least two of the undertakings concerned exceeds 250m Ecus* (where each

one earns more than 2/3 of its total turnover* in the Community* in one and the same Member State*).
Cases where there is a 'distinct market' may be referred to national authorities. National authorities may take supplementary measures to safeguard 'legitimate interests' (public security, prudential rules, media plurality).
A Member State* may ask the Commission* to consider whether a transnational concentration impedes competition* below the fixed thresholds. Thresholds will be revised before the end of 1993 by a qualified majority*. The Commission must be notified of the details of any concentration agreement in the Community* at most one week after it has been signed. The Commission* has one month to decide whether to authorize it or to start the appropriate procedure, which must take no longer than four months. Authorization is refused if the concentration creates or strengthens a dominant position*.
Task force of DG IV of the Commission*.

Concerted Practice A form of coordination between undertakings, which, without having actually signed an agreement, knowingly cooperate with one another rather than allowing themselves to be subject to the risks concomitant with competition* (Judgement* 14/7/19/2, 48/69). Prohibited under art. 85 of the EEC* treaty*.
SEE AGREEMENTS BETWEEN UNDERTAKINGS, AGREEMENTS BETWEEN UNDERTAKINGS.

Conciliation Procedure 1975. Procedure employed between the Council*, the Commission* and the European Parliament* when the last considers that the Council* is departing from its opinions* regarding Community* acts* which have important financial implications. Ad hoc procedure in cases of disagreement on an assent (SEE OPINION).

Condition of Reciprocity Whereby access of imported products to a national market, the granting of advantages, the recognition of approvals and certification are subject to the condition that the exporting Member State* or other Member States* authorize reciprocity*. It may be considered to be a measure having equivalent effect*, contrary to art. 30 of the EEC* treaty* (DIR.* 70/50/EEC, ART. 2, PARA. 3.0).

Confederation of British Industry (CBI) The CBI is the voice of British business. It is an employers' association representing the views of business across the board whether manufacturing or services, large or small companies, individual companies or trade associations. The CBI has a European Community Affairs Group, Centre Point, 103 New Oxford Street, London WC1A 1DU and a CBI Brussels Office, Rue des Deux Eglises 7, Bte 6, B–1040 Brussels, Belgium.

Conference on Security and Cooperation in Europe (CSCE) Intergovernmental conference of 34 states in Helsinki, Finland, between 1972 and 1975. The *Final Act* defined the principles of East-West cooperation including disarmament. Made official by the Paris conference of 19/11/1990.
19/6/1991: admission of Albania.
10/9/1991: admission of the three Baltic republics.
30-31/1/1992: Helsinki II conference. Admission of all the ex-Soviet republics except Georgia (disqualified by civil strife).

Confidentiality Principle accorded to undertakings which are under investigation by the Commission*; refers to their correspondence with their lawyers.

Conformity
SEE EVALUATION OF CONFORMITY.

Conseil de Ministres des Communautés Européennes (Conseil) French term for the Council of Ministers of the European Communities*.

Construction
SEE BUILDING CONTRACTORS OF THE EUROPEAN COMMUNITY.

Consultation Procedure Consultation of the European Parliament* is laid down by the EEC* treaty* (amended by the Single Act*) for, among other things, free movement of goods, CAP*, right of establishment*, transport policy*, association agreements* and in the areas of economic and social cohesion, research* and the environment*.
SEE PROCEDURE.

Consultative Assembly of the Council of Europe Former name of the Parliamentary Assembly of the Council of Europe* until 24/9/1974.

Consultative Committee on the European Social Fund Committee which assists the Commission* in the administration of the European Social Fund* (ESF). 36 members, nominated by governments and by organizations representing workers and employers.

Consumer(s)
SEE CONSUMPTION.

Consumer Credit A Directive* lays down the conditions for harmonizing* legal, regulatory and administrative provisions relating to consumer credit in the Member States* (87/102/EEC, 22/12/1986, OJ* L 42, 12/2/1987). Amended by a Directive* of 22/2/1990 (OJ* L 61 1990) (method for calculating the overall effective rate).

Consumers Contact Committee in the Common Market European consumers' organization: set up in 1962, dissolved on 14/2/1972.
SEE EUROPEAN BUREAU OF CONSUMERS UNIONS.

Consumption The White Paper* lists 96 measures to harmonize* legislation concerning the right to the protection of health* and safety* and of economic interests, the right to compensation for damage, to information*, to education and to representation. Qualified majority* at the Council* (Single European Act, Art. 18). Five-year programmes on consumer protection since 1975.
SEE ADVERTISING, BEUC, COFACE, COMPETITION, CREDIT, ENVIRONMENT, FLAIR, FOODSTUFFS, HEALTH, LABEL, SAFETY.

Contracting Authority Any state, local authority, body governed by public law and association formed by one or more these authorities or bodies governed by public law, which is entitled to award a public works* contract* or a public supply contract*.

Control of the activities of an undertaking.
SEE CONCENTRATION, MERGER.

Controlled Thermonuclear Fusion Community* research* programme on thermonuclear fusion and fusion technology*. Sub-programmes JET*, NET*, TOKAMAK. Budget: 735m Ecus* (JET* and general programme) (1988-1992). OJ* L 222, 12/8/1988 and L 286, 20/10/1988. DG XII of the Commission*.
SEE JOINT RESEARCH CENTRE.

Convention Association agreement with a group of countries.
Conventions signed by the EEC:
20/7/1963: Yaoundé* (1964-1969): cooperation and trade with 17 African countries and Madagascar.
1968: Arusha* (1968-1969): with the East African Community.
28/2/1975: Lomé* I (1975-1979): with 46 ACP* countries: commercial cooperation, free access for their products to the Community* market, price stability for 36 primary products (STABEX*), industrial and financial cooperation, common administration by joint institutions.
31/10/1979: Lomé* II (1981-1985): with 66 ACP* countries: cooperation in mining and energy (SEE SYSMIN), fisheries and employment.
8/12/1984: Lomé* III (1985-1990): financing of STABEX* and SYSMIN*, exemption from customs duty* (GSP*), prohibition of quantative restrictions* and of discrimination with regard to the right of establishment*, 7,160m Ecus* aid (aid, loans, equity capital) for development projects.
15/12/1989: Lomé* IV (1990-1995): 12,065m Ecus* (of which 1,200m as loans from the EIB*); accession of Haiti, the Dominican Republic and Namibia.
SEE ACP, LDC, STABEX, SYSMIN.

Conventional Law Part of secondary Community law*: consists of rules arising from agreements concluded between Member States* or between the Community* and non-member countries*.

Convergence The first stage of economic and monetary union* involves progressive convergence of the economic policies of the Member States*. Decision* of 12/3/1990 and OJ* C 100, 1990. The White Paper* stipulates alignment of national VAT* and excise* rates. See also COM (87) 324 (OJ* C 250, 1990).

Conversion of Production Measures to encourage Community* farmers to convert a part or all of their production to products for which there is not surplus production in the EC.* 25% financing by the EAGGF* (Guidance section).

Cooperation Set of provisions intended to aid LDCs* in their development, in particular by means of commercial, financial and technical conventions*.

Cooperation Agreement Agreement, usually concerning trade*, between the Community* and a state or a group of states,

which does not bind the two parties as completely as an association agreement*. The European Parliament* decides on all international agreements *of major importance*; it may ask the Council* to consult it before the start of negotiations on the conclusion of a trade and cooperation agreement. Examples: 10/1986: agreements with the Maghreb* and Machraq* countries; and with the EFTA* countries; agreement of 27/11/1989 with the USSR (reduction of quantitative restrictions*; 13/3/1990: agreement with the German Democratic Republic; 1/1/1990: outline agreement with the Gulf states came into force.
SEE SINGLE EUROPEAN ACT.

Cooperation Procedure Established by the Single European Act* (art. 149 of the EEC* treaty*), it is a 'shuttle' system (double reading) between the European Parliament*, the Commission* and the Council*, particularly in matters relating to establishing the internal market* (not including taxation*, freedom of movement of persons* and the rights and interests of paid workers), protection of the health* and safety* of workers*, protection of the environment* and public health* (a Member State* may take national decisions derogating from Community* provisions) and decisions relating to the implementation of the ERDF* and the research and technological development framework programme*.

a) The Commission* submits a proposal for a Directive* to the Council* which requests the opinion* of the European Parliament.
b) The Parliament* debates the proposal and submits proposals for amendments*.
c) The Commission* prepares, if necessary, a new proposal taking into account the amendments* submitted by the European Parliament*.
d) The Council* adopts a joint position* which is submitted to the Parliament with an explanatory memorandum*. The Commission* must also submit its observations.
e) The joint position* is given a second reading in the European Parliament*.
f) Conditions for definite adoption of the draft by the Council* depend on the position adopted by the Parliament. There are three possible scenarios:

1) If the Parliament approves the joint position* or makes no decision within three months, the Council* adopts the act* concerned.

2) If the Parliament rejects the joint position*, the Council* may only act in unanimity* at the second reading.
3) If the Parliament proposes amendments to the joint position* by an absolute majority* of its members, the Council* may approve, by qualified majority*, the text as amended by the Commission* taking into account the amendments* proposed by the European Parliament*. It must act in unanimity* if it wishes to amend the new proposal. If the Council* has made no decision within three months, the proposal by the Commission* is deemed to have not been adopted.
A Judgement* of the CJEC* of 22/5/1990 granted the EP* the power to introduce an action annulling a Community* Regulation*; this could lead to the Commission* and the Council* being forced to have recourse to the cooperation procedure.

The figure below is a more detailed representation of the cooperation procedure:

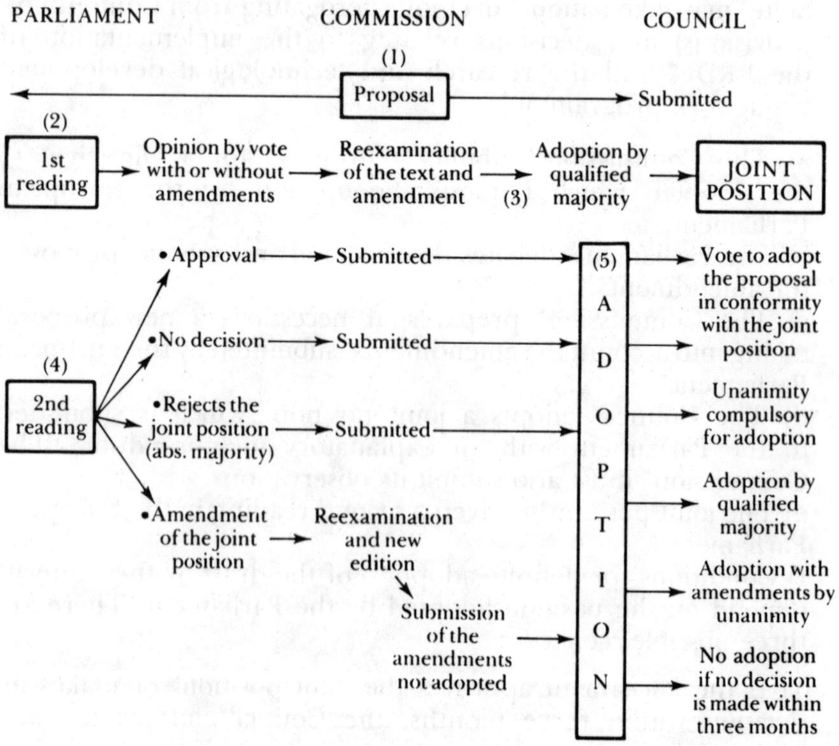

Cooperatives
SEE COGECA, CONSUMPTION, EUROPEAN COMMUNITY OF CONSUMER* CO-OPERATIVES, TRADE.

Coordinating Committee for Executives and Employees of the EEC Body representing the national unions concerned at Community* level (1964).

Coordinating Committee for the Textile Industries in the EEC
SEE COMITEXTIL.

Coordinating Committee for the Textile Unions Sectoral union committee at Community* level.
SEE EUROPEAN TRADE UNION COMMITTEE FOR THE TEXTILE, CLOTHING AND LEATHER INDUSTRIES, EUROPEAN SOCIAL AREA, WORKERS.

Coordination Paysanne Europeénne (CPE) *(European International Coordination)* Association of four Community* defence organizations and those of Switzerland and Austria.

Coordinator Member of a policy working party of the European Parliament* responsible for keeping the work of a parliamentary committee* under review and for ensuring the cohesion of the decisions taken by the members of the policy working party belonging to that parliamentary committee*.

COPA (Comité des Organisations Professionnelles Agricoles de la Communauté Europeénne)
SEE COMMITTEE OF AGRICULTURAL ORGANIZATIONS IN THE EUROPEAN COMMUNITY.

Copenhagen Capital of the Kingdom of Denmark. *14-15/12/1973*: Summit (common energy policy); *7-8/4/1978*: European Council*.

Copyright Exclusive right of an author to exploit a work of his/her invention. Draft regulations by the Commission* concerning rental, loan and reproduction. Protected by art. 36 of the EEC* treaty* which guarantees industrial and commercial property (Judgement* of 21/1/1981, 55 AND 57/80). Right 'exhausted' after the first application (Judgement* of 9/2/1982, 2/10/80). See also Berne Convention.
SEE GREEN PAPER, EUROPEAN PATENT, SOFTWARE.

CORDIS (Community Research and Development Information Service)
SEE VALUE.

COREPER (Comité des Représantants Permanents)
SEE COMMITTEE OF PERMANENT REPRESENTATIVES.

Coresponsibility System where producers participate in the budgetary reponsibility for the disposal of surplus of certain agricultural products (sugar, colza, cereals . . .) by means of levies* on surplus production or reductions in guaranteed prices. For milk this appears in the budget* as 'negative expenditure'.
SEE AGRICULTURAL PRICES, COMMON AGRICULTURAL POLICY, MECHANISMS FOR STABILIZING BUDGETARY EXPENDITURE.

Coresponsibility Levy Levy* initially introduced in 1976 to put an end to the constant increase in milk production by reducing the price received by the producer. The income produced by this levy* is used to fund measures to enlarge the market. It has been extended to cover cereals.
SEE CORESPONSIBILITY, MECHANISMS FOR STABILIZING BUDGETARY EXPENDITURE, OWN RESOURCES.

CORINE Community programme* to compile data on surface water resources, on water quality and on the environment* (OJ* L175, 5/7/1985). 1988-1992. DG XI of the Commission*.

COSINE Project in the EUREKA* programme ('EU 8'): Co-operation for Open Systems Interconnection Networking in Europe: to set up a European information technology* market in conformity with OSI* standards. The Twelve* (minus Italy), plus the EFTA* countries and Turkey. 1987.
SEE COMMUNITY DATA BANKS, INFORMATICS, OSI, TELECOMMUNICATIONS POLICY.

COST (European Cooperation in the field of Scientific and Technical research) Community research* programme* (1970): cooperation with non-member countries on scientific research*; either within Community programmes* (Type A) or separate from them (Type B). Members: the Twelve* and the OECD* countries (except Iceland). DG XII of the Commission*.

Council
SEE COUNCIL OF MINISTERS OF THE EUROPEAN COMMUNITIES.

Council of Europe Intergovernmental European organization for political, cultural, social and legal cooperation, established on 5/5/1949 by the BENELUX* countries, France and the United Kingdom; the following have since joined: Denmark, Ireland, Italy, Norway, Sweden, then Greece, Turkey, Iceland, Germany, Austria, Cyprus, Switzerland, Malta, Portugal, Spain, Liechtenstein and Hungary.
The *Parliamentary Assembly** of the Council of Europe elects the judges for the *European Court of Human Rights** and submits its recommendations to the Committee of Ministers* (one representative per member state) which meets twice a year and addresses its conclusions or recommendations to the member states.
Annual report of the European Parliament* is submitted to the President of the Parliamentary Assembly*. Annual common sittings were held up to 1979. Common meetings are still held by the Bureaux.
Palais de l'Europe, Strasbourg, France.

Council of Ministers of the European Communities (usually called the Council) Foremost legislative body of the European Communities* on matters relating to the EEC* and EURATOM*; it ensures coordination of the economic policies of Member States*, has the power to take decisions and confers on the Commission*, in the acts it adopts, powers for the implementation of the rules it lays down (art. 145 of the EEC* treaty*). In fields relating to the ECSC*, the Council harmonizes the action of the Commission* and that of the governments, which are responsible for the general economic policies of their countries (art. 26 of the ECSC* treaty*). The Council consists of one minister (depending on the subject at issue) from each Member State*.
'General business' Councils (foreign ministers) coordinate and supervise Community* work.
Specialist Councils involve the ministers reponsible for the subject under discussion (finance, agriculture*, industry, transport*, social affairs, development cooperation, arts, environment* etc.)
The *Presidency* is held by each Member State* for six months in rotation according to two six-yearly predetermined cycles (1: B, DK, D, GR, E, F, IRL, I, L, NL, P, UK. 2: DK, B, GR, D, F, E, I, IRL, NL, L, UK, P).
The Council adopts Regulations*, Directives* and Decisions* by simple majority, by qualified majority* or by unanimity*, following proposals by the Commission*.

It gives its *assent* to Commission* decisions on ECSC* matters. Its work is prepared by the Committee of Permanent Representatives* (COREPER).
170 rue de la Loi, 1048 Bruxelles, Belgium. Centre Européen, Plateau du Kirchberg, 2920 Luxembourg.
SEE AMENDMENT, COOPERATION PROCEDURE, EUROPEAN COUNCIL, TROIKA.

Countervailing Charge Charge used to balance out the difference in prices which may exist between international markets and the Community* market, taking customs duties into account.

Court of Auditors Community* institution*, established by the 2nd treaty of Brussels on 22/7/1975 to examine the accounts of all Community* bodies and of EDF* operations to ensure that all revenue was received and all expenditure incurred in a lawful and regular manner and that the financial management of the Community* is sound.
The Court of Auditors replaced the *Audit board* of the EEC* and of EURATOM* and the *Auditor* of the ECSC*, as the increasing size of the Community* budget* needed a permanent review body with more authority.
The Court of Auditors has twelve members, nominated by the Council (after consultation of the European Parliament*). The Court draws up an annual report* after the close of each financial year which is adopted by a majority* of its members and published in the OJ*, together with the replies of the Community institutions* to the Court's observations and any special reports (eg on EAGGF* guarantees or on food aid to LDCs*). The Court may check expenditure incurred by Member States* on behalf of the Community* (agricultural expenditure, collection of customs duties etc.), submit observations on specific questions and deliver opinions at the request of one of the institutions of the Community*. On the other hand the Court may not check substantive transactions carried out by Member States* in relation to own resources* (SEE BUDGET). 29 rue Aldringen, 1118 Luxembourg; 83 rue de la Loi, Bruxelles, Belgium.

Court of Justice Community institution* set up to ensure that Community* law is observed in the interpretation and application of the treaties* and to review Community* regulations*. The ECSC* treaty* established a Court of Justice to ensure that Community* law was observed in implementing it. In 1957 the

treaties of Rome* replaced it with a single Court for the three European Communities*.
The Court of Justice has *thirteen judges* and six advocates-general nominated by common agreement of the governments of the Member States* for six years (renewable; partial renewal every three years). A *President* is elected by the judges every three years. Clerks are chosen by the Court. A *Registrar* is nominated for six years (renewable) by the Court and keeps the records of proceedings. 606 permanent and 40 temporary officials.
The *judgements* of the Court rule on specific cases and give interpretations of disputed articles of the treaties*.
Direct *actions** are brought before the Court *for annulment* or *for failure to act* (control of the legality of Community* acts*), *for liability* (control of the civil liability of the Commission*), *in cases of irregularity* (control of Member States'* observation of Community* obligations); indirect *actions** are brought before the Court by a *request for a preliminary ruling* (interpretation and control of the validity of Community law*), compulsory in cases where the national judge considers that the case can no longer be dealt with under national law.
The *opinion* of the Court is given on the compatibility of national agreements with Community law*.
The Court acts as an arbitration* body within the framework of the ECSC*.
The Court settles disputes in the last instance between Community* institutions* and their employees (see below for the court of first instance). Actions* may be brought before the Court by preferential applicants (Community* institutions*: Commission's* right to bring an action* relating to the application of the treaties* and observation of Community* regulations; governments of Member States*) and by non-preferential applicants (individuals, businesses) under certain conditions.
National courts refer cases *for preliminary ruling*; this makes for uniform application of Community law* and a cohesive European legal system. National courts are competent to apply Community law*.
Procedures: application*, preparation*, hearing*, judgement*, interim ruling*.
The Court ensures that national regulations* present no obstacle to the smooth operation of the common market*, ie to freedom of movement under broadly competitive conditions. Its judgements are universally binding and may not be the object of an appeal or annulment at another level of court.
The Single European Act*, in accepting the possibility of national

exemptions to the harmonization* measures referred to in Art. 100a of the EEC treaty*, lays down that the Court shall remain the supreme judge of their compatibility with the operation of the internal market*.
In 1989 a *Court of the First Instance* was added to the Court (responibilities: staff of Community* institutions*, competition*, steel quotas*, ECSC* levies*).
Plateau du Kirchberg, 2920 Luxembourg.

CPCCI (Conférence Permanente des Chambres de Commerce et d'Industrie de la CEE)
SEE PERMANENT CONFERENCE OF CHAMBERS OF COMMERCE AND INDUSTRY OF THE EEC.

CPE
SEE COORDINATION PAYSANNE EUROPEENNE.

Crafts Total freedom of establishment* for activities not regulated by Member States*; subject to obtaining training* or a diploma stipulated by the host country for other activities subject to the provisions of specific Directives*.

Credit Operation whereby a lender places a sum of money or means of payment at the disposal of a borrower against repayment over a period of time usually agreed by the two parties in advance.
SEE BANK, CONSUMER CREDIT, CREDIT INSTITUTION, MORTGAGE.

Credit Institution Any undertaking whose activities consist in having and receiving deposits of money and in giving credit for its own profit (bank*, savings bank, institution specializing in short-, medium- and long-term credit). Directives* of 18/12/1989 (OJ* L 386, 1989) on credit institutions' *right to trade*, on their *solvency ratio**. Draft Directive* on *guarantees* issued by credit institutions (COM (88) 805, OJ* C 51, 1989).
SEE EUROPEAN FINANCIAL AREA, FREEDOM TO PROVIDE SERVICES, MOVEMENTS OF CAPITAL.

CREST (Comité de la Recherche Scientifique et Technique) *(Scientific and Technical Research Committee)*: Committee consisting of senior officials of the national ministries responsible for scientific policy (content of programmes) and acting as an intermediary between the Commission* on the one hand and the Member States* and the Council* on the other hand.
SEE RESEARCH AND TECHNOLOGICAL DEVELOPMENT FRAMEWORK PROGRAMME.

CROCODILE Club Club of Members of the European Parliament* established on 9/7/1980 in Strasbourg by Altiero Spinelli* to commit the European Community* to advancing towards Political Union.
SEE EUROPEAN UNION.

CRONOS Digital data bank* (European statistics), administered by EUROSTAT*.

CRS (Computerized Reservation System) Proposed Community programme*: code of conduct for the use of computerized reservation systems. Reg.* 89/2299/EEC, 24/3/1989, OJ* L 220, 29/7/1989.

CSCE
SEE CONFERENCE ON SECURITY AND COOPERATION IN EUROPE.

CST (Comité Scientifique et Technique)
SEE SCIENTIFIC AND TECHNICAL COMMITTEE (OF EURATOM).

Customs Authority Any authority responsible for the enforcement of customs regulations*, even if this authority is not part of the customs administration.

Customs Clearance Administrative process which allows goods to be made available to consumers* in a given country. Customs clearance procedures may be considered to be measures having equivalent effect*, contrary to art. 30 of the EEC* treaty*, if they involve restrictions which exceed the norm for such regulations, ie obstacles, delays, unjustified costs, long periods of time (checking, laboratory analyses, tests, technical verification, the granting of authorizations, approval procedures, etc.) or insufficient periods of time (to adapt to new technical requirements, for the necessary certificates or documents) in relation to the normal periods of time for these operations (DIR.* 70/50 EEC).
SEE CUSTOMS ENTRY, FREE CIRCULATION.

Customs Codes Draft Regulation* to establish a Community* Customs Code, consolidating existing legislation and taking into account the Single European Act*. Effective from 1/1/1993.
SEE COMMON CUSTOMS TARIFF.

Customs Control Measures taken to ensure compliance with the laws and regulations which customs authorities* are responsible for enforcing.

Customs Cooperation Council (CCC) Intergovernmental body (Brussels convention, 15/12/1950): coordinates between the 104 member states (EEC* and EFTA*, among others). Headquarters in Brussels, Belgium. Convention of 14/6/1983 on the Harmonized Commodity Description and Coding System (COUNCIL* DECISION* 87/369/EEC, 7/4/1987, OJ* L 198, 20/7/1987).
SEE CUSTOMS (OTHER ENTRIES), STANDARD INTERNATIONAL TRADE CLASSIFICATION.

Customs Debt Obligation for a person to pay the amount of import* or export* duties* applicable, according to the regulations in force, for goods subject to such duties. Reg.* 2144/87/EEC, 13/7/1987 (OJ* L 201, 22/7/1987). Payable by the person in whose name the customs entry* (or any other act having the same legal effect) has been made or by the medium by whom the entry has been made or even by the person not authorized to have done this or by persons having participated in the irregular introduction of goods or who have excluded these goods from customs control. Reg.* 1031/88/EEC, 18/4/1988 (OJ* L 102, 21/4/1988).
See also Reg.* of 22/12/1989: guarantees against payment of a customs debt.

Customs Duty Abolished at the internal frontiers of the Community* on 1/7/1968. Customs legislation has been harmonized* under common commercial policy*.
Regulations* 1224/80/EEC on the value of goods for customs purposes; 80/68/EEC on rules of origin*.
1/1/1990: in relations between Spain and other Member States* (industrial sector) duties became 35% of basic duty, and 40% for Portugal.
DG I of the Commission*.
SEE ACP, ARUSHA, CARNET, CERTIFICATE OF ORIGIN, COMBINED NOMENCLATURE, COMMITTEE ON ORIGIN, COMMON CUSTOMS TARIFF, COMMUNITY GOODS, COMMUNITY TRANSIT, COMPENSATORY LEVY, CUSTOMS CLEARANCE, CUSTOMS CODES, CUSTOMS CONTROL, CUSTOMS COOPERATION COUNCIL, CUSTOMS DEBT, CUSTOMS ENTRY, CUSTOMS OFFICE, CUSTOMS TERRITORY, CUSTOMS WAREHOUSE, DECLARATION OF GOODS, DUMPING, DUTY-FREE, EFTA, EXPORT DUTY, FLORENCE AGREEMENT, FREE CIRCULATION, FRONTIER CONTROL, GATT, HARMONIZED COMMODITY DESCRIPTION AND CODING SYSTEM, IMPORT DUTY, INTRACOMMUNITY MOVEMENT OF GOODS, INWARD PROCESSING, CONVENTION (LOMÉ), NON COMMUNITY GOODS, NON-MEMBER COUNTRY, ORIGIN, OUTWARD PROCESSING, PERSONAL EFFECTS, PRIMARY PRODUCT, PROCESSING UNDER CUSTOMS CONTROL, RETURNED GOODS, SAD, SGP, SINGLE EUROPEAN ACT,

TARIC, TEMPORARY ADMISSION, TEMPORARY STORAGE, TEMPORARY USE, TIR, TRANSIT.

Customs Entry Act by which a person, using the correct procedure, expresses the desire to assign goods to a customs procedure or to bring a customs procedure to an end. Intra-community: may be made by any legal or natural person or association of persons able to do so (in accordance with the regulations in force at the time) by submitting or having submitted to the competent authority, in accordance with the provisions laid down to this end, the goods in question (with the correct documents) which have been produced in the Community*

Customs Office
of departure: the office where intracommunity movement begins.;
of exit: the office through which goods leave the territory of a Member State* after having been subject to temporary use* there;
of entry: the office through which goods enter the territory of a Member State* where they will be used temporarily;
of transit: the office through which goods enter the territory of a Member State* for transit across that State or through which goods leave that State after transit* (or an office of exit from the Community* if goods leave the territory of the Community* by way of a simple transit* operation via the frontier between a Member State* and a non-member country*);
of arrival: any customs office of a contracting party to the Geneva Customs Convention of 14/11/1975 regarding the international transit* of goods. See Reg.* 3/84/EEC, 18/12/1983 (OJ* L 2, 4/1/1984).

Customs Regulations All the provisions for implementing Community* regulations on import*, export*, transit* and storage of goods which are the object of trade between Member States* or between Member States* and non-member countries*. Eg. Reg.* 1468/81/EEC.
SEE CUSTOMS (OTHER ENTRIES).

Customs Territory Territory throughout which the same customs regulations* apply. The customs territory of the Community* includes the territories of the Member States* but not the Faeroe Islands and Greenland (Denmark), Heligoland and Busingen (Germany), the Canary Islands, Ceuta and

Melilla (Spain), the French Overseas Departments (FOD*), the communes of Livigno and Campione and the Italian parts of Lake Lugano (Italy); also included are the Austrian territories of Jungholz and Mittelberg, the Principality of Monaco, the Republic of San Marino, territorial waters surrounding the coasts of the Member States*, inland areas of water and the air space over each Member State*. Community* customs regulations* apply uniformly throughout this territory (except where specific provisions to the contrary apply). Reg.* 2151/84/EEC.
SEE CUSTOMS (OTHER ENTRIES), FREEDOM OF MOVEMENT.

Customs Union Where two or more national customs territories* are replaced by a single common customs territory*; in the EEC* this entails abolition of barriers* to trade between Member States* and the application of a common customs tariff* with regard to non-member countries*. The Commission* White Paper* aims at achieving a true internal market* by 1992.
SEE BENELUX, COMMON MARKET, EFTA, EUROPEAN ECONOMIC COMMUNITY, OBJECTIVE 1992.

Customs Warehouse Any place approved by and under the control of the customs administration for storing goods exempt for a fixed period of time from all forms of taxation (customs duties*, charges having equivalent effect*, agricultural levies*). Goods may be admitted for 5 years, under certain conditions, and must be taxed if they leave the warehouse to be put on the market or must be placed under another customs procedure or be exported. See also Reg.* 2503/88/EEC, 25/7/88 (OJ* L 225, 15/8/1988); Dir.* 69/74/EEC, 4/3/1969 (OJ* L 58, 8/3/1969), 71/235/EEC, 21/6/1971 (OJ* L 143, 29/6/1971), 76/634/EEC (OJ* L 223, 16/8/1976).
SEE DUTY-FREE WAREHOUSE.

D

DAC
SEE DEVELOPMENT ASSISTANCE COMMITTEE.

Data Base Computerized collection of sources of information.
SEE CELEX, EUROBASES, SCAD.

Davignon (Etienne) Former Secretary-general of the Belgian Ministry of Foreign Affairs, author of a report* on European Union*, approved on 27/10/1970, and, as a European Commissioner*, author of a plan to ward off crisis within the ECSC*, introduced in 1977.

Decision
EEC, EURATOM**: Community act* binding in all parts for those to whom it is addressed (Member States*, undertakings or individuals).
*ECSC**: Community act* binding in all parts, which may have general application. Comes into force on the day of notification* or on the day specified in the Directive*.

Decisions of the Court The decisions of the Court of Justice* of the European Communities* are generally considered to be an unwritten source of Community law* because of the Court of Justice's* status as a Community institution* and because it was established by the treaties* to 'ensure that in the interpretation and application of this Treaty the law is observed' (art. 164 of the EEC* treaty*).
SEE JUDGEMENT.

Declaration of Goods The parties concerned use the procedure laid down by the customs administration to indicate which customs procedure to assign to the goods in question and provide any information which the customs administration requires to apply this customs procedure.

Declaration of Origin Note showing the origin of goods, at export*, as indicated by the manufacturer, producer, supplier, exporter or any other responsible person, on the invoice or any other document relating to the goods.
SEE CERTIFIED DECLARATION OF ORIGIN, CUSTOMS ENTRY, ORIGIN.

Decommissioning Nuclear Installations Community* development programme* for managing disused nuclear installations and the radioactive waste* arising from dismantling the installations (to protect people and the environment*). Budget: 31.5m Ecus* (1989-1993). OJ* L 98, 11/4/1989. DG XII of the Commission*.
SEE RADIOACTIVE WASTE.

DECT (Digital European Cordless Phone) Draft Directive* (1990) on improving coordination of wavebands and to introduce the system in the Community* before the end of 1992.
SEE ERMES.

Delegation Provided that the principle of collective responsibility is observed, the Commission* may authorize its members (or some of its officials) to take clearly defined managerial or administrative measures in its name and under its supervision (art. 27 of the Commission's* internal regulations). It may also delegate powers to management and regulatory committees (SEE COMITOLOGY). The treaties* establishing the Communities* authorize the Council* to delegate responsibility for implementing the rules it lays down to the Commission*.

Delocalization of Savings Transfer of financial investments by businesses and individuals to countries where the tax and administrative systems are more favourable.
SEE EUROPEAN FINANCIAL AREA, FREEDOM TO PROVIDE SERVICES, MOVEMENTS OF CAPITAL, STOCK EXCHANGE.

Delors (Jacques) French statesman. President of the Commission of the European Communities* (1985-1992).
SEE MONETARY UNION, REPORT, SINGLE EUROPEAN ACT, WHITE PAPER.

DELTA (Developing European Learning Through Technological Advance) Community programme* for training through advanced information and telecommunications technology*. Budget: 20m Ecus* (1988-1990). Decision* 88/417/EEC, 28/6/1988 (OJ* L 206, 30/7/1988). DG XIII of the Commission*.

De Minimis Rule
SEE AGREEMENTS BETWEEN UNDERTAKINGS.

Denaturing Processing or destroying agricultural products to avoid surplus Community* production.
SEE AGRICULTURAL PRICES, COMMON AGRICULTURAL POLICY.

Derogation A special dispensation or exemption clause which allows specified member states an exemption from enacting all or part of the relevant directive or regulation. It is usually applied to Member States when they require extra time to implement a directive or regulation but on occasions it can be open ended.

DESCARTES (Debugging and Specification of ADA Real-time Embedded Systems)
SEE ESPRIT

Development Assistance Committee (DAC) Intergovernmental body of the OECD*, of which the Community* is a member.
SEE EUROPEAN DEVELOPMENT FUND, LDCs.

DIANE (Direct Information Access Network for Europe)
SEE DIANE GUIDE.

DIANE GUIDE Catalogue of European data bases*, European data banks* and on-line data services. ECHO* on-line service.

DIN (Deutsches Institut für Normung)
(German Institute for Standardization)

Diplomas Mutual recognition* of diplomas, certificates and other titles is laid down by art. 57 of the EEC* treaty*. It has been applied, by means of Directives* (ESPECIALLY DIR.* 89/48/EEC, 21/12/1988, OJ* L 19, 24/1/1989), to the medical and allied professions, to hairdressers and to road transporters. One Directive*, called 'Bac+3', of 22/12/1989 (OJ* L 19, 1989) lays down mutual recognition* of diplomas equivalent to or above degree level (in general, not just by sector).
SEE ARCHITECTS, DOCTORS, FREEDOM OF ESTABLISHMENT, FREEDOM TO PROVIDE SERVICES, NURSES.

Dir. Abbreviation of Directive*.

Direct Investments Any kind of investment by natural persons or by commercial, industrial or financial undertakings which establish or maintain long-term direct relations between the person providing the capital and the head of the undertaking or the undertaking where the capital is invested.
SEE EUROPEAN FINANCIAL AREA, FREEDOM TO PROVIDE SERVICES, MOVEMENTS OF CAPITAL.

Directive Community act*: 'shall be binding, as to the result to be achieved, upon each Member State* to which it is addressed, but shall leave to the national authorities the choice of form and methods' (art. 189 of the EEC* treaty*, art. 161 of the EURATOM* treaty*). Member States* are notified of Directives addressed to them and of the period of time allocated for their implementation.
Publication in the OJ* (L series) is not a condition of applicability. Directives* are often known by the name of the main subject they cover (eg 'Seveso Directive') or by the name of the member of the Commission* who proposed them (eg 'Vredling Directive') and also by the order in which they appeared, where several Directives cover the same subject (eg 'second banking Directive').
SEE COMMISSION, COUNCIL, PROCEEDINGS.

Disabled
SEE EUROPEAN SOCIAL AREA, HANDYNET, HELIOS, HORIZON.

Discharge Act* by which the European Parliament* agrees to the implementation of the previous year's budget*, after having debated it (treaty of Brussels*). In November 1984 the Parliament refused to give a discharge in respect of the 1982 budget*. The discharge is accompanied by the Parliament's observations on the budget*.

Discrimination The EEC* treaty* (art. 48) lays down 'the abolition of any discrimination based on nationality between workers of the Member States*', and the prohibition of restrictions or new restrictions on the freedom of establishment* of nationals of a Member State* in the territory of another Member State* (art. 52 and 53).
SEE FREEDOM TO PROVIDE SERVICES.

Dissemination and Use Community programme* for disseminating and using the results of research* in the fields of science and technology.
SEE VALUE.

Distribution
SEE TRADE.

DOCDEL (Programme for Electronic Publishing and DOCument DELivery) Budget: 18.2m Ecus* (1984-1985). EURODOCDEL European data bank*.

Dock Dues Charge made by the French (FOD*) and Portuguese overseas departments and territories on all goods entering their territories, with exemptions for locally produced products. In adopting the POSEIDOM* programme the Community* has requested these territories to apply the principle of equality of treatment from 2003. Provisional exemptions will apply from 1993.

Doctors Benefit from the principle of freedom to provide services*, under certain conditions relating to medical training*. Affiliation to the relevant professional organization in the host country is compulsory (DIR.* 75/362 AND 75/363 of 16/6/1975, OJ* L 167, 30/6/1975).

Domicile The principle of freedom of movement of workers within the Community* prohibits a Member State from taking into account the domicile of a worker* as a criterion for applying national legislation or for granting advantages (Judgement* 44/72, 12/12/1972; 152/73, 12/2/1974).

Dominant Position (Abuse of) Art. 86 of the EEC* treaty*: 'Any abuse by one or more undertakings of a dominant position within the common market or in a substantial part of it shall be prohibited as incompatible with the common market in so far as it may affect trade* between Member States*'. (See also art. 66 of the ECSC* treaty*).
'Such abuse may, in particular, consist in:
(a) directly or indirectly imposing unfair purchase or selling prices or other unfair trading conditions;
(b) limiting production, markets or technical development to the prejudice of consumers;
(c) applying dissimilar conditions to equivalent transactions with other trading parties, thereby placing them at a competitive disadvantage;
(d) making the conclusion of contracts subject to acceptance by the other parties of supplementary obligations which, by their nature or according to commercial usage, have no connection with the subject of such contracts.'
SEE COMPETITION.

DOMIS Community data base*: directory of sources of information on supplies. ECHO* on-line data service. DG XIII of the Commission*.

DOSES (Development of Statistical Expert Systems) Community programme* intended to improve the collection and exploitation of Community* statistical data* by using advanced information technology. Budget: 4m Ecus* (1989-1993). See also OJ* C 203, 1988; C 170, 1989; L 200, 19/7/1989. ECHO*. DG XIII of the Commission*.

Double Disapproval Principle by which the price of a flight may only be prohibited if it has been vetoed by both the governments concerned. Reg.* of 1990 on tariffs.
SEE TRANSPORT POLICY.

Draft European Standard Experimental European standard* adopted by CEN* or CENELEC*.
SEE AFNOR, BARRIERS, STANDARDS.

Draftsman (of an Opinion) Member of a European Parliament* committee appointed by his/her colleagues to prepare its discussions on a given subject. He/She is also the committee's spokesman in plenary sittings of the Parliament and is responsible for following draft laws through to their adoption (if this occurs).
(SEE SINGLE EUROPEAN ACT).

Draft Standard Document containing technical specifications* for a particular object which are to be adopted according to the national standardization* procedure, resulting from preparatory work and made available for comments from those concerned or for public inquiry.
SEE BARRIERS, NEW APPROACH.

Draft Technical Regulation Technical specifications*, including administrative provisions, elaborated with the intention of implementing them as technical regulations* and still at a stage of preparation where substantial amendments could be made.
SEE BARRIERS, NEW APPROACH.

DRIVE (Dedicated Road Infrastructure for Vehicle safety in Europe) Community research* programme* in the field of informatics* applied to road safety and quality of life of road users, and also to protecting the environment (on-board computers, information infrastructures, talking receivers and transmitters of data and images; road haulage; SME* specializing

in advanced technology). Budget: 60m Ecus* (1988-1991). See also OJ* L 206, 30/7/1988. DG XIII F5 of the Commission*.
SEE AUTOMOTIVE INDUSTRY.

Driving Licence Directive* of 21/6/91 on mutual recognition* (harmonization* of the content of driving tests, medical tests, categories of licences). Universal *European Driving Licence* format (comes into force on 1/1/1996).
SEE MOTOR VEHICLES, SELF-DRIVE VEHICLE HIRE.

Dublin Capital of the Republic of Ireland. Headquarters of the European Foundation for the Improvement of Living and Working Conditions*.
29-30/11/1979: European Council* (UK contribution to the Community budget*);
28/5/1990: Extraordinary European Council* (German reunification; revival of European Union* and Economic and Monetary Union*);
25-26/6/1990: European Council* (aid to the countries of Eastern Europe; environment*; Economic and Monetary Union*).

Dumping When a supplier sells goods abroad at a considerably lower price than the same goods would command on the home market. Policy or measures which have the effect of artificially lowering export* prices in order to remove competition* or to attract customers.
This practice is prohibited by art. 91 of the EEC* treaty*, whether it is direct or in another form (subsidies or excessive credit on exports*, tax relief, etc).
The Commission* or the Council* may fix *anti-dumping duties* or *countervailing duties* with regard to non-member countries* (anti-dumping procedure: Council* Reg.* 1761/87/EEC of 22/6/1987 (OJ* L 167) and 2423/88 of 11/7/1988 (OJ* C 209/1).
1/7/1968: *anti-dumping code* adopted by GATT* (this practice must not cause or threaten to cause material injury to a producer established in the importing country; however, a direct link must be established between the dumping and the injury).
SEE BOOMERANG CLAUSE, COMPETITION.
Social dumping: practice whereby industrial investment is attracted to countries where labour costs are low.

DUNDIS (Directory of United Nations* Data bases* and Information Systems)

Duty
SEE CUSTOMS DUTY,

Duty-Free Exemption from duty, up to a certain fixed level. *Customs*: exemption from customs duty* on the import* of goods into a country.
There is a limit to the amount of goods tourists may purchase in the various Member States* of the Community* without paying duty. Application of the principle of the freedom of movement of goods* means that they no longer apply after 1/7/1999. The duty-free principle applies to all indirect taxes on personal effects when an individual changes his/her place of residence or marries, on inherited personal effects and on temporary imports* of vehicles, to the single VAT* rate on goods for charitable or philanthropic organizations and low value samples (DIR.* OF 8/7/1985, OJ* L 183, 16/7/1985).
SEE TEMPORARY EXPORT.
*CAP**: fixed-rate reduction applied to the actual monetary gap* in order to obtain the applied monetary gap*.

Duty-Free Warehouse Warehouse on Community* customs territory* where non-Community goods* are considered as not being on Community* customs territory* as regards the application of import duties* and measures relating to commercial policy on imports*, as long as they are not put into free circulation* or placed under another customs procedure*.
Public customs warehouse: managed by customs authorities* or other authorities or by other natural or legal persons and open to all importers;
Private customs warehouse: for the sole use of certain specified persons. Reg.* 2504/88/EEC, 25/7/1988 (OJ* L 225, 15/8/1988).
SEE CUSTOMS WAREHOUSE.

E

EABS (Euroabstracts) Community* data base* summarizing Commission* scientific and technical publications every month.
SEE ENERGY, ENVIRONMENT, NUCLEAR ENERGY.

EAC (European Association for Cooperation)

EAEC European Atomic Energy Community.
SEE EURATOM

EAGGF (European Agricultural Guidance and Guarantee Fund) Community* fund established in 1964.
Guidance Section. Objective: to increase agricultural productivity via technological progress and the optimum use of production factors. Administers the Community* funds intended to give aid, by means of co-financing, to measures of structural policy* or (up to 1979) to the financing of individual projects (agricultural reparcelling, electrification, processing and marketing methods and installations). Advisory committee.
Guarantee Section: established to finance Community* market interventions (SEE COMMON MARKET ORGANIZATIONS): stabilization of agricultural markets, refunds* for exports* to non-member countries* to promote sales of Community* products on world markets, food aid, Monetary Compensatory Amounts (MCA*). Monies from the EAGGF Guarantee Section are part of compulsory expenditure*.
Regulations* (EEC) 17/64, 159/72, 375/77, 219/78, 1361/78, 3073/82.
SEE AGRICULTURAL PRICES, COMMON AGRICULTURAL POLICY, EARLY RETIREMENT, SET ASIDE, SINGLE EUROPEAN ACT, STRUCTURAL POLICY,

EAST EUREKA* project (software* factories): Denmark, Finland, France, Italy, Norway, United Kingdom. Budget: 141m Ecus* over six years.

Early Retirement A Regulation* encourages 'main-occupation' farmers over 55 years old to cease all agricultural activity by stopping production or by restructuring*. The EAGGF*

guidance section is involved in the financing of these measures.
SEE COMMON AGRICULTURAL POLICY, EUROPEAN SOCIAL AREA, STRUCTURAL POLICY.

Eastern Europe
SEE COMECON, EUROPEAN COUNCIL, EUROPEAN FOUNDATION FOR VOCATIONAL TRAINING, PHARE.

EBCG (European Biotechnology* Cooperation Group) Assessment of the biotechnology* research programme*.

EBN
SEE BIC, EUROPEAN BUSINESS INNOVATION CENTRE NETWORK.

EBRD
SEE EUROPEAN BANK FOR RECONSTRUCTION AND DEVELOPMENT.

EC
SEE EUROPEAN COMMUNITY.

ECAC
SEE EUROPEAN CIVIL AVIATION CONFERENCE.

EC Declaration of Conformity Compulsory declaration with which a manufacturer or his/her agent in the Community* ensures and declares that his/her product fulfils the obligations in the Directive* concerning that product.
SEE BARRIERS, CERTIFICATION OF CONFORMITY, EC TYPE EXAMINATION, STANDARDS, NEW APPROACH.

ECDIN (Environmental Chemicals Data Information Network) Community* data base* on chemical products and their effects on the environment* and on health*. Administered by the JRC*.
SEE CHEMISTRY.

ECE (UN) Economic Commission for Europe of the United Nations (ECOSOC). Geneva, Switzerland.

ECHO (European Commission Host Organization) Community* host computer.
SEE ARCOME, DIANE, DOMIS, EABS, ECHO CUSTOMER SERVICE, ELISE, ENREP, EURISTOTE, EURODICAUTOM, IES-DC1–3, IRSOFT, MISEP, PABLI, RURALNET, SESAME, TED.

ECHO Customer Service Community* data base* service (TED*-PABLI*-EABS*). 117, route d'Esch, 1471 Luxembourg.

ECHR
SEE EUROPEAN CONVENTION ON HUMAN RIGHTS, EUROPEAN COURT OF HUMAN RIGHTS.

ECISS (European Committee for Iron and Steel Standardization) Committee of national standards* bodies.
SEE CEN, EUROPEAN COAL AND STEEL COMMUNITY, IRON AND STEEL POLICY.

ECLAIR (European Collaborative Linkage of Agriculture and Industry through Research) Community programme* of basic research*: the application of biotechnology* in the agro-industrial sector (preparation of agricultural products for industry* and of industrial products for agriculture; development of agricultural and industrial methods which are less damaging to the environment*). Budget: 80m Ecus* (1989-1993). See also OJ* L 62, 3/3/1989. DG XII of the Commission*.
SEE AGRICULTURE.

ECLAS Bibliographical data base* established in 1978 as an automated catalogue of the Commission's* central library. Public access via EUROBASES*. Research documentation; official publications of the EC* in all the different language versions; official documents (except the 'COM' series) and European Parliament* working papers; publications of other intergovernmental organizations, commercial, university and official publications; policy proposals and statistics; a selection of articles and periodicals.

ECMT
SEE EUROPEAN CONFERENCE OF MINISTERS OF TRANSPORT

ECMWF
SEE EUROPEAN CENTRE FOR MEDIUM-RANGE WEATHER FORECASTS.

Economic Commission for Europe
SEE ECE (UN).

Economic and Monetary Union (EMU)
SEE ECONOMIC UNION, MONETARY UNION.

Economic and Social Committee (ESC) 189 member consultative assembly (France, Germany, Italy, United Kingdom: 24; Spain: 21; Belgium, Greece, Netherlands, Portugal: 12; Denmark, Ireland: 9; Luxembourg: 6). Members are nominated for 4 years (renewable) by the Council* following proposals from national governments and consultation of the professional organizations concerned.
The Chairman, elected for two years, chairs the Bureau elected by the Committee and coordinates its work.
Three opinion groups: Employers, Workers, Other interests.
Nine sections: agriculture*, economic and financial affairs, energy* and nuclear* affairs, environment*, public health*, consumption*, external relations*, industry*, trade*, crafts* and services*, regional development, social affairs, transport* and telecommunications*.
Opinions, or own-initiative opinions**, adopted by section, then in plenary sitting, following examination by study groups who submit draft opinions and reports to the monthly plenary sitting.
Experts may be consulted and plenary sitting debates held with Commissioners* or Directors of the Commission*.
The ESC also organizes socio-professional conferences on various subjects.
2 rue Ravenstein, Bruxelles, Belgium.

Economic Union Term used to describe the fulfilment of the following objectives: the single market*, competition* policies designed to strengthen market mechanisms, structural adjustments, regional development, coordination of macro-economic policies, coupled with compulsory budgetary rules. Often linked to Monetary Union*.
SEE EUROPEAN ECONOMIC AREA, EUROPEAN ECONOMIC COMMUNITY, FREEDOM OF MOVEMENT, FREE TRADE, OBJECTIVE 1992.

ECOSOC
SEE ECONOMIC AND SOCIAL COMMITTEE.

ECPDR
SEE EUROPEAN CENTRE OF PARLIAMENTARY DOCUMENTATION AND RESEARCH.

ECSC
SEE EUROPEAN COAL AND STEEL COMMUNITY.

ECSC Consultative Committee Committee of 96 members (Manufacturers, workers, consumers, businessmen) consulted (compulsorily in certain cases) by the Commission* on matters relating to coal* and steel* policy. Own-initiative opinions*. See art. 18 of the the treaty of Paris (ECSC*).

ECSC Funds Instrument for financial intervention on the common coal and steel market (treaty* of Paris*). ECSC* loans. Aid for research*. Aid for readaptation. The Commission* (DG XVIII, consultation of DG II, IV, V, and XVI) takes decisions relating to loans. Audit by the Court of Auditors*.

ECSC Loans Loans laid down in art. 54 of the treaty* of Paris*.
SEE EUROPEAN COAL AND STEEL COMMUNITY.

ECSC Research (or Steel Research) Community research* programmes*: technological research* in steel production; financial research for the iron and steel* industry. Budget: 30m Ecus* (OJ* C 203, 12/8/1986, C 108, 6/5/1986). DG XII, XIII (steel), DG XVII (coal) of the Commission*.

EC Type Examination Procedure by which an approved body states and certifies that a representative example of the product in question conforms to the provisions of the appropriate Directive*.
SEE EC DECLARATION OF CONFORMITY, STANDARDIZATION.

Ecu (European Currency Unit) European unit of account defined by a rate on the exchange market, calculated from the exchange rates of the currencies which make it up. The basket of currencies* which make up the Ecu includes all the currencies of the Member States*. The weighting of each currency takes into account the proportion each Member State* represents of the GNP of the EEC* and of intra-community trade. This is revised every five years or on request by a Member State* if the exchange rate of one of the currencies varies by more than 25%.
Composition of the Ecu basket of currencies since 21/9/1989: (weighting coefficients):

1E	DM	FF	HFL	FB	L	KR	£I	£	DR	FLUX	PE	EP
=	30.1	19	9.4	7.9	10.15	2.45	1.1	13	0.8	7.9	5.3	0.8

The Ecu is issued for profit by the central banks of the EMS*, in return for the deposit of 20% of their gold and dollar reserves with the European Monetary Cooperation Fund (EMCF*). The Ecu plays the role of currency denominator in the exchange

rate mechanism of the EMS* (fixing central rates*) and for operations in the intervention and credit mechanisms it is the basis for establishing a divergence indicator and a means of settlement between the monetary authorities of the EEC*. The Ecu is the basis for Community* accounting, for the common customs tariff*, for intra-community payments, for agricultural prices*, for loans and subsidies from Community* funds*, for statistics*, for Community* credits to Member States*, for fines imposed on businesses by the Commission*, for repaying debts between central banks. It is the accounting currency of the European Investment Bank (EIB)*. Fluctuations of 2.25% above and below the central rate are allowed (6% for the Spanish Peseta).
The Ecu is used as a unit of account for private settlements both inside and outside the Community*. Banknotes and bonds (Eurobonds) have been issued in Ecus by European institutions and undertakings of Member States* or non-member countries*. Some large business groups use the Ecu as the unit of account for their European subsidiaries. The stability of the Ecu in relation to national currencies lends security to financial and commercial operations (the Ecu has been quoted on the Paris stock exchange since 1974).
Use of the Ecu remains subject to certain restrictions; once they are lifted the Ecu would become a wholly separate currency, issued and administered by a European central bank. This presupposes a common monetary policy.
SEE ASSOCIATION FOR THE MONETARY UNION OF EUROPE, COMMITTEE FOR THE MONETARY UNION OF EUROPE, ECU BANK ASSOCIATION, EUROPEAN ECONOMIC AREA, MONETARY UNION.

Ecu Bank Association Association of about one hundred banks* around the world to promote the use of the Ecu* in international transactions and to facilitate its use on the market. 4, rue de la Paix, 75008 Paris, France.
SEE ASSOCIATION FOR THE MONETARY UNION OF EUROPE, COMMITTEE FOR THE MONETARY UNION OF EUROPE.

ED European Democrats (Conservatives in the European Parliament*).

EDC
SEE EUROPEAN DOCUMENTATION CENTRES.

EDF (European Development Fund) Fund created in 1957 to help the ACP* countries with financial and technical cooperation under the Lomé* conventions*, which fixed the amount of appropriations and the intervention procedures for the areas concerned. Subsidies and special loans approved by the European Investment Bank*. Decision* by the Commission* following a proposal by the ACP* countries and agreed by the EDF committee (representatives of Member States*). Used to finance investments and cooperation projects. Public works* and supply contracts* (CONDITIONS: OJ* L 39, 14/2/72; L 214, 13/8/73; L 287, 14/10/73), public services contracts, open to European undertakings and those of the ACP* countries. Open, restricted and accelerated procedures.
The Court of Auditors* audits its operations.
DG VIII of the Commission*. 170 rue de la Loi, 1049 Bruxelles, Belgium.

Education Education and training* policy is not a specific area of Community* responsibility, but 'access to such forms of education is laid down in the treaties*' (Judgement* of 13/7/1983, 152/82).
SEE EQUAL TREATMENT, EUROPEAN SOCIAL AREA, SOCIAL SECURITY BENEFITS.

EEA
SEE EUROPEAN ECONOMIC AREA.

EEC
SEE EUROPEAN ECONOMIC COMMUNITY.

EEC Committee for the Wine, Aromatic Wine, Sparkling Wine and Liqueur Wine Industries and Trades Body representing producers and distributors at Community* level.

EEIG (European Economic Interest Grouping) Legal structure allowing several businesses in different Member States* of the Community* to pool their resources in order to attain specific objectives (research* and development, tenders for public contracts*, group purchases of raw materials, pooling of services). May employ no more than 500 workers. Management by corporate decision or by managers who represent the grouping to third parties. Fiscal transparency. Regulation* 2137/85/EEC, 25/7/1985, applicable on 1/1/1989 (OJ* L 199/1, 31/7/1985). DG III of the Commission*.
SEE COMPANY LAW, REWARD.

EFICS (European Forestry Information and Communications System) Established by a Council* Regulation* of 29/5/1989 (1612/89, OJ* L 165, 15/6/1989).
SEE FORESTRY POLICY.

EFTA
SEE EUROPEAN FREE TRADE ASSOCIATION.

EHLASS (European Home and Leisure Accidents Surveillance System) Community programme* to prevent accidents at home and during leisure activities (1988-1990).

EIB
SEE EUROPEAN INVESTMENT BANK.

EIC European Insurance Committee.
SEE ALSO EURO INFO CENTRES.

EIIA (European Information Industry Association) Federation uniting users, manufacturers and service centres, as well as government organizations involved in the information industry, for promoting exchanges between members and with similar organizations in other groups of countries. Luxembourg. 1989. P.O. Box 19, Wilmslow, Cheshire SK9 2DZ.

EIMAG European Information Market Development Group

EINECS (European INventory of Existing Chemical Substances)
SEE COPA, EUROPEAN CENTRE OF PUBLIC ENTERPRISES, EUROPEAN SOCIAL AREA, EUROPEAN SOCIAL CHARTER, INTERNATIONAL LABOUR ORGANIZATION, ROUND TABLE OF INDUSTRIALISTS, UNION OF INDUSTRIES OF THE EUROPEAN COMMUNITY.

EIPA (European Institute of Public Administration) Study seminars for officials of the administrations of the Twelve* and of the Communities*. OL Krouweplein 22, P.O. Box 1229, 6201 BE Maastricht, Netherlands.

Electricity Draft Regulation* on the transfer of electricity on transeuropean networks* (COM (89) 332, OJ* C 8, 1990). Transparency of prices (DIR.* OF 29/6/1990, OJ* L 185, 1990).
SEE EXCLUDED SECTORS, LIAISON GROUP FOR THE EUROPEAN ENGINEERING INDUSTRIES, PUBLIC CONTRACT.

Electromagnetic Compatibility Council* Directive* on harmonization* (89/336/EEC, 3/5/1989, OJ* L 139, 16/7/1989).
SEE NEW APPROACH.

Electronic Payment Recommendation* by the Commission* on a 'European Code of Conduct' (8/12/1987, OJ* L 365, 24/12/1987). Agreement on 9/10/1987 between the main European banks to accept each other's payment cards.

Electronics
SEE INFORMATICS, LIAISON GROUP FOR THE EUROPEAN ENGINEERING INDUSTRIES.

Eligibility for Employment 'Any national of a Member State* shall, irrespective of his place of residence, have the right to take up an activity as an employed person and to pursue such activity within the territory of another Member State* in accordance with the provisions laid down by law, regulation or administrative action governing the employment of nationals of that state. He shall, in particular, have the right to take up available employment in the territory of another Member State* with the same priority as nationals of that state' (REG.* 1612/68/EEC, 15/10/1968, OJ* L 257, 19/10/1968).
SEE FREEDOM OF MOVEMENT, EUROPEAN SOCIAL AREA.

ELISE (European Local Initiative System of Exchanges) Employment* in Europe; exchange of information between regions* on manpower and employment organizations. Access via ECHO*, Brussels.

EMBL
SEE EUROPEAN MOLECULAR BIOLOGY LABORATORY.

EMCF (European Monetary Cooperation Fund) Instrument used by the Community* to operate the EMS* and which allows it to use the Ecu*. Each Member State* in the EMS* contributes 20% of its gold and dollar reserves to the EMCF. The amount of Ecus* created is adjusted every quarter as a function of changes in gold and dollar reserves and variations in their prices.

Employers' Federation of the French Iron and Steel Industry Representation to the EC*. 45, rue de Treves, 1040 Bruxelles, Belgium.

Employment
SEE COMMON AGRICULTURAL POLICY, EAGGF, ECSC FUNDS, ELIGIBILITY FOR

EMPLOYMENT, ELISE, EUROPEAN SOCIAL AREA, EUROPEAN SOCIAL CHARTER, STANDING COMMITTEE ON EMPLOYMENT, STRUCTURAL FUNDS, STRUCTURAL POLICY, POLICY TRAINING.

EMS
SEE EUROPEAN MONETARY SYSTEM.

EMU (Economic and Monetary Union)
SEE ECONOMIC UNION, MONETARY UNION.

EMUG (European MAP Users Group) Group of European manufacturers, modelled on the Manufacturing Automation Protocol (MAP), to define operating standards* and basic standards*.
SEE OSI.

EN
SEE EUROPEAN STANDARD.

ENDOC On-line directory of environment information and documentation centres in Member States*. Access via ECHO*, Brussels.

Energy Common energy policy covers, apart from coal* (SEE ECSC) and nuclear energy* (SEE EURATOM), the supply and consumption of energy in the Community* (global and sectoral objectives, reports by the Commission*), deregulation of distribution (particularly of electricity* and gas*), improvement of the transparency of markets and prices, energy programmes (SEE NON-NUCLEAR ENERGY), cooperation on supply and consumption (oil reserves), rational use of energy, alternative forms of energy, protection of the environment* and safety*, coordination of relations with non-member partners, right of transfer between networks*, two draft Directives* on electricity* and gas*, aid for modernization, investment in production, transport and distribution infrastructures, safety reserves of oil and natural gas (DIR.* L 308 of 23/12/1968). *1988*: report by DG XVII of the Commission* on the obstacles in the way of achieving a single energy market.
Provisionally, energy is an *excluded sector** for public contracts*.
SEE AGRICULTURE, COAL, ENVIRONMENT, EURATOM, EUROPEAN COAL AND STEEL COMMUNITY, EUROPEAN INVESTMENT BANK, EUROPEAN PARLIAMENT, EUROPEAN REGIONAL DEVELOPMENT FUND, IMP, JET, JOULE, NEW COMMUNITY INSTRUMENT, RECHAR, REWARD, SCIENCE, SESAME, STRUCTURAL FUNDS, THERMIE, VALOREN, WASTE.

ENREP Directory of research* projects on the environment* in the Community*. DG XI of the Commission*. Access via ECHO*, Brussels.

Entry for Consumption Customs procedure which allows goods to remain on a customs territory* after any import duties* and charges have been paid and all customs formalities have been completed. Council* Decision* 86/103/EEC.

Entry into Free Circulation The same as 'placing on the market', but not yet defined in the Community*.

ENVIREG Community programme*: regional action to protect the environment* and promote socio-economic development.

Environment Aid* is available for businesses to enable them to conform to new environmental standards* (communication* from the Commission*, 7/11/1974). Four year programmes by the Commission*.
19-21/10/1972: Paris summit*.
22/11/1973: Council* declaration (OJ* C 1 139, 13/6/1987); 17/5/1977: 2nd programme (1977-1981).
2/1976: Barcelona convention (to protect the Mediterranean) (accession of the EC* on 25/5/1977).
3/12/1976: Bonn convention (on chemical pollution of the Rhine) (accession of the EC* on 25/5/1977).
1985: Vienna convention on protecting the ozone layer (cf. Decision* of 16/9/1987 and Regulation* 3322/88/EEC.
1985: Single European Act*: unanimity* required in the Council* to amend or reject an opinion* of the European Parliament*. Venture capital, aid* and loans* made available to businesses to help them protect the environment.
10/6/86: Decision* to include the environment in RTO Framework* (OJ* L 159, 14/6/1986).
1987: Montreal protocol (chlorofluorocarbon emissions).
1987-1992: 4th action programme*; the Council* of environment ministers (Delphi) calls upon the Commission* to study the relation between the development of the internal market* and environment policy.
7/5/1990: Regulation* establishing a *European Environment Agency**.
The Community* has taken protective measures relating to: the effects of nuclear energy*, protection of the ozone layer,

prohibition of PCPs, pollutants in exhaust gas emissions (DIR.* 70/220 ON DIESEL ENGINES, DIR.* OF 9/6/1989 ON CARS; SEE HEAVY GOODS VEHICLES), the export of toxic waste, air and water pollution, packaging, labelling and the use of dangerous substances (Seveso Directive* of 24/6/1982) fertilizers used in agriculture (Directive* of 4/6/1991); on a more general level there are measures to conserve and improve the environment, to protect health, and on rational use of natural resources.

There are draft Directives* making businesses legally reponsible for damage to persons or to the environment caused by their waste* and on protection of flora and fauna. Assessment of the effects of certain public and private works: refineries, nuclear power stations, storage and disposal of radioactive waste*, motorway construction, construction of tracks for high-speed trains and of airports (DIR.* of 27/6/1985, OJ* L 175, 5/7/1975).

Directive* on freedom of access to information relating to the environment (OJ* L 158, 1990).

The possibility of 'environmental labelling' is currently being considered.

1988 was decreed 'environment year'.

The EC* takes part in the work of the United Nations Environment Programme.

DG XI of the Commission*. 13 advisory committees and 2 management committees.

SEE AGRICULTURE, AQUARIUS, BLUE ANGEL, CHEMISTRY, CLIMATOLOGY, COMMUNITY BUREAU OF REFERENCES, CORINE, DECOMMISSIONING NUCLEAR INSTALLATIONS, ECDIN, ECLAIR, ECONOMIC AND SOCIAL COMMITTEE, EINECS, ENDOC, ENERGY, ENREP, ENVIREG, ENVIRONMENT PROGRAMME, ENVIRONMENT PROTECTION, EROS, EURENVIRON, EUREKA, EUROPEAN COAL AND STEEL COMMUNITY, EUROPEAN ENERGY CHARTER, EUROPEAN PARLIAMENT, EUROPEAN REGIONAL DEVELOPMENT FUND, GENETICALLY MODIFIED ORGANISMS, HEAVY GOODS VEHICLES, LABEL, LIFE, MAJOR INDUSTRIAL RISKS, MEDSPA, NETT, NEW COMMUNITY INSTRUMENT, NORCAR-TRAMET, NUCLEAR ENERGY, PACKAGING, RADIATION PROTECTION, RADIOACTIVE WASTE, SINGLE EUROPEAN ACT, STANDARDS, STEP, STRUCTURAL FUNDS, TELEMAN, UNANIMITY, WASTE.

Environment Programme Community programme* to develop the scientific and technical knowledge necessary to allow the Community* to fulfil its responsibilities towards the environment: participation in the 'Global Change' programme – international research into the greenhouse effect; environmental technology and engineering; social and economic aspects of these matters; integrated research* projects. Budget: 414m Ecus* (1990-1994).

EOTC (European Organization for Testing and Certification) Body for establishing a common set of rules for quality assurance in Europe with international reliability. In 1991 the twelve members of the EOTC signed a memorandum of understanding defining a set of benchmarks for assessing companies and their products. Underpinning the agreement is a European Standard, EN 45011/2, which specifies the criteria that quality certification bodies should apply to their own operations.
SEE EVALUATION OF CONFORMITY, OVERALL APPROACH.

EP
SEE EUROPEAN PARLIAMENT.

EPC
SEE EUROPEAN PATENT CONVENTION, EUROPEAN PLASTIC CONVERTEUR.

EPO
SEE EUROPEAN PATENT OFFICE, EUROPEAN PATENT ORGANIZATION.

EPP (European People's Party) Christian Democrat group in the European Parliament*.

Equal Opportunity in Business Principle whereby businesspersons are granted equal opportunities in the common market*.
SEE COMPETITION.

Equal Treatment Under the principle of freedom of movement*, workers* of Member States* of the Community* who move to another Member State* are treated the same as nationals of that Member State*; this prohibits any form of discrimination against them, in particular with regard to employment*, remuneration, working conditions and social security* and tax benefits.

Equity Capital *Credit institutions**: non-consolidated equity capital; capital, reserves and profits after the annual accounts; revaluation reserves; funds for general banking risks; value adjustments; various liabilities (for cooperatives and funds); fixed term preferential cumulative shares and conditional loans.
Less: book value shares held by the institution; intangible assets; significant negative results from the current financial year; holdings in other financial institutions* above 10% of the capital

of the latter, and conditional credit. How equity capital is used, as well as the fixing of minimum ceilings and other deductions is left to the judgement of individual Member States*. Dir.* 89/299/EEC, 17/4/1989 (OJ* L 124/18, 5/5/1989) and Dir.* 86/635/EEC.
SEE EUROPEAN FINANCIAL AREA, SOLVENCY RATIO.

Equivalent Effect
SEE MEASURE HAVING EQUIVALENT EFFECT

ER European Right group in the European Parliament*.

ERASMUS (EuRopean Community Action Scheme for the Mobility of University Students) Community action programme* for students from Member States*: 1. European university network; 2. Grants; 3. Mutual recognition* of qualifications; 4. Supplementary measures. Budget: 85m Ecus* (1987-1989); 192m Ecus* (1990-1992). 15, rue d'Arlon, B-1049 Bruxelles, Belgium.
SEE MUTUAL RECOGNITION, TRAINING POLICY.

ERDF (European Regional Development Fund) Structural fund* established on 1/1/75 to support national aid for regions with development problems, in order to avoid regional disparities within the EEC*. Since 1989 its priorities are to intervene to aid growth and adjustment in economically deprived areas and to help declining industrial regions reconvert (investments in industry, crafts and SME*, energy*, infrastructures, technological innovation, the environment*, job creation and preservation, management consultancies, feasibility studies). See also art. 130 c) and 130 e) of the EEC* treaty*. The Fund helps finance Community programmes*, national programmes of Community* interest, measures to promote endogenous development potential, investment projects and studies.
Subsidies are conditional upon national contributions. Decisions for the application of the Fund are taken by a qualified majority* of the Council* (cooperation procedure*). National administrations receive the requests for finance from the fund and pass these on.
Reg.* 724/75/EEC, 3325/80/EEC, 1787/84/EEC, 42052/88/EEC, 4253/88/EEC, 4254/88/EEC.
DG XVI of the Commission*, Committee of the European Regional Development Fund, Committee for regional development and reconversion.
SEE EUROPEAN INVESTMENT BANK, EUROPEAN SOCIAL FUND, INTEGRATED

MEDITERRANEAN PROGRAMMES, REGIONAL POLICY, SINGLE EUROPEAN ACT, STRUCTURAL POLICY.

ERMES (European Radio MEssaging System) Joint position*, 9/5/1990. Allocation of frequencies by June 1991.
SEE DECT.

EROS (European River Ocean System) Community programme* to provide basic information to help find a realistic compromise between economic development and protection of the environment* and its biological resources.

ERTP Project in the EUREKA* programme: support for projects relating to road transport (technical standards*, road signs, infrastructure).

ES 2 (European Silicon Structures) Project in the EUREKA* programme ('EU 16'): custom integrated circuits (chips). Belgium, France, Netherlands, United Kingdom, Sweden, Switzerland. Budget: 94m Ecus* (1987-1990).

ESA
SEE EUROPEAN SPACE AGENCY.

ESC
SEE ECONOMIC AND SOCIAL COMMITTEE.

ESF
SEE EUROPEAN SOCIAL FUND.

ESF (European Software Factory) Project in the EUREKA* programme ('EU 43'): to work out a 'reference structure' for managing software* production. 18 subprojects. Berlin.

ESO European Southern Observatory, European Organization for Astronomical Research in the Southern Hemisphere.

ESOC (European Space Operations Centre)
SEE EUROPEAN SPACE AGENCY.

ESPRIT (European Strategic Programme for Research and Development in Information Technology) ESPRIT 1: Budget of 23m Ecus* (1984-1987). ESPRIT 2: Budget of 1600m Ecus* (1987-1991): research* and development, basic research*

(microelectronics, data processing systems, office technology). OJ* L 67, 1984, L 118, 6/5/1988.
SEE AMADEUS, INFORMATICS, SCIENCE, TELEMATICS.

ESRIN (European Space Research INstitute)
SEE EUROPEAN SPACE AGENCY.

ESRO
SEE EUROPEAN SPACE RESEARCH ORGANIZATION.

Essential Requirements Fundamental requirements on health*, safety*, protection of the environment*, etc., mentioned in art. 36 of the EEC* treaty* as permissible justifications for restricting the movement of products. They are the legal basis for harmonization* in the 'new approach'* Directives*.
SEE CE, HARMONIZATION.

ESTEC (European Space Research and TEchnology Centre)
SEE EUROPEAN SPACE AGENCY.

ETIC (European Tape Industry Council) Professional coordinating body representing the industry at European level.

ETP (Executive Training Programme) Community programme* for training* young executives in the language, culture and business environment of Japan.

ETSI (European Telecommunications Standards Institute) Established by CEPT* in January 1988 to work out European standards* so that a telecommunications* product or service can be used in all member countries without modification. A majority (71%) of the general assembly, the technical committees and the working parties voted in its favour. Sophia-Antipolis (Alpes-Maritimes, France). BP 52, 06561 Valbonne Cedex, France.
SEE ISDN, STANDARDS, TELECOMMUNICATIONS POLICY, VIDEOTEX.

ETUC European Trade Union Confederation.

ETUI
SEE EUROPEAN TRADE UNION INSTITUTE.

EUA
SEE EUROPEAN UNIT OF ACCOUNT.

EUDISED (EUropean Documentation and Information System for EDucation)

EUI

SEE EUROPEAN UNIVERSITY INSTITUTE.

EUMETSAT (EUropean Organization for the Exploitation of METeorological SATellites) Established in 1986 by the Twelve* plus Austria, Finland, Norway, Sweden, Switzerland and Yugoslavia. Darmstadt-Eberstadt, Germany.

EUR 1, EUR 2 Movement certificates for goods, adopted by the EEC* and the EFTA* from 1973. Since 1986 'approved exporters' have been able to have EUR 1 certificates valid for a year or to replace EUR 2 with a simple declaration of origin* on the invoice (applicable to EUR 1 since 1987).

EURAM (EUropean Research in Advanced Materials) Community research* programme*. Budget: 167m Ecus* (1988-1992). May involve EFTA* countries. OJ* C 186, 16/7/1988. DG XII of the Commission*. Merged with BRITE* to form BRITE/EURAM.

EUROTOM (EURopean ATOMic Energy Community) One of the three European Communities, established by the treaty of Rome* of 25/3/1957 (came into effect 1/1/1958) to 'contribute to the raising of the standard of living in the Member States* and to the development of relations with other countries by creating the conditions necessary for the speedy establishment and growth of nuclear industries' (art. 1) for peaceful use.
Objective: to establish a common energy* market. Specific actions favouring energy supply, research*, safety* and protection of people and the environment*. The Community* has been authorized to take out loans up to 4000m Ecus* (Decision* 77/271/EURATOM; 27/4/1990). A Supply Agency and a Joint Research Centre* (JRC) were also established. Rue de la Loi 200, 1049 Bruxelles, Belgium. DG XVII of the Commission*.

EUREKA Programme set up on the initiative of France on 17/7/1985, uniting 19 European countries (the Twelve*, EFTA* and Turkey) and the Commission* to strengthen cooperation between industry and research* institutes in the field of advanced technology and public works* projects: robotics, biotechnology*, energy*, new materials, lasers, telecommunications*, transport*.

In 1989 there were 302 projects. 89 have been added since. EUREKA is oriented towards the needs of the market with emphasis on creating new products and new markets. Financed both privately and publicly by each of the countries involved. *Organization*: conference of ministers (coordination, approval, responsibility for the projects); High Representatives of the member countries (information, contacts between businesses, finance problems); secretariat in Brussels (collection and dissemination of information, finding partners, attendance at meetings of EUREKA bodies); national coordinators. *Interministerial conferences* (approving projects for EUREKA): *17/7/1985*: Paris; *5-6/11/1985*: Paris; *30/6/1986*: London; *17/12/1986*: Stockholm; *14-15/9/1987*: Madrid; *15/6/1988*: Copenhagen; *18-19/6/1989*: Vienna. Coordinating agency for European Research.
Secretariat: ave des Arts 19H, Boîte 3, B-1040 Bruxelles, Belgium.
SEE COSINE, DRIVE, EURENVIRON, JESSI, RESEARCH POLICY.

EUREKA Broadcasting Project for cooperation between European countries in broadcasting*. Set up by the President of France in April 1988. A report was submitted to the European Council* of Rhodes (2-3/12/1988).
SEE HDTV, TELEVISION WITHOUT FRONTIERS.

EURENVIRON Umbrella project adopted for one year by the EUREKA* conference in Vienna in 1989 to implement programmes to counter pollution (except that arising from nuclear energy*).
SEE ENVIRONMENT.

EURET (EUropean REsearch in Transport) Community research* programme* on transport* in Europe: to develop a transport system which will satisfy the needs of the internal market*, by optimizing networks and logistics. Budget: 25m Ecus* (1990-1993). See also OJ* C 318, 20/12/1989. DG VII of the Commission*.

EURIPA European Information Providers.

EURIS Host computer for EURONET* (1980), used in particular for the CELEX* system.

EURISTOTE Data base* of university theses and studies on European integration. DG X of the Commission*.

Euro 92 French Ministry of Industry's data base* on the internal market, the elaboration and implementation of Community* rules and on Community programmes*.

Eurobarometers Opinion polls carried out by the Commission* on samples of 500 people. 'Flash Eurobarometers' when required; 'Standard Eurobarometers' twice a year. OJ* C 55, 7/3/1980.

EUROBASES Official host computer for Commission* data banks* (access to CELEX*, ECLAS*, INFO 92*, RAPID*, SCAD*). 200, rue de la Loi, 1049 Bruxelles, Belgium. Not to be confused with EUROBASE (SEE MINITEL).

EUROCONTROL (European Organization for the Safety of Air Navigation) 72, rue de la Loi, 1040 Bruxelles, Belgium.

EUROCOOP
SEE EUROPEAN COMMUNITY OF CONSUMER COOPERATIVES.

EUROCOTON
SEE COMMITTEE OF THE COTTON AND ALLIED TEXTILE INDUSTRIES OF THE EEC.

Eurocreation French agency for youth initiatives in Europe to give technical and financial assistance to new businesses started up by young people (technology*, farming, communications*, tourism*). 3, rue Debelleyme, 75003 Paris, France.
SEE SME.

EURODICAUTOM Data bank* of scientific and technical terminology (equivalent terms in the official EC* languages). Access via ECHO*. DG IX of the Commission*.

EURODOCDEL (European Document Delivery)
SEE DOCDEL.

EUROFED Name of the federal structure of central banks in the second stage of the Delors* plan.
SEE EUROPEAN SYSTEM OF CENTRAL BANKS, MONETARY UNION.

EUROFORM Commission* initiative (1990) to align national training* policy for the better use of human resources and to formulate international programmes. Budget: 300m Ecus*.

Euroguichets
SEE EURO INFO CENTRES.

EUROGUIDE French Ministry of European Affairs' data base* (general information on the EC* and the single market*).
SEE MINITEL, OBJECTIVE 1992.

Euro Info Centres (EIC) Created by the Commission* since 1987 to provide businesses with reliable and up-to-date information on Community* activities, sources of information and events, and to help them with programmes*, aid, etc. Each Euro Info Centre runs a regional sub-network, attends trade fairs and congresses, disseminates information and passes on comments to businesses. DG XXIII of the Commission*.

Eurolaser Umbrella project in the EUREKA* programme ('EU 6'): development of a 25 kW CO_2 laser cell. 9 member countries. 1988-1991.

Euromanager Association of managers who are under 30. 13, rue Duroc, 75007 Paris, France.
SEE SME.

EURONALP
SEE MINITEL.

EURONET European telecommunications* network (EURONET DIANE*, 13/2/1980). Transmits information on patents (SEE EUROPEAN PATENT OFFICE) and scientific, technical, social and economic information. Non-governmental advisory committee (EURONET User Forum). Managed by the telecommunications* administrations of the Twelve* and of the EFTA*.

Euronorm Standard* elaborated and approved by the Iron and Steel Nomenclature Coordination Committee and the Commission*.
SEE ECISS.

EUROPACE (EUROpean Programme of Advanced Continuing Education) Cooperation between universities and businesses in rapid-growth areas. Remote training* via satellite (Porta COM system) and electronic communications. Administered by an international association (representatives of the founding businesses and from universities). Paris. Final stage: September 1989.

Europartenariat Business Cooperation Centre* project to bring important financial support, via the ERDF*, to under-developed regions or regions undergoing industrial redevelopment and to encourage cooperation and partnership between businesses in these areas. 1990: Wales. A directory of projects is available via BCNET* and Euro Info Centres*.
SEE SME.

European Association of Clothing Industries Rue Montoyer 47, B-1040 Bruxelles, Belgium.

European Atomic Energy Community (EAEC)
SEE EURATOM.

European Bank for Reconstruction and Development (EBRD) Financial institution devised by the European Council* of Strasbourg (8-9/12/1989) and established 29/5/1990 in Paris to encourage the transition to open market economies and to promote private initiative and the spirit of enterprise in the countries of Central and Eastern Europe by adopting and implementing the principles of pluralist democracy. Agreement applicable before 31 March 1991. 10,000m Ecus* capital, 51% controlled by Member States* of the EC* and with the participation of the member countries of EFTA* and EIB* and of other countries (Australia, Bulgaria, Canada, Cyprus, Czechoslovakia, Egypt, Hungary, Israel, Japan (8.5%), Malta, Morocco, Mexico, New Zealand, Poland, Romania, South Korea, Turkey, United States (10%), CIS (6%) and Yugoslavia). The Community* has twelve seats on the *Board of Directors* (out of 23). *President* elected for four years by a simple majority of the Board of Governors. *General Assembly* (finance ministers of the 42 shareholding countries).
Loans for the economic infrastructures (up to 40%) of eligible countries (limited for 3 years for the CIS); financial advice; assistance in privatizations, mergers*, acquisitions and in setting up joint ventures; business development in the production sector; mobilization of national and foreign capital and of management teams. Specific investment programmes and financial support for projects. Energy Operations Policy. Headquarters in London. President: Jacques Attali (1990-1995).

European Broadcasting Area
SEE BROADCASTING.

European Bureau of Consumers' Unions (BEUC) Group of consumers' associations and consumer institutes of the Twelve*, representing the interests of consumers* in the Community* (1962) and grouping together the organizations of the Six*. Has published a consumer* protection programme. 29, Rue Royale, 1000 Bruxelles, Belgium.
SEE COMPETITION, CONSUMPTION, HEALTH, SAFETY.

European Business Innovation Centre Network (EBN) About one hundred members in the Member States* of the EEC*. Rue Belliard 205, Boîte 2, 1040 Bruxelles, Belgium.

European Centre for the Development of Vocational Training (CEDEFOP) Body established on 10/2/1975 to promote the development of vocational training* and in-service training* by experience and training* programmes. Administered jointly by governments, employers and unions. Bundesallee 22, 1000 Berlin 15, Germany.

European Centre for Medium-Range Weather Forecasts (ECMWF) Intergovernmental organization grouping together the Twelve* (excluding Luxembourg) and Austria, Finland, Sweden, Switzerland, Turkey and Yugoslavia. Brussels* Convention 11/10/1973.

European Centre of Parliamentary Documentation and Research Centre established in 1977 to promote the exchange of information between parliaments, cooperation on documentation, parliamentary libraries and research facilities, subject to the authority of the conference of presidents of European parliamentary assemblies, the President of the European Parliament* and the President of the Parliamentary Assembly of the Council of Europe*. Karl Reiner Ring 3, 1017 Wien, Austria.

European Centre of Public Enterprises (CEEP) Body grouping together 58 public enterprises from Community* countries (1965). Information conferences, studies of public policy and Community programmes*. Rue de la Charité 15 (bte 12), B–1040 Bruxelles, Belgium.

European Centre of Retail Trade (CECODE) Body representing the retail trade industry at Community* level (1965). 6 countries represented.
SEE TRADE.

European Civil Aviation Conference (ECAC) European professional body (1954), 3 bis, Villa Emile Bergerat, 92522 Neuilly, France.
SEE AERONAUTICS.

European Coal and Steel Community (ECSC) One of the three European Communities*, established by the treaty* of Paris* on 18/4/1951 (came into force 25/7/1952) to reduce customs barriers, to progressively abolish quota restrictions and to coordinate the policies of the Member States* (the Six* at that time) in the area of coal* and steel*; to pool resources and markets, under the control of a High Authority*, and to commit Member States* irreversibly to liberalizing trade*, foreshadowing the European Economic Community* (EEC). The treaty* laid down rules on competition* (art. 65 and 66) and employment policy to facilitate the necessary changes. With the signing of the EEC* and EURATOM* treaties*, the Parliament and the Court of Justice* became common to the ECSC, the EEC* and EURATOM.
1/1/1967: *merger of the executive institutions* (a single Commission* and a single Council*). On the other hand the ECSC Consultative Committee was preserved.
Mechanisms of the ECSC: budget* financed by levies* on the production of coal* and steel*; a total ban on official aid*; control of non-discrimination on prices and their publication, and the option for the Commission* to impose minimum and maximum prices; production quotas* fixed in cases of overproduction; social measures favouring mobility and reemployment; a system of loans* (SEE ECSC FUNDS); cooperation between the Commission* and the industries concerned in administering the coal* and steel* common market*; voluntary-restraint agreements with non-member countries* and reciprocal agreements with EFTA* countries.
Arbitration* by the Court of Justice* as provided for in the treaty*.
The Commission* has the right to make the final decision with regard to anti-dumping* and anti-subsidy measures (definitive right to decide on the institution by way of a recommendation*). Its recommendations* have the same force as Directives* of the EEC* and of EURATOM*. DG XVII of the Commission*.

European Commission
SEE COMMISSION OF THE EUROPEAN COMMUNITIES.

European Commission of Human Rights Institution established by the European Convention on Human Rights (examination of claims, amicable settlements, actions brought before the European Court of Human Rights*).

European Committee for Electrotechnical Standardization
SEE CENELEC.

European Committee for the Study of Salt Committee of 13 professional organizations from 13 countries (EEC* + Austria, Switzerland, Turkey).
SEE SALT.

European Community (EC) Name used increasingly frequently, especially since the Single European Act*, for the three Communities* established by the treaties* of Paris* (ECSC*) and of Rome* (EEC*, EURATOM*) to underline the unity of spirit and initiative.

European Community of Consumer Cooperatives (EUROCOOP) European body grouping together federations and commercial groups from five Community* countries (the Six* minus Luxembourg). 1966. Rue Archimède 17a, 1040 Bruxelles, Belgium.
SEE CONSUMPTION, TRADE.

European Company
SEE PUBLIC LIMITED LIABILITY COMPANY IN EUROPEAN LAW.

European Confederation of Agriculture (CEA) Body representing European agriculture* at the OECD* and in the Community* (1948).
SEE COPA.

European Confederation of Christian Trade Unions European body (1958): national professional federations and confederations.

European Confederation of Pulp, Paper and Board Industries (CEPAC) (1963). Representative in the Community* and at GATT*. Rue Defacoz 1, 1050 Bruxelles, Belgium.

European Confederation of Wood-Working Industries (CEIBOIS) Representative European body at Community* level and at the OECD* (1952). An executive Commission is responsible for representation in the Community*. Rue Royale 109-111, 1000 Bruxelles, Belgium.

European Conference of Ministers of Transport (ECMT) Intergovernmental conference: coordination in the field of internal transport* (1953). 18 member countries, including the Twelve*. Secretariat attached to the OECD* secretariat: 19 rue de Franqueville, 75775 Paris Cedex 16, France.

European Conference of Postal and Telecommunications Administrations (CEPT) Intergovernmental conference: coordination in the field of post and telecommunications* services. Technical role with regard to standardization*.

European Container Glass Federation (FEVE) Avenue Louise 89, 1050 Bruxelles, Belgium.

European Convention on Human Rights
SEE COUNCIL OF EUROPE, EUROPEAN COURT OF HUMAN RIGHTS.

European Council Meeting of the heads of state and of government of the Member States* and the President of the Commission* (assisted by the foreign ministers of the Member States* and by one member of the Commission*), established on 10/12/1974 (Paris* summit) and made official by the Single European Act* (adopting the substance of the Stuttgart* declaration); it is the supreme body of political cooperation*, stimulating and coordinating Community* activities. Its decisions are made official by the Council of the European Communities*. Its President is the current President of the Council*. It submits a report to the Parliament after each meeting and once a year on the state of the European Union*.
The European Council met three times a year between 1975 and 1986 and has met twice a year since (except for extraordinary meetings).
1-2/12/1975 Rome (decided that the European Parliament* should be elected by universal suffrage);
7-8/4/1978: Copenhagen (date of the first elections to the European Parliament*);
6-7/7/1978: Bremen (EMS*);
5/12/1978: Brussels (EMS*);
9-10/3/1979: Paris (EMS*);
29-30/12/1979: Dublin (UK contribution to the budget*);

27-28/4/1980: Luxembourg (UK contribution to the budget*);
19/6/1983: Stuttgart (revival of European Union*);
6/1984: Fontainebleau (UK contribution to the budget*);
30/6/1985: Milan (adoption of the White Paper*);
2/12/1985: Luxembourg (preparation of the Single European Act*);
27-28/6/1988: Hannover (liberalization of movements of capital*);
2-3/12/1988: Rhodes (introduction of the Single European Act*);
26-27/6/1989: Madrid (monetary union*);
8-9/12/1989: Strasbourg (monetary union*; European social charter*; Eastern Europe*);
28/5/1990: Dublin (extraordinary meeting: German reunification; aid to Eastern European countries; European Union*; political cooperation*; economic and monetary union*; European economic area*);
25-26/6/1990: Dublin (convening of two intergovernmental conferences on European Union* and economic and monetary union*; environment*; Eastern Europe*; European social charter*; convening of a summit in Paris for 19/11/1990 within the framework of the CSCE*);
13/12/1990: Rome (European Union*; economic and monetary union*; European social area*; taxation*; transport policy*; regional policy*; environment*; association with EFTA* and the countries of Eastern Europe*);
6/1991: Luxembourg (European Union*; economic and monetary union*).
9–10/12/1991: Maastricht (Netherlands) (European Union*; Economic and Monetary Union*; realization of the internal market; Eastern European countries).
6/1992: Lisbon (European Union*; Economic and Monetary Union*; realization of the internal market).
12/1992: Edinburgh (realization of the internal market).

European Council of Chemical Manufacturers' Federations (CEFIC) Body representing national federations at the OECD*. Avenue Louise 250, 1050 Bruxelles, Belgium.

European Council for Nuclear Research
SEE CERN.

European Court of Human Rights Palais des Droits de l'Homme – BP 431 Q6, 67006 Strasbourg Cedex, France.
SEE PARLIAMENTARY ASSEMBLY OF THE COUNCIL OF EUROPE.

European Documentation Centres (EDCs) Based in the academic institutions and main libraries within the regions of the EC's member countries, these provide an information and documentation service to stimulate development of the study of Europe.

European Economic Area (EEA) Extended cooperation project between the Member States* of the Community* and the EFTA* countries; the association is more structured than in current bilateral agreements, with common decision-making and administrative bodies. The project was devised by a group of senior officials from the Commission* and from the EFTA* countries. On 19/12/1989 the ministers of foreign affairs of the countries concerned decided to hold formal negotiations on the subject in the first half of 1990.
Agreement signed in Luxembourg in October 1991 between the Twelve* and the seven EFTA* countries, creating a trading area comprising 380 million people and accounting for 43% of world trade. Free movement of goods, capital, workers and services. This followed 16 months of negotiations and will come into being at the same time as the EC* single market on 1 January 1993. EFTA* is to accept existing EC* legislation. It will have no vote in the Council* but will be consulted on new legislation. There is to be an EEA council, comprising the EC* Council* and one representative from each of the EFTA* governments, and an EEA court to safeguard common regulations. The court will work in conjunction with the CJEC*.
Tariff and trade controls are to be lifted in all sectors but energy, agriculture, coal and steel.
The United Kingdom, France and Germany retain existing fishing rights to North Sea cod. Poorer EC* Member States* with no rights in the North Sea are granted cod quotas of 6000 t in 1993, increasing to 11,000 t in 1997. This is to be shared between Spain and Portugal, but Ireland has also requested participation.
Iceland and Norway were granted a ban against foreign investment in their fishing industries.
The EFTA* countries are to pay low interest loans of 1,500 m Ecus and give grants of 500 m Ecus to Greece, Portugal, Ireland and parts of Spain for development.
Switzerland will have safeguards against real estate investment until 1995 and similar rules will apply until 1996 for Finland, Iceland and Austria.
Switzerland is obliged to build tunnels under the Gotthard and

Loetschberg passes and Austria a new tunnel under the Brenner pass.
Switzerland will retain its 28 t heavy goods vehicle limit and Austria will keep its own rules for cutting pollution by 60% over 12 years.
Future plans include a possible incorporation of Eastern European countries.
SEE CUSTOMS UNION, FREEDOM OF MOVEMENT, RELEVANT COMMUNITY PATRIMONY.

European Economic Community (EEC) One of the three European Communities (with ECSC* and EURATOM*), established by the Treaty of Rome*, signed on 25-3-1957. Its aim was to set up a general common market* between the Member States* (the Six* at that time) with common economic, commercial, social, financial and fiscal policies, incorporating customs union* and economic and monetary union*, and ensuring free movement of goods, people and capital between Member States*.
1/1/1958: The Treaty of Rome* comes into force.
1/1/1973: Accession of Denmark, the Republic of Ireland and the United Kingdom. Free trade agreements between the EEC* and EFTA* come into force.
1/1/1981: Accession of Greece.
1/1/1986: Accession of Spain and Portugal.
SEE ALSO EURATOM, EUROPEAN COAL AND STEEL COMMUNITY, EUROPEAN COMMUNITY, SINGLE EUROPEAN ACT.

European Economic Interest Grouping
SEE EEIG.

European Energy Charter EC* project. Objectives: development of trade; cooperation and coordination; protection of the environment and operational safety; access to resources; conditions of exploitation; code of conduct, etc.

European Environment Agency Agency established by the Twelve* on 28/11/1989: information and coordination of studies (European Space Agency*, Council of Europe*, EUROSTAT*, OECD*). Budget: 30m Ecus*. 14 member administrative board (one per Member State* and two for the Commission*). Multiannual programmes following consultation of a 9 member scientific committee and the Opinion* of the Commission*. European network for monitoring information on the environment. Possible participation of non-member countries*. Reg.* of 7/5/1990, OJ* L 120, 1990.

European Environmental Bureau (EEB) Association for the protection of the environment*.

European Federation of Financial Analysts Societies (FEAAF) European professional federation (1962). Paris. Members in Belgium, France, Germany, Netherlands, United Kingdom, Switzerland.

European Financial Area
SEE BANK, BASEL-NYBORG AGREEMENTS, EQUITY CAPITAL, FREEDOM TO PROVIDE SERVICES, INSURANCE, MOVEMENTS OF CAPITAL, PROSPECTUS, RIGHT OF ESTABLISHMENT, SOLE APPROVAL.

European Footwear Confederation Rue François-Bossaerts 53, 1030 Bruxelles, Belgium.

European Foundation for the Improvement of Living and Working Conditions Community* body set up in Dublin in 1976 to contribute to improving working conditions by developing and disseminating information in this field. Representatives from the Commission*, from the Member States* and from the two sides of industry, as well as experts in the field sit on the Administration Board. Loughlinston House, Shankill, Co. Dublin, Republic of Ireland.

European Foundation for Vocational Training Part of the aid package for Eastern Europe decided at the European Council* in Strasbourg (8-9/12/1989) in the context of the 'group of 24': coordination to help the countries of Eastern Europe (Poland and Hungary first of all) evaluate their needs and pass on their requirements to Community* training* centres, universities and businesses; organization of training* programmes. Berlin (SEE CEDEFOP). Budget: 6000m Ecus* per year (1/7/1990 – 31/12/1990).
SEE PHARE.

European Free Trade Association (EFTA) Intergovernmental organization established by the treaty of Stockholm (4/1/1960). Participant nations: Austria, Norway, Sweden, Switzerland, Finland, Iceland and Liechtenstein. Denmark, the United Kingdom and Portugal, who also signed the establishing treaty, left on accession to the Community*. Bilateral agreements with the

EEC* and the ECSC* which established, on 1/1/1984, a *free-trade area** for industrial products (abolition of customs duties* and all quantitative restrictions* or measures having equivalent effect*). *18/7/1990*: decision of the EC* to open negotiations with a view to concluding a closer association agreement* with EFTA designed to establish a *European economic area** (SEE LUXEMBOURG DECLARATION).
The agreements with the EEC* specify alternative percentage rules which allow products to be designated as being of origin in the country of manufacture where the percentage of imported goods in the finished product does not exceed 30-40%.
SEE ORIGIN, SAD.
Bodies: Council, Secretariat, committees and working groups. 9-11, rue de Varembe, CH-1211 Genève 20, Switzerland.

European Fund for Multilingual Broadcasting
SEE BABEL.

European High Speed Train (HST) European network of high speed trains.
SEE TRANSPORT POLICY.

European Industrial Cleaning Federation Avenue des Nerviens, 117b, 1040 Bruxelles, Belgium.

European Institute for Transuranic Elements One of the four establishments of the Joint Research Centre*. Karlsruhe, Germany.

European Investment Bank (EIB) Independent finance institution of legal personality (art. 129, EEC* treaty) established to finance infrastructure investment projects, which contribute to the balanced development of the Community*, from resources obtained on the capital market.
Resources: contributions from Member States (57,600m Ecus* capital on 1/1/1991) and repayment of previous loans.
Long-term loans, mostly to the regions of the ERDF*: regional development, advanced technology, SME*, environmental protection, communications* infrastructures, development* cooperation.
Board of Governors (ministers nominated by Member States*), Board of Directors (members nominated by Member States* and by the Commission*), Management Committee and Audit Committee. 100 bd Konrad Adenauer, 2950 Luxembourg.

SEE ACP, EUROPEAN BANK FOR RECONSTRUCTION AND DEVELOPMENT, INTEGRATED MEDITERRANEAN PROJECTS, STRUCTURAL FUNDS, PHARE.

European Molecular Biology Laboratory (EMBL) Intergovernmental organization (Austria, Denmark, France, Germany, Israel, Italy, Netherlands, Sweden, Switzerland). 1973. Heidelberg, Germany.

European Monetary System (EMS) System of monetary cooperation which came into effect on 13/3/1979 by applying a European Council* Resolution* of 5 December 1978.
Objectives: to make Europe an area of internal and external monetary stability; to be the framework for increased economic cooperation between the Member States* of the EEC* who take part in the system; to contribute on a global scale to reducing instability in currencies of non-member countries* and to spread the impact of external monetary crises over all the currencies in the system.
24/4/1972-12/3/1979: the 'European currency snake' fixes the maximum fluctuation of the exchange rates of the currencies of the Benelux* countries, Germany, Italy and Denmark at 2.25% (Norway until 12/12/1978).
5/12/1978: adoption of the European Monetary system (participant countries: Benelux*, France, Denmark, Germany; associate members: Spain (19/6/1989) and (in part) the United Kingdom, Greece and Portugal.
13/3/1979: the system comes into effect.
12/3/1985: system strengthened by the board of management of the central banks by improving the opportunities for using the official Ecu*.
28/2/1986: the single European Act* makes the EMS official and recommends developing the Ecu*.
2/1987: the Commission* proposes strengthening the common constraints on exchange rates and on the EMS.
12/9/1987: the Basel-Nyborg agreements* introduce greater symmetry for interventions by central banks.
28/6/1988: the European Council* in Hannover gives a committee presided over by Jacques Delors* the task of proposing concrete stages which would lead to Monetary Union*.
5/1/1990: the Italian Lira fluctuates to the same extent as other countries.

8/10/1990: United Kingdom joins (6% fluctuation margin). Central banks should not allow their currencies to fluctuate more than 2.5% above (ceiling rate) or below (minimum rate)

a central rate expressed in Ecus*. They guarantee this margin taken from a *divergence indicator*. Each of them deposits 20% of their gold and currency reserves with the European Monetary Cooperation Fund (EMCF*) and in return is credited with the equivalent amount in Ecus* which it can use to settle any debts within the EMS.
The EMCF* grants very short term loans (90 days), short term loans (3 months) and medium term loans (2 to 5 years) in order to maintain monetary stability. Monetary realignments* within the EMS are decided by unanimity* (all the participating states are bound by the new parity structure). The EMS has reduced fluctuations between European currencies, produced greater convergence of inflation rates and less variation in the exchange rates between the partners in the system.
10–11/12/1993: European summit meeting at Maastricht* agreed a treaty creating Economic and Monetary Union* to be signed *2/1992* and to come into effect in *1993*.
SEE EUROPEAN FINANCIAL AREA.

European Organization for Nuclear Research
SEE CERN.

European Parliament One of the four main Community institutions, with the Council*, the Commission* and the Court of Justice*.
18/4/1951: the treaty* of Paris* gives the ECSC* a 78 member Common Assembly*. It met in Strasbourg from September 1952 to 1958, in which year the treaties* of Rome* establishing the European Economic Community* (EEC) and the European Atomic Energy Community* (EURATOM) replaced it with the *Assembly of the European Communities*, with responsibility for all three Communities (3/1958: 142 members; 1973: 198 members, following the accession of Denmark, Ireland and the United Kingdom);
7/1979: 410 members elected by direct universal suffrage (decision taken by the Paris* summit of December 1974, adopted in September 1976, came into effect on 1/7/1978);
1/1/1981: 434 members, following the accession of Greece;
1/1/1986: 518 members, following the accession of Spain and Portugal;
22/4/1970: treaty* of Luxembourg*; *22/7/1975*: treaty* of Brussels* (giving the assembly greater budgetary powers);
1/7/1987: the Single European Act* confirms the name *European Parliament* (which the Assembly had given itself in 1958 and

1962) and extends its powers: opinions*, assent on proposals for accession and on association agreements*; cooperation procedure* with the Council*. The Parliament may start proceedings to annul a Community* Regulation* if its interests are injured (CJEC* Judgement* of 22/5/1990).
The Parliament adopts the Community* budget* after having drawn it up jointly with the Council*; it may reject it, amend of its own authority the distribution of non-compulsory expenditure*, increase the amount of the budget within certain limits (fixed each year with the Commission* and the Council*), and propose amendments to compulsory expenditure*. It gives a discharge* to the Commission* to implement the budget*.
It may request starting a *conciliation procedure** with the Council* if it is in disagreement with it concerning a proposal by the Commission*, the adoption of which would have significant financial consequences.
It enjoys *general control* over the activities of the Community institutions* with the power to pose written and oral questions* to the Commission* and the Council*, to force the Commission* to resign by passing a motion of censure* against it and the power to adopt own-initiative resolutions*. The Commission* and the Council* are represented at committee meetings and at open sittings. Since 1981 the President of the European Council* gives a report to the Parliament of the work of the European Council* and the President of the Commission* presents its programme to the Parliament and asks for a vote of confidence. Emergency debates on topical matters.
Every three months the European Political Cooperation* president takes part in a colloquy with the Political Affairs Committee of the Parliament and every year a debate is organized on its results and future actions, not including questions* posed by members of the Parliament in this area. A *joint assembly* with representatives of the 66 ACP* countries examines economic and development problems concerning the Lomé Convention*.
Administration: One President, 14 Vice-presidents and five Quaestors are elected for two and a half years.
This *Bureau** is, with the chairmen of the political groups in the Parliament (Communist, Rainbow, Socialist, European People's Party (Christian Democrats), European Democratic Alliance, Liberal, Democratic and Reformist, European Democrats, European Right) an *enlarged Bureau**, which lays down the agenda for the plenary sittings which are held in Strasbourg one week in every month, except in August, and for two weeks in October or November. Extraordinary sittings held in Brussels, Belgium.

18 committees meet in Brussels for two or three days every month to prepare reports on proposals by the Commission*, to examine draft Opinions* and to prepare own-initiative Resolutions*. The Parliament may delegate its powers of decision to a committee (art. 37 of its rules of procedure). It lays down its own rules of procedure.
2/1984: 'draft European Union treaty' (Spinelli* report*) for co-decision with the Council*.
Presidents since 1979: Simone Veil (1979-1982), Pieter Dankert (1982-1984), Pierre Pfimlin (1984-1987), Lord Plumb (1987-1989), Enrique Baron (1989-1993).
General Secretariat: Centre Européen, Plateau de Kirchberg, BP 601, 2920 Luxembourg and 89-91, rue Belliard, 1040 Bruxelles, Belgium.
SEE AMENDMENT, QUAESTOR, QUESTION.

European Parliamentary Assembly
SEE COMMON ASSEMBLY.

European Patent Patent* awarded by the European Patent Office (Munich) to protect an invention in all states party to the Munich Convention of 5/10/1973 (the Twelve* – less Ireland and Portugal – Austria, Liechtenstein, Monaco, Norway, Sweden, Switzerland) which established a European system for granting patents (same protection as national patents).
SEE COMMUNITY PATENT, PATENT FOR INVENTION, RESEARCH POLICY.

European Patent Convention Convention adopted by 13 European states (EEC* and EFTA*) in Munich in 1973: to rationalize procedures for issuing patents* by establishing a common judicial system.
SEE EUROPEAN PATENT OFFICE.

European Patent Office (EPO) Office established in 1973 (Munich convention) to issue patents valid throughout Europe. Munich, Germany.
SEE COMMUNITY PATENT, EUROPEAN PATENT.

European Patents Organization (EPO) Intergovernmental organization (1977) responsible for European Patents*. Austria, Belgium, France, Germany, Italy, Liechtenstein, Luxembourg, Netherlands, Sweden, Switzerland, United Kingdom. Based in Munich, Germany.

European Plastic Converteur (EPC) Rue Capouillet 19, 1060 Bruxelles, Belgium.

European Political Cooperation (EPC) Cooperation between Member States* to coordinate their foreign policy. Meetings of foreign ministers under the presidency of the country which presides over the Council* (made official by the Single European Act*).
18/7/1961: Bad-Godesberg-Bonn: heads of state and government of the Six* commit themselves to hold regular meetings (commitment unfulfilled due to the rejection of the Fouchet* report);
1-2/12/1969: Summit* in The Hague* (adoption of the principle of political cooperation);
27/10/1970: approval of the Luxembourg* report (Davignon* report): creation of an instrument for voluntary harmonization* of foreign policy by frequent intergovernmental consultation;
23/7/1973: Copenhagen* summit* (additional report to the Davignon* report adopted by the foreign ministers of the Nine*: 4 meetings per year and continuous consultation);
9-10/12/1974; 1981: London report;
1983: Stuttgart: formal declaration on European Union*;
1987: following the Single European Act*, the establishment of the position of Secretary (permanent) for political cooperation (Brussels*), assisted by officials appointed in rotation by the foreign minister of the country holding the presidency (SEE COUNCIL, TROIKA).
25-26/6/1990: the Dublin* summit* discusses strengthening of EPC within the framework of European Union (convening of an intergovernmental conference to produce a result before 31/12/1993).
Common declarations by foreign ministers on political issues. The President replies, on behalf of the foreign ministers, to questions* from members of the European Parliament*. The President presents his programme at the beginning of his mandate and an annual report on EPC. He/she monitors, with the Commission*, cohesion between Community* common policy and actions or guidelines agreed within the framework of EPC. The European Parliament* debates matters relating to EPC.
SEE COMMON FOREIGN AND SECURITY POLICY, REPORT.

European Regional Development Fund
SEE ERDF.

European Research and Development Committee (CERD) Committee of experts at the Commission*.

European Social Area The objective is to harmonize* the social legislation of the Member States* in order to avoid social dumping* and the disadvantages associated with non-competitiveness in relation to non-member countries* because of very high labour costs in the Community* and in order to increase mobility within the Community*.
21/1/1974: action programme (hygiene, health* and safety*).
1975: CEDEFOP* established in Berlin.
6/1984: European Council* of Fontainebleau.
1/1985: Val Duchesse meeting (ESC*, UNICE*, CEEP*).
2/1985: Single European Act* (qualified majority* in the Council* for the harmonization* Directives*).
28/6/1988: European Council* of Hannover.
3/12/1988: European Council* of Rhodes.
8-9/12/1989: European Social Charter*.
See also art. 117-128 of the EEC* treaty*.
SEE CASSTM, DUMPING, ELIGIBILITY FOR EMPLOYMENT, EMPLOYMENT, EUROPEAN SOCIAL FUND, FAMILY BENEFITS, SOCIAL SECURITY BENEFITS, STRUCTURAL POLICY, TRAINING, WORKING CONDITIONS.

European Social Charter Text adopted in December 1989 (See also COM (89) 471) by the European Council* to obtain from 11 Member States* of the Community* minimum commitments concerning the right to employment*, social security*, education* and training*, of association, negociation and to conclude collective agreements, of freedom of movement, of men and women to equal treatment*, to information, consultation and worker participation*, to protection for elderly people and to flexible retirement and rights relating to working conditions*. This charter refers to a more detailed action programme which defines 42 initiatives, all of which should have been adopted by the end of 1991. The charter was a priority of the Italian presidency of the Council* (2nd half of 1990). 13/9/1990: resolution* of the European Parliament*.

European Social Fund (ESF) Community fund* set up by the EEC* treaty* (art. 123-128) to aid actions against long-term unemployment and for the professional integration of persons under 25 years by vocational training*, accompanied if necessary by vocational guidance and recruitment premiums for newly

created stable employment and aid for creating independent businesses.
Priorities: transnational operations, advanced technology, women, migrant workers, disabled workers.
Administered by DG V of the Commission* (Tripartite Consultative Committee on the European Social Fund: government, employers, trade unions). Council* Decisions* 66/71, 801/71. Reg.* (EEC) 2950/83, 3283/85, 3284/85, 2052/88, 4253/88, 4255/88.
SEE COMMON AGRICULTURAL POLICY, CONSULTATIVE COMMITTEE ON THE EUROPEAN SOCIAL FUND, EUROPEAN SOCIAL AREA, INTEGRATED MEDITERRANEAN PROJECTS, REGIONAL POLICY.

European Social Fund Committee
SEE CONSULTATIVE COMMITTEE ON THE EUROPEAN SOCIAL FUND.

European Space Agency Private body grouping together the European Space Research Organisation (ESRO)* and the European Space Vehicle Launcher Development Organization (ELDO) to ensure and promote cooperation in European space research for peaceful ends. *Members*: Austria, Denmark, France, Germany, Ireland, Italy, Norway, the Netherlands, Spain, Sweden, Switzerland, United Kingdom. *Associate member*: Finland. Coordination of scientific and technical programmes; launch and control of satellites and rockets, exploitation of data collected. Examples: Ariane programme, Hermes shuttle. 1900 staff.
Administrative headquarters: 8, rue Mario Nikis, 75015 Paris, France. Technical centres throughout Europe.

European Space Research Organization (ESRO) Organization set up in 1964 to coordinate space research* programmes in European countries. Merged with the European Space Vehicle Launcher Development Organization (ELDO) to form the European Space Agency* (ESA).

European Standard (EN) Standard* adopted by qualified majority* by CEN* and CENELEC* to replace the corresponding national standard*. Before coming into force it may be preceded by the publication of a Draft European Standard*. Reference to European Standards is laid down in the Directives* concerning public contracts* and in technical harmonization* Directives*.
SEE CE.

European System of Central Banks (EUROFED) Financial institution proposed in 1989 by the Delors* committee to achieve the objective of a single monetary policy: federative structure independent of the national central banks.
SEE MONETARY UNION.

European Technical Approval Favourable technical assessment of the aptitude for use of a product (public works contracts*) carried out by the body established for this purpose by a Member State*.
SEE ACCREDITATION.

European Telecommunications Standards Institute
SEE ETSI.

European Testing and Approval Organization Organization set up by the EC*, EFTA*, CEN* and CENELEC* (letter of intent of 18/5/1990) to ensure efficient coordination of agreements on mutual recognition* of test and approval certificates and to ensure the circulation of information and to promote agreements in the private sector. Starts at the end of 1992. *Parties involved*: consumers, trade unions, businessmen, European testing and certification* organizations, European standardization* bodies in the EC* and EFTA*.
SEE OVERALL APPROACH, WORKERS.

European Trade Union Committee of the Textile, Clothing and Leather Industries Committee representing the unions of the workers in these industries at European level. Rue Joseph Stevens 8, Bruxelles, Belgium.
SEE COMITEXTIL, EUROPEAN SOCIAL AREA.

European Trade Union Institute (ETUI) Research institute founded on 10/2/1978 by the European Trade Union Confederation. Publishes works in areas affecting trade union activity and organizes training courses for trade unionists. Subsidized by the Community* (convention of 7/6/1978). 662, Boulevard de l'Impératrice, 1000 Bruxelles, Belgium.

European Training and Promotion Centre for Farming and Rural Life (CEPFAR) Association established by COPA*, the General Committee for Agricultural Cooperation in the EC*, the European Council of Young Farmers of the European Community* and the European Federation of Associations of

Farm Workers. It is supported by the Community*. Brussels, Belgium.

European (Political) Union The Council* and the European Council* have repeatedly laid down the objective of political union and have commissioned prominent personalities to write reports on the subject.
10-11/2/1961 (Bonn*): the Six* commit themselves to establishing political union.
19/10/1961: 1st Fouchet* Plan.
4/12/1961: 2nd Fouchet* Plan.
18/1/1962: 3rd Fouchet* Plan.
14/4/1962: negotiations on the Fouchet* Plan adjourned.
1-2/12/1969 (The Hague*): European integration relaunched.
27/10/1970 (European Council* of Luxembourg*): Davignon* Plan adopted.
19-21/10/1972: Summit of the Nine* in Paris: union by 1980.
14/2/1974: Spinelli* draft treaty adopted by the European Parliament*.
16-17/10/1974: 1st Bertrand report* to the European Parliament*.
3/1975: Marjolin* report*.
26/6/1975: Ortoli* report*.
10/7/1975: 2nd Bertrand report*.
29/12/1975: Tindemans* report* (progressive reform and 'qualitative change').
29-30/11/1976 (European Council* of The Hague*): annual reports by the ministers of foreign affairs and by the Commission* on short-term achievable progress in European Union.
19/6/1983: European Council* of Stuttgart* (revival of the Community*).
6/1984: European Council* of Fontainebleau*.
30/6/1985: European Council* of Milan* (preparation of the Single European Act*).
2/12/1985: European Council* of Luxembourg* (adoption of the Single European Act*).
25-26/6/1990: European Council* of Dublin*: objective to have a ratified treaty before 31/12/1992 (following an intergovernmental conference).
14/12/1990: intergovernmental conference in Rome*.
9–10/12/1991: examination of the draft treaty at the European Council* of Maastricht.
10–11/12/1991: European summit meeting at Maastricht* agreed a treaty creating European Political Union to be signed 2/1992.

SEE TREATIES OF MAASTRICHT.
SEE EUROPEAN POLITICAL COOPERATION, SINGLE EUROPEAN ACT.

European Unit of Account (EUA) Unit of account replaced by the Ecu* on 1/1/1981 (REG.* 3308/80/EEC-EURATOM, 16/12/1980). See also art. 10 of the financial Regulation* of 21/12/1977, applicable to the general EC* budget* (REG.* 2779/88/EEC, OJ* L 33, 30/11/1988) for acts relating to customs. Amounts which are expressed in units of account are considered as being in Ecus* from 1/1/1979, with the exception of amounts which are to be converted according to representative exchange rates.

European University Institute (EUI) Institute for research and postgraduate education established by the Member States* of the Community* (convention of 19/4/1972) in Florence, Italy. Issues doctorates of the same standard as national doctorates. Badia Fiesolana, Via dei Roccetini 9, 50016 San Domenico di Fiesole, Italy.

Europêche (Association of National Organizations of Fishing Enterprises of the EEC) Rue de la Science 23-25, Boîte 15, 1040 Bruxelles, Belgium.

EUROPOLIS EUREKA* project (control systems for urban and inter-urban traffic): Denmark, France, Italy, Spain. Budget: 128m Ecus* over 7 years.

Eurosecurities Securities which are distributed by a syndicate, at least two of whose members are based in different states, and which are bought in one or more states other than that of the issuer, and which may only be signed or acquired in the first instance via the intermediary of a credit institution* or another financial institution*. Dir.* 89/298/EEC (OJ* L 124/8, 5/5/1989).

EUROSIDIC (European Scientific Information Dissemination Service, now *European Association of Information Services)* Association of private and public bodies to exchange information on production.

EUROSPORTELLO Confindustria (Italian Employers' Association) computer network on Community* matters.

EUROSTAT
SEE STATISTICAL OFFICE OF THE EUROPEAN COMMUNITIES.

EURO TECH ALERT Community* information system of study reports on research* financed by various Member States* of the Community*.
SEE SPRINT.

EUROTECNET Community programme*: vocational training* and new information technology (SME*).

EUROTRA Advanced design machine translation programme. Community programme*, part of the 4th action plan to improve the transfer of information between the official languages of the Community*. 10m Ecus* (1989-1990). Decisions* 410/89, 29/6/1989 (OJ* L 200, 13/7/1989) and of the 5/6/1990. Eurotra III: updated in line with international evolution in translation practice. DG XIII/B of the Commission*.
SEE LINGUA, SYSTRAN, TRAINING POLICY.

EUROTRAC Project in the EUREKA* programme ('EU 7'): transport and transformation of pollutants in the air over Europe. 17 member countries.
SEE ENVIRONMENT.

EURYDICE Education information network in the Community* (cooperation in higher education, cultural and vocational training* for migrant workers, development of foreign language teaching).

EUTELSAT European satellite telecommunications* organization established by the European Space Agency* at the instigation of the members of the European Conference of Postal and Telecommunications Administrations (CEPT*). 1964. 26 member states. 33 avenue du Maine, 75015 Paris, France.
SEE EUMETSAT, IMMARSAT, INTELSAT.

Evaluation of Conformity Ways in which a product is considered to be in conformity to standards*. Memorandum* by the Commission* (COM (89) 209, OJ* C 231, 1989). Joint position* established by the Council* on 20/6/1990, Decision* pending. There will be nine modules for awarding the 'CE' mark for an industrial product. Quality standards* of the EN 29.000 series will be extended for products, and those of the EN 45.000 series for the technical bodies responsible for the evaluation procedures.
SEE CERTIFICATE OF CONFORMITY, EOTC, OVERALL APPROACH.

EVCA (European Venture Capital Association) DG XIII of the Commission*. Clos du Parnasse 11F, 1040 Bruxelles, Belgium.

EWOS (European Workshop on Open Systems) Established in December 1987 under the aegis of CEN*.

Exception on Grounds of Illegality Legal channel allowing a defendant to bring an appeal* before the Court of Justice* of the European Communities* against an individual action, thus questioning the legality of the rules behind the implementation of this action.

Exception Procedure Procedure for awarding public contracts* by which the contracting authority* may negotiate with a supplier without publishing a contract notice (where a previous open procedure* or restricted procedure* has failed; where there is just one suitable supplier in the Community*; in the case of objects to be made for research* or testing purposes; in the case of unforeseen events; for additional deliveries; for supplies quoted and purchased on a stock exchange*; for supplies which have been declared to be secret).

Exchange Control Interventions by official authorities on the exchange market by buying or selling currencies or by limiting the convertibility of currencies to protect the balance of payments. Abolished in the Community* with the liberalization of movements of capital*.
SEE EUROPEAN FINANCIAL AREA.

Exchange Rate Mechanism Mechanism within the EMS* which helps to preserve monetary stability. Participating Member States* accept that they must keep the market rate for their currency within set limits either side of their bilateral central rate*.

Excise Indirect tax on certain petroleum products, alcoholic drinks and tobacco. The White Paper* provides for the standardization* of excise within the harmonization* of indirect taxation* (COM (87) 321, 324; COM (89) 525, 526, 527). Directive* of 19/12/1972 (OJ* L 303, 31/12/1972) on tobacco (See also COM (87) 325 and COM (87) 326). The Strasbourg European Council* (8-9/12/1989) decided that, in principle,

products subject to excise would move between authorized warehouses under suspension of taxes.
SEE BARRIERS, CONVERGENCE, TAXATION, VAT.

Excluded Sectors Sectors of industry (water, energy*, telecommunications*, transport) which are provisionally excluded (until 1/1/1993 and 1/1/1996 for Spain, 1998 for Portugal and Greece) from the principle of opening up public contracts*. Exemptions will still exist after these dates for water distribution, prospecting for and production of oil and natural gas, electricity supply, air and sea transport and public works contracts* not exceeding 5m Ecus* and public supply contracts* not exceeding 400,000 Ecus* (600,000 Ecus* for telecommunications*). Community preference* for EC* undertakings. Directive* of 17/9/1990.
SEE COMPETITION.

Exclusive Purchase Agreement Agreement* which obliges a person wishing to resell to purchase exclusively from one fixed supplier. Subject to the rules governing agreements between undertakings* in Member States* of the Community*.
SEE COMPETITION.

Exclusive Rights Right by which someone is the sole exploiter of products and goods. Subject to the prohibition of measures having equivalent effect* (art. 30-34 of the EEC* treaty) in so far as it makes imports* or exports* more difficult or more costly in relation to sales of national products or to other imports* or exports*.

Exemption Exemption from the prohibition of agreements between undertakings*, granted by the Commission* in some cases (*individual exemption*), or, following authorization by the Council*, granted for certain categories of agreements if they fulfil certain conditions (*exempting regulations*) under competition* law. The parties involved must notify the Commission* of their agreement in advance in order to be able to receive an *individual exemption*. Horizontal agreements (SEE AGREEMENTS BETWEEN UNDERTAKINGS) which receive a category exemption: specialization agreements (REG.* 417/85/EEC OF THE COMMISSION*), research* and development agreements (REG.* 418/85/EEC OF THE COMMISSION*). Vertical agreements which receive a category exemption: sole distribution* agreements (REG.* 1983/83/EEC OF THE COMMISSION*), exclusive purchase agreement* (REG.*

1984/83/EEC OF THE COMMISSION*), agreements on the distribution, sales and after-sales service of motor vehicles (REG.* 123/85/EEC OF THE COMMISSION*), franchise* agreements (REG.* 4087/88/EEC OF THE COMMISSION*), licensing of patent rights agreements (REG.* 2349/84 OF THE COMMISSION*), know-how licensing agreements (REG.* 556/89/EEC OF THE COMMISSION*). An exemption is granted for a fixed period of time which may be extended.

Exhibitions and Fairs Display signs indicating that imported goods* may not be sold in a Member State, because they do not conform to national standards* or regulations, are considered as measures having equivalent effect*, in contravention of art. 30 of the EEC* treaty*.
SEE MEASURE HAVING EQUIVALENT EFFECT.

Export Transport and sale of goods from one state to the customs territory* of another state or group of states.
SEE COMMON COMMERCIAL POLICY, COMMON CUSTOMS TARIFF, COMMON MARKET, CUSTOMS UNION, FREE-TRADE AREA, IMPORT, TEMPORARY EXPORT.

Export Declaration Form to be filled in and submitted to a customs office* by a natural or legal person wanting to export goods from the customs territory* of the Community*. The correct form must be signed and accompanied by the documents required for the purpose of applying the specific export duties* and other provisions governing the export* of the goods in question. Dir.* 81/177/EEC, 24/2/1981 (OJ* L 83, 30/3/1981).
SEE CUSTOMS (ALL ENTRIES).

Export Duties *Agriculture* agricultural levies* and other export charges laid down by the Common Agricultural Policy* or by specific procedures applicable to certain goods produced by processing agricultural products. Dir.* 81/177/EEC, 24/2/1981 (OJ* L 83, 30/3/1981).

EXPROM Community programme* to help businesses get to know the Japanese market. ETP* sub-programme.

Extensification Voluntary reduction of agricultural production of surplus products. Community* financial incentives.
SEE AGRICULTURAL PRICES, COMMON AGRICULTURAL POLICY, CORESPONSIBILITY.

Extensification (Programme) Community programme* to reduce production of certain products by at least 20% without increasing production in another sector. EAGGF* provides 25% of funding. Reg.* of 25/5/1988.
SEE COMMON AGRICULTURAL POLICY, QUOTA, RESTRUCTURING, STRUCTURAL POLICY.

F

Fairs
SEE EXHIBITIONS AND FAIRS.

Family Benefits Member States* must pay family benefit to the families of all nationals of the Community* having regular employment on their territory, wherever the place of residence of their family might be (Judgement* of the Court of Justice* of 15/1/1986, confirmed in 3/1989, Council* Decision* of 30/10/1989).
SEE EUROPEAN SOCIAL AREA, SOCIAL SECURITY BENEFITS, WORKERS.

FAMOS Project in the EUREKA* programme: robotics in manufacturing industries.

FAO
SEE FOOD AND AGRICULTURE ORGANIZATION OF THE UNITED NATIONS.

FAR (Fisheries and Agricultural Research) Community* research programme* to promote interdisciplinary research into a rational use of resources. Development of aquaculture and new methods for the use of resources which have not been widely researched. Budget: 30m Ecus* (1988-1992). See also OJ* L 134, 4/11/1987. DG XIV of the Commission*.

FAST (Forecasting and Assessment in Science and Technology) Sub-programme of the MONITOR* programme, to measure the impact of technology on economic and social development. Budget: 14m Ecus*. See also COM (88) 386 F. DG XII of the Commission*.
SEE SAST, SPEAR.

FEAAF (Fédération Européenne des Associations d'Analystes Financiers)
SEE EUROPEAN FEDERATION OF FINANCIAL ANALYSTS' SOCIETIES.

Federation of the Pharmaceutical Industry Associations in the EEC (GIIP) (1959). Brussels, Belgium.

Fee Charge made by a Member State* of the Community* for a service rendered, if the service brings an individual business-person real benefit (not all the persons carrying out the same kind of business), failing which the fee may be considered to be a charge having equivalent effect*, which thus impedes competition*.

FEVE (Fédération Européenne du Verre d'Emballage)
SEE EUROPEAN CONTAINER GLASS FEDERATION.

FFSRS Data base* of EEC* studies on the structure of agricultural production (EUROSTAT*).

FIGED (Fédération Internationale des Grandes Entreprises de Distribution)
SEE INTERNATIONAL FEDERATION OF RETAIL DISTRIBUTORS.

Financial Aid Production aid (paid by the Community* to farmers who agree to cultivate certain products, or designed to directly support farmers in less-favoured regions).
SEE COMMON AGRICULTURAL POLICY, INTEGRATED MEDITERRANEAN PROGRAMMES.

Financial Engineering Availability of venture capital for undertakings.
SEE DRIVE, ECSC FUNDS, ERDF, EUROPEAN INVESTMENT BANK, EVCA, NEW COMMUNITY INSTRUMENT.

Financial Instruments Funds which allow the Community* to intervene according to policy.
SEE AID, BUDGET, COMMON AGRICULTURAL POLICY, EMPLOYMENT, ENERGY, ENVIRONMENT, EUROPEAN SOCIAL AREA, REGIONAL POLICY, RESEARCH POLICY, RESTRUCTURING.

Financial Solidarity Basic principle behind the Common Agricultural Policy* (CAP), whereby the costs of the policy are shared. The EAGGF* finances expenditure on a common basis, irrespective of the product or Member State* concerned.

Fine The Commission* of the EC* may, by way of a Decision*, impose fines or penalty payments* for infringements of Community Law* (for example competition law*).

Fiscal Barriers
SEE BARRIERS.

Fisheries Policy Community* policy based on the fisheries Common Market Organization*: marketing (quality) standards*, common pricing system, trade arrangements with non-member countries* (common customs tariff*), tariff quotas according to the supply situation on the Community* market. *Agreement of 25/1/1983*: Community* system for conserving and administering resources (Total Allowable Catch (TAC), mesh size for fishing nets, authorized fishing areas), access in coastal areas within twelve miles of the coast (except where historical rights dictate otherwise); CMO* (implementation: 1/1/1983); structural measures (REG.* 4/10/1983). Annex E of the Stockholm* convention excludes certain products from the free-trade* system between the EFTA* countries.
SEE FAR, FISHERIES PROGRAMME, FRONTIER CONTROL.

Fisheries Programme Community programme* to coordinate fisheries research* (management of the fisheries business, technology*, aquaculture, improving fisheries products). Budget: 30m Ecus* (1988-1992). OJ* L 314, 4/11/1987. DG XII and DG XIV of the Commission*.
SEE FISHERIES POLICY.

FLAIR (Food-Linked AgroIndustrial Research programme) Community* research* programme* in the field of food science and technology (adapting foods to the needs of the market: quality, safety* etc.). Budget: 25m Ecus* (1989-1993). DECISION* 411/89/EEC, 20/6/1989 (OJ* L 200, 13/7/1989). DG XII of the Commission*.
SEE FOODSTUFFS.

Florence Agreement Agreement on the duty-free importation of certain objects of an educational, scientific or cultural nature, formulated on the initiative of UNESCO* and signed on 26/11/1976. Applicable in the EC* following the Decision* of the Council* of 8/5/1979 (79/505/EEC, OJ* L 134, 1979).

FOD (French Overseas Departments) They receive development cooperation aid from the EEC* (SEE DOCK DUES, EDF, POSEIDOM). The Commission* has adopted a further 250m Ecus* programme (1989-1993) to assist the most outlying areas of the Community* (French, Portuguese and Spanish departments).

Food
SEE AGRICULTURE, COMMON AGRICULTURAL POLICY, CONFERENCE OF AGRI-FOODSTUFF INDUSTRIES, FAO, FOODSTUFFS, FLAIR, FOOD EUROPEAN WORKING GROUP.

Food Aid Certain goods in public storage are delivered free by the Community* to LDCs*, either in a bilateral capacity or via international organizations.
SEE FOOD AND AGRICULTURE ORGANIZATION OF THE UNITED NATIONS, UNO.

Food and Agriculture Organization of the United Nations (FAO) Specialist UN* institution (Rome). Objectives: to improve levels of nutrition throughout the world and to increase agricultural efficiency.

Food European Working Group Association of European teachers and researchers (economic research on the food industries). 16, rue Claude Bernard, 75231 Paris, France.

Foodstuffs Freedom of movement is ensured (except where essential requirements* state otherwise) by the harmonization* of national regulations by means of Directives*. From 1/1/1993 any plastic surface intended to come into contact with foodstuffs to conform to a Directive* from the Commission* (February 1990).
SEE AGRICULTURE, COMMON AGRICULTURAL POLICY, CONSUMPTION, FOOD.

Footwear
SEE EUROPEAN FOOTWEAR CONFEDERATION.

FORCE Community programme* on continuing education for adults. Aid for innovation; grants for teacher training; transnational pilot schemes; sectoral study. Budget: 24m Ecus* (1991-92).

Foreign Relations
SEE COMMON COMMERCIAL POLICY, COMMON CUSTOMS TARIFF, ECONOMIC AND SOCIAL COMMITTEE, EUROPEAN PARLIAMENT, EUROPEAN POLITICAL COOPERATION, NON-MEMBER COUNTRIES.

Foreign Trade
SEE CUSTOMS (ALL ENTRIES), EXPORT, FOREIGN RELATIONS, GATT, IMPORT.

FOREST (FOrestry sector RESearch and Technology) Community programme* on research* and technology in forestry: to increase resources and the competitiveness of the forestry industries; wood and cork technology; manufacture of pulp and paper. Sub-programme of the research* and development programme on renewable raw materials. COM (88) 795 F (OJ* C 52, 1/3/1989); COM (89) 247 F-SYN 188 (OJ* C 164, 16/7/1989). 1990-1992. DG XI of the Commission*.
SEE FORESTRY POLICY.

Forestry Policy There are Community* provisions for the protection, development and optimization of forestry in the Member States*. Cork comes under the CAP*, other forestry products under the Common Customs Tariff*. Reg.* (EEC) 3528/86, 3529/86, 17/11/1986 (OJ* L 326, 21/11/1986); 1609/89, 29/5/1989 (OJ* L 165, 15/6/1989); 1610/89, 1611/89, 1612/89, 29/5/1989 (OJ* L 165, 15/6/1989); Dir.* 66/404/EEC, 14/6/1966 (OJ* 125, 11/7/1966); 71/161/EEC, 30/3/1971 (OJ* L 087, 17/4/1971).
SEE ATMOSPHERIC POLLUTION, EFICS, ENVIRONMENT, FOREST, CEI-BOIS.

Fouchet (Christian) French statesman, author of reports* on European Political Cooperation*.

Fourth Resource The contribution made by each Member State* of the Community* to the budget*, proportional to its GDP; introduced by the Brussels* agreement of February 1988.

Franchise Rights of industrial and intellectual property concerning trade marks, trade names, signs, designs and models, patent and know-how copyrights for use in the sale of products or services to end users. Agreement by which a business (the *franchisor*) grants another business (the *franchisee*) the right to exploit the above rights under conditions of mutual commitment, against payment for the franchise. The judgement* of the Court of Justice* of 26/1/1986 ('Pronuptia') recognized that a franchise does not in itself infringe competition* law, provided that the clauses in the agreement ensuring protection of know-how and other knowledge provided by the franchisor, or which maintain and control their identity and reputation, are not in contravention of Community law*. On the other hand clauses relating to pricing (imposed prices) and to market shares are subject to an application for exemption* (art. 85.3 of the EEC* treaty*). The franchisor must prove that the agreement 'contributes to improving the production or distribution of goods or to promoting technical or economic progress, while allowing consumers a fair share of the resulting benefit, and does not impose on the undertakings concerned restrictions which are not indispensable to the attainment of these objectives, nor afford such undertakings the possibility of eliminating competition in respect of a substantial part of the products in question'. The Commission* has worked out a Regulation* on category exemptions* (4087/88/EEC, OJ* L 359, 1988) for this type of agreement, but not including industrial franchises. It accepts measures necessary for protecting the trade mark of the franchisor, and its know-how if this gives the franchisee a competitive advantage. Other permissible clauses: exclusive supply, territorial exclusivity, non-competition. The know-how must be secret, substantial and identified.

Free Circulation Authorization for the import* to a Member State* of goods already imported to another Member State*, following completion of customs formalities and collection of duties and charges having equivalent effect which allow them to circulate freely throughout the Community*. The principle of free circulation comes in art. 9.2 of the EEC* treaty*, but is corrected by article 115 (defined further by two Commission* Decisions*: 80/47 of 20/12/1979 and 87/433 of 22/7/1987) which gives the Commission* the power to authorize Member States* to take protective measures to avoid deflections of trade or unfair competition*, or where differences between measures of commercial policy in Member States* lead to economic difficulties in one or more Member States* (abuse of free circulation). The Commission* evaluates the impact on the sector affected by these indirect imports* and determines in what measure these imports* may continue, and for how long. SEE CUSTOMS (ALL ENTRIES).

Freedom of Establishment The EEC* treaty* (art. 52 to 58) lays down the abolition of all restrictions on the freedom for nationals of a Member State* to establish themselves in the territory of another Member State* as self-employed persons. The principle is extended to cover the establishment of agencies, branches* or subsidiaries* by nationals of a Member State* on the territory of another Member State*. Exceptions are made for activities of official authority, or those decreed by the Council* or for reasons of public order or public health*. Directives* have been adopted in the area of freedom of establishment to harmonize* divergent national legislation currently in force in

Member States*. These Directives* concern certain categories of services (medicine, law, architecture, other professional services, financial services), in the agricultural, mining and energy sectors, in manufacturing industry, public works* contracts*, transport, commercial, financial and cinematographic activities, positions of responsibility in trade unions.
SEE FREEDOM TO PROVIDE SERVICES.

Freedom of Movement The principle of *freedom of movement of workers* for nationals of Member States* of the Community* is laid down in the EEC* treaty* (art. 48 to 51) and repeated in the Single European Act*. Regulation* 1612/68 forms the basis for the regulations on this matter.
1/1/1985: European passport and driving licence.
9/12/1989: interim report of the 'coordinating group': draft conventions on the removal of duty and visa* requirements at frontiers; on *request for asylum*; on the transfer of *repressive measures*; on the recovery of maintenance due to minors. This area is excepted from qualified majority* voting in the Council*.
27/3/1990: a judgement* of the CJEC* fixes the framework within which *freedom to provide services** is to operate in conjunction with freedom of movement.
28/6/1990: adoption of three Directives* on the right of residence* of students, retired persons and non-employed persons. They come into effect on 30/6/1992. Nationals of Member States* of the Community* remain subject to police controls and fiscal supervision at intra-community frontiers.
SEE COMETT, ERASMUS, DUTY-FREE, FREEDOM OF ESTABLISHMENT, FREEDOM TO PROVIDE SERVICES, RIGHT OF ASYLUM, SINGLE EUROPEAN ACT, YES.

Freedom to Provide Services Whereby an undertaking which is established in a Member State* may freely do business in another Member State*. Restrictions in this respect must be abolished (art. 59 to 66 of the EEC* treaty*). The White Paper* provides for the freedom to provide financial services (banks*, insurance*, investment of securities, mortgages, stockbroking), transport services, as well as mutual recognition* of diplomas* and freedom of establishment* for professional occupations. Adopted by qualified majority* by the Council* (SEE SINGLE EUROPEAN ACT). *Insurance*: 'Passive' freedom to provide services, where a customer contacts, of his own initiative, an insurer who is not established in his Member State*; 'active' freedom to provide services, where an insurer who is not established in a Member

State* tries to sell insurance there (see proposal for a Directive* from the Commission* to the Council* of 23/12/1989).
SEE ARCHITECTS, DOCTORS, FREEDOM OF ESTABLISHMENT, LAWYERS, NURSES.

Free Trade Ideology behind and practice of free movement of goods between all countries.
SEE COMMON COMMERCIAL POLICY, CUSTOMS UNION, EUROPEAN ECONOMIC COMMUNITY, EUROPEAN FREE TRADE AREA, FREEDOM OF MOVEMENT, FREE-TRADE AGREEMENT, FREE TRADE AREA, GATT, PREFERENTIAL AGREEMENT, WHITE PAPER.

Free-Trade Agreement Agreement between the EEC* and EFTA* on common trade policy.
SEE EUROPEAN ECONOMIC AREA, FREE TRADE, PREFERENTIAL AGREEMENT.

Free-Trade Area (or Tariff Union) Conglomerate customs territory*, made up of several smaller customs territories*, in which goods produced on these territories move freely from one to the other without being subject to any customs duty nor to quota* restrictions, but where there is no common customs tariff* nor common commercial policy towards third countries.
SEE CUSTOMS UNION, EUROPEAN FREE TRADE AREA, FREE TRADE, GATT, ORIGIN.

French National Council of Employers (CNPF) French employers' organization covering industry*, trade* and service* industries. European affairs office: 31 avenue Pierre I de Serbie, 75116 Paris, France. Delegation in Brussels: 45 rue de Trêves, 1040 Bruxelles, Belgium.

Frontier Control Administrative control of movements of persons*, capital*, vehicles, goods* etc., carried out at a frontier by the competent authorities (Customs* and police). The EEC* treaty* and the White Paper* lay down progressive abolition of controls at intracommunity frontiers, except where they are for legitimate reasons (receipt of possible customs duties*, VAT* and excise duties*, verification of conformity*, safety*, hygiene and public morality). Where this is not the case (controls only on imported products, especially strict controls of certain products, controls involving restrictions which exceed the authority of such a control, or controls whose nature goes beyond what is required to carry out the control) they may be considered to be measures having equivalent effect*, contrary to art. 30 of the EEC* treaty*. The same applies to 'double controls', imposed on the import of a product, when identical, similar or equivalent controls have

already been carried out by official or recognized authorities or bodies in the exporting state.
SEE COMMON CUSTOMS TARIFF, COMMUNITY TRANSIT, CUSTOMS CLEARANCE, CUSTOMS CONTROL, DUTY FREE, FREEDOM OF MOVEMENT, HEALTH, ORIGIN, PLANT, ANIMAL AND OTHER HEALTH CONTROLS, SAFETY, TRANSPORT POLICY.

Frontier Transit Note Customs document required of hauliers at each crossing of a Community* frontier to ensure that the goods are not sold in transit* before reaching their European country of destination. Abolished 1/7/1990 (COUNCIL* DECISION* OF 22/2/1990, OJ* L 151, 1990).

G

GALILEO EUREKA* project on improved reservation facilities for air travel.
SEE AMADEUS.

Gas Directive* of 31/5/1991 on transeuropean networks (COM (89) 334, OJ* C 247, 1989), and investment projects (COM (89) 335, OJ* C 250, 1989, C 8, 1990) and a Directive* on the transparency of prices (DIR.* of 29/6/1990, OJ* L 185, 1990).
SEE ENERGY.

Gas Appliances Directive* (25/6/1990) on the harmonization* of the safety*, performance, energy* efficiency and rationalization of production of cooking, heating, hot water, refrigeration, lighting and domestic or professional (but not industrial) washing appliances; safety*, monitoring and regulating mechanisms to be integral parts of gas appliances. (OJ* L 196, 1990) SEE CERTIFICATE OF CONFORMITY, NEW APPROACH.

GATT (General Agreement on Tariffs and Trade) Signed by the leading economic powers in Geneva on 30/10/1947. It provides guidance on customs and world trade policy with the intention of promoting the development of international trade. This agreement, which has 95 member states and is applied by a further 30, has created a de facto organization, based in Geneva. Although it has no actual legal powers, it formulates recommendations on commercial and customs regulations, intervenes as an arbitrator to regulate commercial disputes between nations, proposes solutions to the problem of organizing international markets and organizes multilateral trade negotiations (MTN): Geneva (1947), *Torquay round* (1955-1958), *Dillon round* (1960-1962), *Kennedy round* (1963-1967), *Tokyo round* (1973-1979), *Uruguay round* (1986-1990). *Rules*: fair trade; non-discrimination between contracting parties and the application between them of the most favoured nation clause*; reasonable settlement of commercial disputes by committees of experts; special treatment for less developed countries (LDCs*); compensation to countries injured by the establishment of customs unions* between certain countries (as in the case of the Community*, which has permanent representation at GATT).

Director: Arthur Dunkel. Centre William-Rappard, 154, rue de Lausanne, 1211 Genève 21, Switzerland.
SEE COMPETITION, FREE TRADE, MEASURE HAVING EQUIVALENT EFFECT, MULTI-FIBRE ARRANGEMENT.

Generalized System of Preferences (GSP) Preferential customs system granted unilaterally since 1/1/1971 by Member States* of the EEC* to 128 Less Developed Countries* (LDC); reduced or zero rates of import duty* on their industrial products and, in some cases, their agricultural products (with a quota* system for sensitive products). Under review for the period 1991-2000.
SEE COMMON AGRICULTURAL POLICY, CONVENTION.

Genetically Modified Organisms
SEE GMO.

GIIP (Groupement International de l'Industrie Pharmaceutique des pays de l'EEC)
SEE FEDERATION OF THE PHARMACEUTICAL INDUSTRY ASSOCIATIONS IN THE EEC.

GIRP (Groupement International de la Répartition Pharmaceutique des pays de la Communauté Européenne)
SEE INTERNATIONAL GROUP FOR PHARMACEUTICAL DISTRIBUTION IN THE COUNTRIES OF THE EUROPEAN COMMUNITY.

Glass
SEE EUROPEAN CONTAINER GLASS FEDERATION.

GMO (Genetically Modified Organisms) Directive* of 23/4/1990 on protecting the environment* and persons against the risks concomitant with the use and dissemination of GMO: 'confined' use (laboratory use); protection against dissemination by pesticides, breakdowns of chemical products. Notification procedure, coupled with authorization for each individual instance of use. The national authority responsible notifies Member States*, via the Commission*, of any such authorization (OJ* L 117, 1990).
SEE BIOLOGY, BIOTECHNOLOGY.

GNG (Group of Negotiations on Goods) Part of GATT*.

GNS (Group of Negotiations on Services) Part of GATT*.

Goods for Temporary Export Goods under outward processing* arrangements.
SEE CUSTOMS (ALL ENTRIES).

Green Central Rate (or Green Ecu) Central rate* multiplied by the corrective factor, for applying the switchover* mechanism.

Green Currency
SEE GREEN EXCHANGE RATE.

Green Ecu
SEE GREEN EXCHANGE RATE.

Green Exchange Rate (or Agricultural Conversion Rate) Representative exchange rate, fixed for each Member State* by the Council*, which is used to convert the agricultural prices* fixed each year by the Council* into each national currency. It is called the green exchange rate because it only covers agricultural products.
SEE AGRICULTURAL PRICES, COMMON AGRICULTURAL POLICY.

Green Paper Discussion paper worked out by the Commission* on a given subject. Eg: copyright; COM (88) 172; European telecommunications* policy (1987); European standardization* policy (1990); postal services (1991), etc.
A green paper in 1985 on the 'prospects for the Common Agricultural Policy*' gave rise to a Commission* policy document ('A Future for European Agriculture'), following consultation of organizations representing farmers and consumers* and the Community institutions*.
SEE COMMON AGRICULTURAL POLICY.

Green Parities
SEE GREEN EXCHANGE RATE.

Grounds Compulsory part of general ECSC* Decisions* and EEC* and EURATOM* Regulations* giving the background to the adoption of the act*, its general objectives and the proposals and opinions* required by the treaties*.

Group Taxation *23/7/1990*: adoption of three Directives* (OJ* L 225, 1990) on deferred taxation of capital gains produced by mergers*, divisions, contribution of assets, exchanges of shares between companies operating in different Member States*

('mergers' Directive*); on abolition of double taxation and all *deduction at source* on dividends distributed by a subsidiary* to its parent company in another Member State* and the possibility of exemption for a transitional period for Greece, Germany and Portugal ('parent companies–subsidiaries' Directive*); on the *arbitration procedure* (abolition of double taxation on profits adjustments by associated businesses which carry out transactions at internal prices: *transborder operations*); draft Directive* on the possibility for a parent company to take into account negative results of institutions or subsidiaries* situated in another Member State*.
SEE COMPANY LAW.

GS (Geprüfte Sicherheit) *(Safety-tested)*: German safety* mark.
SEE STANDARDS, TECHNICAL SPECIFICATIONS.

GSP
SEE GENERALIZED SYSTEM OF PREFERENCES.

GTO (Gate Turn-Off) Project in the EUREKA* programme ('EU 24'): development of a new generation of thyristors (electronic components used as interrupters in high voltage circuits).

Guarantee Sum required before an import* or export* licence* is issued. Covers imports* or exports* during the period of validity of the licence*.

Guaranteed Bank Deposits A guarantee system is provided for in a proposal for a Directive* on the stabilization and liquidation of credit institutions* (COM (85) 788.)

Guaranteed Thresholds System adopted to limit surplus agricultural production, by reducing the cost to the budget* of storing and selling surplus products. Above a certain threshold producers must provide all or part of the additional costs involved in selling their produce.
SEE COMMON AGRICULTURAL POLICY.

GUE (Gauche Unitaire Européenne) European Unitarian Left group in the European Parliament*.

Guidelines Constraint on the annual growth rate in agricultural expenditure: since 1988 the objective for the EAGGF* guarantee section is for a maximum of 74% rate of increase in the Community's* Gross Domestic Product. Early warning system set up by the Commission*.

SEE COMMON AGRICULTURAL POLICY, MECHANISMS FOR STABILIZING BUDGETARY EXPENDITURE.

H

HALIOS EUREKA* project (1989): construction of three deep-sea vessels for industrial fishing (France, Ireland, Spain).

HANDYNET EC* computerized information system on the problems faced by disabled people. Decision* 231/88/EEC, 18/4/1988 (OJ* L 104, 23/4/1988) establishing the HELIOS* programme. DG V of the Commission*.
SEE EUROPEAN SOCIAL AREA.

HAR Mutual recognition* system adopted by the members of CENELEC* for cables.
SEE HAR-CENELEC.

HAR-CENELEC Agreement (12/2/1974) between European manufacturers of cables and low voltage conductors on common marking.
SEE CENELEC, STANDARDIZATION, STANDARDS.

Harmonization Approximation, coordination. Of the adaptation of national legislation and regulations of Member States* which 'directly affect the establishment or functioning of the Common Market*' (art. 100 to 102 of the EEC* treaty*). Harmonization of legislation is usually effected by means of Directives*.
SEE BANK, BROADCASTING, CEN, CENELEC, EUROPEAN FINANCIAL AREA, EUROPEAN SOCIAL AREA, EUROPEAN STANDARD, EXCISE, FRONTIER CONTROL, INSURANCE, MUTUAL RECOGNITION, NEW APPROACH, SINGLE EUROPEAN ACT, SINGLE LICENCE, STANDARDIZATION, STANDARDS, WHITE PAPER.

Harmonization Document CEN/CENELEC* standard* which must be applied at national level, by publishing it and its HD number and by withdrawing any national standard* which contradicts it (on the same subject and with requirements such that that which is in conformity with the national standard* is not in conformity with the corresponding HD and vice-versa). Abolished on 1/1/1993 except for some trade with Spain and Portugal (provisionally) and for trade with the EFTA* countries.
SEE BARRIERS.

Harmonized Commodity Description and Coding System Nomenclature comprising headings and sub-headings and the relevant numerical codes, section notes, chapter notes and sub-heading notes and the general rules for interpreting the system. An international convention on the harmonized system was signed in Brussels on 14/6/1983. The CCC* Committee on a Harmonized Commodity Description and Coding System, made up of representatives of each of the signatories, meets at least twice a year. See also Council* Decision* 87/369/EEC.
SEE CUSTOMS COOPERATION COUNCIL.

HD
SEE HARMONIZATION DOCUMENT.

HD-MAC European standard* for HDTV* broadcasting, supported by the CSCE* of 19/6/91.

HDTV (High Definition TV) A number of developments in the field of television (technology, product and broadcasting) have led to improvements in home television viewing. The technical standard* chosen in Europe for HDTV with the International Radio Consultative Committee* is 1250 lines and 25 frames per second. The Japanese standard* is 1125 lines and 30 frames per second. An EEIG* ('1250 Vision') was set up, on the initiative of the Commission*, on 11/7/1990 by broadcasting companies, telecommunications* operators and 14 European manufacturers to coordinate production of available HDTV equipment and to make the European standard* an international one. Regular satellite broadcasts in about 1995.
SEE EUREKA, HDTV (PROGRAMME), HD-MAC, MAC, TELEVISION WITHOUT FRONTIERS.

HDTV (High Definition TV)(Programme) Project in the EUREKA* programme to develop a high definition television system. France, Germany, Netherlands, United Kingdom. Budget: 180m Ecus* (1990-1994). Decision* 89/337/EEC (OJ* L 142, 25/5/1989). DG XIII of the Commission*.
SEE BROADCASTING, HDTV, TELEVISION WITHOUT FRONTIERS.

Health Exceptions are made to measures to harmonize* legislation relating to health because of essential requirements*.
16/12/1988: Directive* on exposure to chemical, physical and biological agents (OJ* L 356, 1988).

12/6/1989: Framework Directive* to promote the health and safety* of workers* in the work-place (OJ* L 183, 1989).
3/11/1989: Directives* on minimum health and safety* provisions in the work-place and for the use of machines*, equipment and installations (OJ* L 353, 1989).
22/12/1989: Directives* on bulk prepackaging of certain liquids, the use of certain hazardous substances and preparations and cosmetic products.
29/5/1990: Directives* on handling heavy loads and on visual display units (VDU*) (OJ* L 156, 1990).
29/6/1990: Directive* on the protection of workers* exposed to carcinogenic agents (OJ* L 196, 1990).
SEE AIM, ATYPICAL WORK, BIOMEDICAL RESEARCH AND HEALTH, DOCTORS, ENVIRONMENT, EUROPEAN SOCIAL AREA, FLAIR, FOOD LABELLING, HEALTH (PROGRAMME), MAJOR INDUSTRIAL RISKS, MEDICAL IMPLANTS, MEDICINAL PRODUCTS, MEDICINE AND PUBLIC HEALTH, NURSES, PREVENTIVE MEDICINE, RADIOACTIVE WASTE, SAFETY, STD, VDU, VETERINARY MEDICINAL PRODUCTS, WORKING CONDITIONS.

Health (Programme) Community programme* to coordinate research* and development in the fields of medicine and health*. Budget: 65m Ecus* (1987-1991). OJ* L 334, 24/11/1987. DG XII of the Commission*.

Hearing 1) Oral phase of proceedings brought before the Court of Justice* of the European Communities*. After the written phase (application* and preparation*) the case is put before the judges in an open hearing. An in camera hearing may be decided of its own motion or on the request of the parties concerned. The oral phase consists, in the terms of the proceedings, of the report of the judge who acts as Rapporteur, hearing the parties, councils and lawyers, and the opinion of the Advocate-General, in the official language* of his choice, after a period of three to four weeks.
2) Contribution to a hearing of the Court of Justice* of the EC*.

Heavy Goods Vehicles Proposals by the Commission* (5/1990) on compulsory anti-pollution standards* for Diesel vehicles (1/7/1992 for new models; 1/1/1993 for all new vehicles; stricter standards from 1/10/1996 for new vehicles; 1/10/1997 for all new vehicles).
SEE ENVIRONMENT.

HELIOS (Handicapped people in the European community Living Independently in Open Society) Community programme* to promote the integration of disabled people in society. Budget: 19m Ecus* (1988-1991). Decision* 88/231/EEC (OJ* L 104, 23/4/1988).
SEE HANDYNET.

HERMES Computerized network for transmitting data to monitor the traffic of goods and for passengers to reserve seats on trains, set up by the International Union of Railways*.
SEE TRANSPORT POLICY.

High Authority Executive body of the ECSC*, replaced on the 1/7/1967 by the Commission* of the European Communities* which assumed all its duties.
10/8/1952: officially operational: 9 members. Based in Luxembourg.
SEE TREATY OF PARIS (art. 8 to 19).

Horizon Initiative by the Commission* (1990) to increase job opportunities for disabled people. Budget: 120m Ecus*.

HTM-DB (High Temperature Materials Data Bank) Data base* of systems for evaluating the mechanical properties of certain materials and their application at high temperatures. Joint Research Centre*.

Human Capital and Mobility Community programme* designed to ensure better management of intellectual resources in research* and development by training post-doctoral researchers for high-level research*, particularly in basic research* in the exact sciences; by encouraging mobility (training courses in other Member States*). Budget: 518m Ecus* (1990-1994). COM (90) 165.
SEE SCIENCE.

Human Genome (Analysis of) Community programme* for the use and improvement of biotechnology* for studying the human genome, for improving understanding of genetic mechanisms and for preventing and treating diseases. Integrated approach involving the ethical, social and legal aspects of the subject. Budget: 15m Ecus* (1989-1993). See also OJ* C 27, 2/2/1989; C 308, 2/12/1989. DG XII of the Commission*.
SEE BIOMEDICAL RESEARCH AND HEALTH

Human Science and Technology for LDCs Community programme* to increase cooperation between European scientists and those from LDCs*: agriculture*; medicine, health* and nutrition. Budget: 1.11m Ecus* (1990-1994).

I

IARC (International Agricultural Research Centres) Established under the aegis of the FAO* and the World Bank (International Bank for Reconstruction and Development*).

IATA (International Air Transport Association) Association governed by Canadian law with responsibility for harmonizing the logistics of flights and for establishing a common tariff system. Bilateral treaties between states refer to these tariff agreements.

IBRD
SEE INTERNATIONAL BANK FOR RECONSTRUCTION AND DEVELOPMENT.

ICAO (International Civil Aviation Organization)
SEE EUROPEAN CIVIL AVIATION CONFERENCE.

ICCE
SEE INTERNATIONAL COUNCIL OF COMMERCIAL EMPLOYERS.

ICONE (Index Comparatif des Normes nationales et Européennes) (*Comparative index of national and European standards)* Community* data base*. DG XIII of the Commission*.
SEE SPRINT.

IDA
SEE INTERNATIONAL DEVELOPMENT ASSOCIATION.

IDIS (Interbourse Data Information System) Project to interconnect by computer the European stock exchanges*: real time transmission of quotations and transmission of the best prices offered and asked for these securities (already in place); direct on-screen negotiation and harmonization* of settlement procedures; extension to the Zurich stock exchange* (to be completed).
SEE TELECOMMUNICATIONS POLICY.

IDO (Integrated Development Operation)
SEE INTEGRATED PROGRAMMES.

IDP Integrated Development Programme.

IDST (Information et Documentation Scientifique et Technique)
SEE SCIENTIFIC AND TECHNICAL INFORMATION AND DOCUMENTATION.

IEC International Electrotechnical Commission.

IES-DC1 Data bank* on research* and development programmes and European projects (telecommunications*, information technology industries, innovation). DG XIII of the Commission*.

IES-DC2 Data bank* on electronic mail (addresses of departments concerned) in EEC* and EFTA* countries. DG XIII of the Commission*.

IES-DC3 Data bank* of addresses of persons and institutions participating in European research* and development programmes. DG XIII of the Commission*.

IIB (Institut International des Brevets)
SEE INTERNATIONAL PATENT INSTITUTE.

ILAC (International Library Accreditation Conference) International test laboratories.

Illustrative Nuclear Power Station Design and Construction in the EC (PINC) Community programme* to develop the nuclear power station design and construction industry at the same time as the single market* is established. COM (84) 653 F; COM (85) 401 F; COM (89) 347. DG XVII of the Commission*.

ILO
SEE INTERNATIONAL LABOUR ORGANIZATION.

IMF
SEE INTERNATIONAL MONETARY FUND.

IMMARSAT International organization created to ensure satellite link-ups with ships.

Immigration
SEE FREEDOM OF MOVEMENT, SCHENGEN.

IMO
SEE INTERNATIONAL MARITIME ORGANIZATION.

IMP
SEE INTEGRATED MEDITERRANEAN PROGRAMMES.

IMPACT (Information Market Policy ACTions) Community research* programme* to develop the information market based on data bases*; implementation of a coordinated policy and plan of priority actions to develop a market of information services at Community* level. Budget: 100m Ecus* (1991–1995. Decision* 88/524/EEC, 26/7/1988 (OJ* L 288, 21/10/1988). DG XIII/B of the Commission*.

Impact Report Document produced by the departments of the Commission* for the use of the European Commissioners*, showing the foreseeable consequences (in particular on SME*) of an expected Community* intervention, to achieve the maximum benefit and to minimize unjustified constraints as far as possible with regard to the desired objective of the intervention.

Import Introduction of goods onto the customs territory* of a state or a group of states.
SEE BARRIERS, COMMON CUSTOMS TARIFF, COMMON MARKET, CUSTOMS (ALL ENTRIES), EXPORT, FREE-TRADE AREA, PARALLEL IMPORT, SUBSIDIZED IMPORTS.

Import Duties or Taxes All customs duties* and other duties, taxes and dues which are collected on the import* of goods, excepting dues and taxes whose amount is limited to the approximate cost of services rendered.
Agriculture customs duties and taxes having equivalent effect; agricultural levies* and other import* taxes laid down by the Common Agricultural Policy* or by specific procedures applicable to certain goods produced by processing agricultural products. Reg.* 2144/87/EEC, 13/7/1987 (OJ* L 201, 22/7/1987).

Imported Goods Non-Community goods* subject to inward processing* arrangements in suspension of customs duties or subject to the formalities for free circulation* and those under the refund system*. Reg.* 1999/85/EEC.
SEE CUSTOMS (ALL ENTRIES).

Import or Export Licence Document authorizing a businessperson to import* or export* an agricultural product into or out of a non-member country* within a fixed period of time and after deposit of a guarantee*. It is issued by the authorities in the state in which the operation will take place. The Commission* may refuse an export* licence if it believes that it would endanger the availability of supplies of the product concerned in the Community*.
SEE COMMON AGRICULTURAL POLICY, EAGGF, GATT, LEVY, REFUND.

Import Timetable National provision limiting the import* of certain products to a specific period in the year. Regarded as being like a measure having equivalent effect* (DIR.* 64/486/EEC, 28/7/1964, OJ* 20/8/1964).

Ind. Non-attached Members of the European Parliament* (those who belong to no particular group).

Industrial Cleaning
SEE EUROPEAN INDUSTRIAL CLEANING FEDERATION.

Industrial and Materials Technology Community research* programme* in the field of materials and raw materials recycling and manufacturing. Objectives: to develop new high performance industrial materials; to improve the materials cycle; distribution technologies and small-scale and mass production technologies. Budget: 663.3m Ecus* (1990-1994). COM (90) 156.

Industrial Policy See under the names of the various industries.
SEE ALSO COMMUNITY PROGRAMMES, COMMUNITY RULES, COMPETITION, ECLAIR, ECSC FUNDS, EUROPEAN INVESTMENT BANK, HARMONIZATION, KANGAROO, NEW APPROACH, NEW COMMUNITY INSTRUMENT, PUBLIC CONTRACT, RESEARCH POLICY, SQUALPI, STANDARDS, UNION OF INDUSTRIES OF THE EUROPEAN COMMUNITY.

Industrial Research and Development Advisory Committee (IRDAC) Community* scientific committee working with industry.

INFO 92 Commission* data base*: programme to abolish physical, technical and fiscal barriers*.
SEE EUROBASES.

Informatics Aid to SME* for information technology.
SEE AID, DATA BASE, CADDIA, CALL, COCOS, DRIVE, ESPRIT, ES 2, EUREKA, EURO INFO CENTRES, IDIS, IR-SOFT, MINITEL, OSI, RESEARCH, SNA, SOFTWARE, SPAG, SWIFT, TED, VDU, VIDEOTEX.

Information *Shareholders*: SEE COMPANY LAW; *Workers*: SEE EUROPEAN SOCIAL AREA, REPRESENTATION; *Consumers*: SEE CONSUMPTION, SAFETY.

Information Technology A quarter of the budget of the 1990-1994 Research and technological development framework programme is for information technology.
SEE COSINE, ESPRIT, IES-DC1, INFORMATION TECHNOLOGY INDUSTRIES, INFORMATION TECHNOLOGY (PROGRAMME).

Information Technology Industries
SEE ACE, AIM, BAP, BRITE, BROADCASTING, COMETT, COMMUNICATION, DATA BASE, DELTA, DOCDEL, DOSES, DRIVE, ECHO, ECLAIR, ESPRIT, EUREKA, EUROPACE, EUROTRA, FAR, FLAIR, HDTV, IDST, IES-DC1, IMPACT, INFORMATICS, ISDN, JOULE, LINGUA, MAST, MONITOR, PETRA, PIIC, PROMETHEUS, RACE, SCAD, SPRINT, STAR, STEP-EPOCH, TELECOMMUNICATIONS POLICY, TELEMAN, TELEVISION WITHOUT FRONTIERS, VALUE, VIDEOTEX, YES.

Information Technology (Programme) Community programme* to strengthen the technological foundations of the EC* and to promote wider access to the technologies used in the business world, in production and in the home: microelectronics, data processing systems and software*, advanced home and office technology systems, peripherals, integrated production by computer, computer engineering, basic research*. Budget: 1,352m Ecus* (1990-1994).

Infrastructure Policy Community* aid* for large-scale projects. See also COM (89) 238 (OJ* C 270, 1988). DG III of the Commission*.
SEE DRIVE, ERDF, ECSC FUNDS, EVCA, FINANCIAL ENGINEERING, NEW COMMUNITY INSTRUMENT.

Insider Information Confidential information, ie unknown to the general public, the nature of which could have a significant effect on a quotation on a stock exchange* if it were made known. A Directive* prohibits the use for profit of privileged information, the communication of such information to a third

party or recommendation to buy or sell securities on the strength of such information (13/11/1989, OJ* L 334, 1989).
SEE EUROPEAN FINANCIAL AREA, STOCK EXCHANGE.

INSIS (INter inStitutional Information System) Integrated system using the latest electronic technology to exchange information between the various administrations of the Community institutions* and between these and the Member States*. Budget: 6-7m Ecus* per year (1983-1992). Decision* 82/869/EEC, 13/12/1982 (OJ* L 368, 28/12/1982). DG XIII of the Commission*.
SEE INFORMATION, ISDN.

'Inst' Procedure Procedure introduced in 1964 by the EFTA* Council, by which EFTA* countries notify each other in advance of any new technical regulation* and of any amendment to an existing technical regulation*.
SEE BARRIERS.

Institute for Regional Cooperation in Intra-Community Frontier Regions Economic and cultural cooperation between Lorraine (France), Luxembourg and the Saar and the frontier areas in the Palatinate (Rheinland-Pfalz, Germany). Based in Luxembourg.

Institutional Cooperation
SEE COOPERATION PROCEDURE.

Insurance A Directive* of 23/6/1988 (88/357/EEC, OJ* L 172, 4/7/1988) set 1/7/1990 for the *freedom to provide services** in high risk non-life insurance (insurance contracted by undertakings) under the conditions of the law in the country of contract; in small risk insurance (insurance contracted by individuals) under the conditions of the risk country. The aim of the White Paper* was to completely liberalize insurance services on 31/12/1992. Work on *harmonization** of the general conditions applicable to contracts and the rules for calculating technical reserves is currently in progress.
20/6/1990 Agreement in principle on a Directive* on *life insurance* (comes into force 1/1/1993): freedom to provide services*; sales via sales representatives permitted, following authorization* by the state of residence of the underwriter, in the whole Community*, the contract being subject to the law of this state; possibility for the insured to choose to benefit

from the regulations of his state of residence if he takes out a policy with a company established in another state (passive freedom to provide services*); group insurance (authorities or undertakings for their staff); under discussion: tax system of the state of residence of the insured applies; reciprocity clause with non-member countries* (establishment of subsidiaries or acquisition of holdings by non-Community nationals) COM (90) 46.
Directive* of 14/5/1990 (OJ* L 129, 1990) on the harmonization* of legislation on third party insurance in *motor vehicle insurance* (compensation for victims of accidents whilst abroad), to come into force on 1/1/1993 (exemptions for Greece, Spain and Portugal until 1999). In progress: liberalization of motor vehicle insurance. (OJ* C 65, 1989).
1991: Directive* on the harmonization of the annual and consolidated accounts* of insurance companies.
1991: creation of an Insurance Committee*.
DG XV of the Commission*.
SEE AUTOMOTIVE INDUSTRY, EUROPEAN FINANCIAL AREA, INSURANCE COMMITTEE, MERGER, MOTOR VEHICLES.

Insurance Committee Permanent committee set up by the Council* at the Commission* to assist it in the implementation of its powers regarding supervision of competition*, to inform it on access to markets in non-member countries*, to give opinions* on the implementation of existing Directives* and on proposals for new Community* legislation. Comes into effect on 1/1/1992.
SEE INSURANCE.

Integrated Development Operation (IDO)
SEE INTEGRATED PROGRAMMES.

Integrated Programmes To optimize concerted Community* actions by additional use of the various relevant financial instruments.
SEE EUROPEAN INVESTMENT BANK, EUROPEAN REGIONAL DEVELOPMENT FUND, EUROPEAN SOCIAL FUND, INTEGRATED MEDITERRANEAN PROGRAMMES, STRUCTURAL FUNDS.

Integrated Mediterranean Programmes (IMP) Large-scale integrated development programmes (1986-1992) to restructure the economy in rural areas of the south of France, and parts of Italy and Greece. Reg.* 2088/85/EEC, 23/7/1985 (OJ* L 197, 27/7/1985).

ERDF*, ESF*, EAGGF* (Guidance), EIB*, NIC* subsidies and specific ad hoc interventions. Agriculture*, fisheries* and connected activities, agri-foodstuffs industries, energy*, crafts* and industry*, services*.
Advisory committee (representatives of Member States* and the EIB*). DG XXII of the Commission*.
SEE COMMON AGRICULTURAL POLICY, STRUCTURAL POLICY.

INTELSAT (INternational TELecommunication SATellite organization) International satellite telecommunications* consortium (1964). 117 member countries, including the Twelve*. Based in Washington, USA.
SEE EUTELSAT, INTERNATIONAL LABOUR ORGANIZATION.

Intergovernmental Conference Conference of the representatives of the governments of the Member States* convened to prepare a revision of the treaties* establishing the Communities*.
29/6/1985 (Milan): intergovernmental conference convened for the *Single European Act**.
25/6/1990 (Dublin): two intergovernmental conferences convened on *Political Union* and *Monetary Union*.
14/12/1990: work begins.
9–10/12/1991: examination by the European Council* of Maastricht.

Interim Protective Measure Temporary measure intended to maintain the status quo and in no way prejudicial to the final outcome of a matter.
SEE COMPETITION.

Interim Ruling Procedure to request the Court of Justice* of the European Communities* to suspend application of a Community* act* or to request any other provisional measures. As in national law, it is to obtain a provisional settlement in legal proceedings in order that the rights and interests of the parties involved are fully protected while awaiting the final judgement*. The *request* must be in the form of a separate appeal* and must be notified to the other party.
The *interim ruling order* is decided by the Court or by its President, following submission by the parties of written and oral observations, and following preparation*. The order is notified to the parties involved and may not be subject to an appeal*. It is in no way prejudicial of the final decision of the

Court nor of the validity of the judgement in law of the parties involved.

Interim Storage Status of goods admitted onto the customs territory* of the Community* without being immediately subject to customs procedure. A declaration of contents must be made. Dir.* 68/312/EEC.

Internal Market
SEE COMMON MARKET, EUROPEAN ECONOMIC COMMUNITY, SINGLE EUROPEAN ACT, SINGLE MARKET.

International Air Transport Association
SEE IATA.

International Bank for Reconstruction and Development (IBRD or World Bank) Specialized agency of the United Nations*: investments in the 152 member countries. Headquarters in Washington (USA). Specialist subsidiary for loans to LDCs*, the International Development Association (IDA).

International Commission for the Protection of the Rhine against Pollution 1963. France, Germany, Luxembourg, Netherlands, Switzerland plus the Community*. Elaboration of conventions. Koblenz, Germany.

International Council of Commercial Employers Body representing employers in the commercial sector in international organizations.
SEE TRADE.

International Crafts Federation International professional body (1947), represented in the Community* by the Community Crafts Union.

International Development Association (IDA)
SEE INTERNATIONAL BANK FOR RECONSTRUCTION AND DEVELOPMENT.

International Federation of Agricultural Producers 1946. Based in Washington. Office at the OECD* in Paris.

International Federation of Retail Distributors (FIGED) Body representing the profession in international organiza-

tions (1956). Members in Austria, Belgium, France, Germany, Italy, Netherlands, Spain and Switzerland.
SEE TRADE.

International Federation of Retail Watchmakers, Jewellers and Goldsmiths of the Member States of the EEC International body (1959), affiliated to the Committee of Commercial Organizations in the EEC Countries*.
SEE TRADE.

International Federation of Small and Medium-Sized Enterprises Based in Paris. Liaison office in Brussels.
SEE INDUSTRY, SME.

International Group for Pharmaceutical Distribution in the Countries of the European Community (GIRP) Body representing the profession in the Community* (1960). Paris.

International Labour Office (BIT)
SEE INTERNATIONAL LABOUR ORGANIZATION.

International Labour Organization (ILO) Specialized agency of the United Nations Organization* (1946). 150 member states. *Conventions and recommendations* for improving working conditions* and social justice. World technical cooperation programmes.
The International Labour Office (BIT) is its permanent secretariat. 4, route des Morillons, 1211 Genève 22, Switzerland.

International Maritime Organization (IMO) Specialized agency of the United Nations Organization*: safety* at sea*, prevention of pollution. 125 countries, including the Twelve*. London.

International Monetary Fund (IMF) Specialized agency of the United Nations* (Bretton Woods 1944): international monetary cooperation. 147 countries, including the Twelve*. 19 and H Street N.W., Washington D.C. 20431, U.S.A..

International Panel on Climate Change United Nations*. Research into climatic change. Conference in Geneva with representatives from the EC*.

International Patent Institute (IIB)
SEE COMMUNITY PATENT, EUROPEAN PATENT.

International Radio Consultative Committee (CCIR) Dependent body of the United Nations*. Plenary session every 4 years. 6/1990: recommendation for a single world standard* for HDTV*.

International Union of Railways (IUR or UIC) Body created in 1922, with 83 members (active, associate or affiliated): EEC*, EFTA*, Eastern European countries, Maghreb* and Machraq* countries. Its aim is to standardize and improve railway stock and the operation of railways. 14, rue Jean Rey, 75015 Paris, France.
SEE HERMES.

International Wholesale and Foreign Trade Centre Representative body of national wholesale trade federations at Community* level (1949). Brussels, Belgium.
SEE TRADE.

INTERREG Proposed Community programme* on trans-frontier regions.

Intervention Mechanisms Mechanisms to support prices by official intervention: withdrawal of a market, action regarding storage of goods (in order to regularize supply over the year), creation of new markets.

Intracommunity Movement of Goods System applying to goods sold and/or transported from one Member State* to one or more other Member States* for temporary use.
SEE CARNET.

INTRASTAT Statistical system relating to intra-Community trade. Also, ongoing group of proposals from the Commission for post-1992 trade statistics.

Investment Services Proposal for a Directive* concerning the liberalization of investment services (brokerage) for securities: banks*, specialized securities dealers, financial advisers, runners). See COM (89) 629, COM (90) 141 (OJ* C 42, 1990); COM (89) 778 (OJ* C 43, 1989). Minimum capital requirements; prudential rules (reserves to cover risks).
SEE FREEDOM TO PROVIDE SERVICES, SOLVENCY RATIO.

Investments in Securities
SEE CIUTS, EUROPEAN FINANCIAL AREA, INVESTMENT SERVICES.

Inward Processing Customs system suspending import* duties, which allows goods to be imported from non-member countries* into the Community* to be subject to one or more processing operations before being re-exported in a more advanced state of production (SEE COMPENSATING PRODUCT) (import duties* are suspended or repayable). Reg.* 1999/85/EEC, 16/7/1985 (OJ* L 188, 20/7/1985); 3677/86/EEC, 24/11/1986 (OJ* L 351, 12/12/1986).
SEE CUSTOMS (ALL ENTRIES), OUTWARD PROCESSING, PROCESSING.

Ionization Draft Directive* on harmonization* of the legislation of Member States* of the Community* on foodstuffs* and ingredients treated by ionization: freedom of movement*, while guaranteeing a high level of consumer protection (list of foods which may be ionized; prior authorization and official monitoring of the units of ionization used; labelling* rules; non-member countries*).
SEE CONSUMPTION, HEALTH.

IRDAC
SEE INDUSTRIAL RESEARCH AND DEVELOPMENT ADVISORY COMMITTEE.

IRIS Community programme*: vocational training* for women*. 1988-1992.

Iron and Steel Policy Based on the ECSC* treaty*, iron and steel policy was for a long time derived from the principle of production quotas* (art. 58 of the EEC* treaty*) which was replaced, from 1/7/1988, by a system of monitoring and detailed forward programmes. Official aid* has been authorized in exceptional circumstances (research on production costs, improvement of the quality and performance of products, environmental and working conditions*).
SEE ECSC FUNDS, EMPLOYERS' FEDERATION OF THE FRENCH IRON AND STEEL INDUSTRY.

IR-SOFT Data base* of software* programmes for micro-computer users.

ISDN (Integrated Services Digital Network)
SEE OPEN NETWORK PROVISION.

ISO (International Standards Organization)
SEE TECHNICAL SPECIFICATIONS.

ISO/IEC Standard Compulsory European standard* for members of CEN*/CENELEC*. National standard* from a harmonized* standard* which has been published in the OJ*.
SEE BARRIERS, NEW APPROACH.

ISO-TOP Group of industrialists based on the American Technical and Office Protocol (TOP) set up to create a consensus of opinion in Europe on international standardization* of office technology, telecommunications* equipment and CAD (Computer Aided Design).

ITSTC Conciliation body for CEN*, CENELEC* and CEPT* to study problems relating to standardization* and certification in information technology*.

ITER (International Thermonuclear Experimental Reactor) Project carried out under the aegis of the International Atomic Energy Agency by EURATOM*, Canada, Japan, the Commonwealth of Independent States and the USA. Decisions* 229/388 of the Commission*, 26/2/1988 (OJ* L 102, 21/4/1988); 528/388 of 29/9/1988 (OJ* L 291, 25/10/1988).
SEE NUCLEAR ENERGY.

IWFTC
SEE INTERNATIONAL WHOLESALE AND FOREIGN TRADE CENTRE.

JESSI (Joint European Submicron Silicon Initiative) Research programme in the EUREKA* programme ('EU 127'), involving Belgium, France, Germany, Italy, Netherlands and United Kingdom, in the field of advanced microelectronics. Budget: 3,800m Ecus* (1989-1997).
SEE AERONAUTICS, HDTV, INFORMATICS, TELECOMMUNICATIONS POLICY.

JET (Joint European Torus) Sub-programme of the Controlled Thermonuclear Fusion* Community programme*. Study of the scientific feasibility of nuclear fusion as a source of energy.

JNRC
SEE JOINT RESEARCH CENTRE.

John-Paul II Pope (elected in 1978), author of several speeches on Europe (Santiago de Compostela, 9/11/1982; speech to the office of the Commission*, 20/5/1985; to the Council of Europe* and the European Parliament*, 27 and 28/10/1988) and the encyclical *Slavorum apostoli*, about Saints Cyril and Methodius, published on the occasion of the 1100th anniversary of Methodius' death.

Joint Nuclear Research Centre
SEE JOINT RESEARCH CENTRE.

Joint Position Cooperation Procedure*: position adopted by the Council* on a proposal by the Commission* about which the European Parliament* has already given an opinion*.

Joint Research Centre (JRC) Community* nuclear research centre established under the EURATOM* treaty (art. 8) to ensure that 'the research* programmes* and other tasks assigned to it by the Commission* are carried out' and that 'a uniform nuclear terminology and a standard system of measurements are established'. It has set up a Central Bureau for Nuclear Measurements* and schools to train specialists. The JRC has four establishments.

JOULE (Joint Opportunities for Unconventional or Long-term Energy supply) Community research* programme* on non-nuclear energy* (including new forms of energy and renewable energy sources) and the rational use of energy*. Budget: 122m Ecus* (1989-1992). Decision* 89/236/EEC (OJ* L 98, 11/4/1989). DG XII/E of the Commission*.

JRC
SEE JOINT RESEARCH CENTRE.

Judgement Decision by the Court of Justice* of the European Communities*.
SEE DECISIONS OF THE COURT.

Judicial Cooperation Cooperation between a national judge and a Community* judge: preliminary jurisdiction by the Court of Justice* of the EC* on a referral from a national court regarding the validity and interpretation of Community law*.
SEE APPEAL.

K

Kangaroo Name of an informal group of members of the European Parliament*, who have been working since 1983 to obtain the support of sectors of industry and commerce in order that the Commission* define strategy with regard to specific sectors. Millbank Tower, London SW1T 4QS.

L

Label Mark of guarantee, certifying that a product has been manufactured in conformity with certain precise conditions. Mutual recognition* scheme between Member States* of the Community* for foodstuffs*, subject to certain conditions (COMMUNICATION* FROM THE COMMISSION*, OJ* C 271, 24/10/1989). Use of a common label by several businesses need not be notified to the Commission* if it is used to describe products of a certain quality and if every competitor may participate under the same conditions (OJ* C 75, 29/7/1968). Proposal for a *European environmental label.* (COM(91)37).
SEE AGREEMENTS BETWEEN UNDERTAKINGS, BLUE ANGEL, CONSUMPTION, REGISTERED DESIGNATION OF ORIGIN.

Languages
SEE BROADCASTING, ERASMUS, EUROTRA, HEARING, LINGUA, YES.

Large Credit Risks Excessive concentration of credit risks on one client. Considered by the Commission* to be a commitment of 15% or more of equity capital* (RECOMMENDATION* 87/62/EEC, 22/12/1986, OJ* L 33, 4/2/1987).
SEE PRUDENTIAL SUPERVISION.

Large-Scale Equipment Community programme*: support and aid* for the use of European scientific equipment and installations. Budget: 30m Ecus* (1989-1992). OJ* L 98, 1989. DG XII of the Commission*.

Lawyer The freedom to provide services* and equality of treatment* are guaranteed by Directive* 77/249 of 22/3/1977 (OJ* L 78, 26/3/1977), subject to the conditions laid down for lawyers established in the Member State* concerned.

LDCs
SEE LESS DEVELOPED COUNTRIES.

LDR Liberal, Democrat and Reformist group in the European Parliament*.

LEADER Community programme* to improve the economic potential of rural areas.
SEE INTERREG, REGIS.

LEDA (Local Employment Development Action) Community programme* implemented in cooperation with the OECD* programme LEI*. DG V/A1 of the Commission*.
SEE EUROPEAN SOCIAL AREA.

LEI (Local Employment Initiatives) Community programme* to support women who set up businesses.

Less Developed Countries (LDCs) Many such countries receive various forms of aid from the Community*, which also uses the EDF* to contribute to the financing of some public contracts*.
SEE ACP, CENTRE FOR INDUSTRIAL DEVELOPMENT, CONVENTION, EUROPEAN INVESTMENT BANK, GENERALIZED SYSTEM OF PREFERENCES.

Levy
SEE BUDGET, COMMON AGRICULTURAL POLICY, COMPENSATORY LEVY, CORESPONSIBILITY LEVY.

Liability
SEE APPEAL.

Liaison Committee of the Architects of United Europe European professional association (1959). Rue de Livourne 158, 1050 Bruxelles, Belgium.

Liaison Committee for the European Engineering Industries (COLIME) Community* group established within the Liaison Group for the European Engineering Industries* in 1953.

Liaison Committee of the European Federations of the Perfume, Cosmetics and Toiletries Industry (COLIPA) Rue de la Loi 223, 1040 Bruxelles, Belgium.

Liaison Committee of the Non-Ferrous Metal Industries in the EC Takes initiatives on unanimous decision with regard to the Community*. Rue Montoyer 47, 1040 Bruxelles, Belgium.

Liaison Committee for Professional Carriers of the European Communities Professional body belonging to the International Road Transport Union (IRU): carriers of goods, carriers of persons and carriers on their own account. Rue d'Arlon 108, 1040 Bruxelles, Belgium.

Liaison Group for the European Engineering Industries (ORGALIME) (1947). Groups together 27 associations in 13 European countries. 99, rue de Stassart, 1050 Bruxelles, Belgium.

Liaison Office of the Ceramic Industries of the Common Market (Cérame Unie): 18, rue de Colonies, 1000 Bruxelles, Belgium.

Licence Administrative document authorizing either the export* or the import* of goods.
SEE CUSTOMS (ALL ENTRIES), EXCHANGE CONTROL, TEMPORARY EXPORT.
Administrative authorization allowing the bearer to trade or carry out a regulated activity for a fixed period of time (import, export licence*).
Authorization to exploit a patent for invention*.
Single banking licence (SEE SINGLE LICENCE).
Community licence: document, issued by the Community institutions, granting authorization.
Single Community licence: whereby any credit institution* approved by a Member State* may do business freely in other Member States*, either by establishing branches or by providing services (DIR.* 89/646/EEC, OJ* L 386, 30/12/1989).
SEE FREEDOM OF ESTABLISHMENT, FREEDOM TO PROVIDE SERVICES, MOVEMENTS OF CAPITAL.

Licensing of Patent Rights Agreement Agreement whereby an undertaking which is proprietor of a patent authorizes another undertaking (licensee) to exploit the patented invention (manufacture, use, put on the market).
SEE COMPETITION, EXEMPTION.

LIFE Financial instrument created by the Council* to allow the implementation of an environmental policy. Incorporates the programmes MEDSPA*, NORSPA, ACE*-Technology and ACNAT.

LINGUA Community programme* to promote knowledge of the languages of the Community* among students and teachers in the EC*: inter-university cooperation; continuing education for teachers; vocational training* and technical education; school exchanges; promotion of languages in SME*. Budget: 250m Ecus* (1990-1994). Decision* 489/88/EEC, 28/7/1989 (OJ* L 239, 16/8/1989). DG V of the Commission*.

LNE (Laboratoire National d'Essais) French national test laboratory.

Local Content Definition of the minimum part of a product, which is to be produced in a Member State*, which allows non-member country* producers to market the product in the Community* after they have established an industrial plant there. For example, the local content of motor vehicles. The GSP* is soon to allow LDCs* to incorporate products of Community origin in the products which they manufacture without losing the GSP* designation for products which are processed and then exported to the EC*.

Lomé Agreement
SEE CONVENTION.

Lomé Convention
SEE CONVENTION.

Luxembourg Capital of the Grand Duchy of Luxembourg. *Luxembourg Agreement*: agreement made in the Council* on 28/1/1966 after France refused to take part for six months because of a disagreement over the method of financing the Common Agricultural Policy* proposed by the President of the Commission*, Walter Hallstein (SEE OWN RESOURCES).
Reestablished in practice the rule of unanimity* in the Council* 'when, in the case of decisions which are to be taken by majority* voting on proposals from the Commission*, very important interests of one or more partners are at stake'. The members of the Council* make an effort to arrive, within a reasonable period of time, at solutions which are acceptable to all 'in respect of their mutual interests and of those of the Community*, in conformity with art. 2 of the Treaty'. This has been seldom used since the signing of the Single European Act*, which reestablished qualified majority* voting for most proposals submitted to the Council*.
22/4/1970: treaty of Luxembourg, which came into effect on 1/1/1971 (increased budgetary powers for the European Parliament*).
SEE BUDGET, OWN RESOURCES, TREATY OF BRUSSELS.

2/4/1984: EEC*/EFTA* summit meeting (declaration opening the way for a 'European economic area'*).
27-28/4/1980: European Council* (UK contribution to the budget*).
SEE EUROPEAN POLITICAL COOPERATION.
6/1991: European Council* (European Union*; Economic and Monetary Union*).

M

Maastricht (The Netherlands) European summit agreed treaties creating European Political Union* and Economic and Monetary Union* to be signed 2/1992 and to come into effect 1993.
SEE TREATIES OF MAASTRICHT.

MAC/Packet Family of Standards Technical specifications for satellite transmission systems. Dir.* 86/529/EEC, 3/12/1986 (OJ* L 311, 6/11/1986).
SEE HDTV.

Machines Directive* of 14/6/1989 on the safety* of machines (89/392/EEC, OJ* L 183, 1989), applicable on 1/1/1993: harmonization* of national legislation to ensure the same degree of protection for users throughout the EC* territory. Special measures for mobile construction plant, lifting gear, machines used in medicine, models used in exhibitions and fairs*. Elaboration of specific technical standards* is carried out by CEN* and CENELEC* with a view to recommending harmonized standards* to Member States*. EC Declaration of Conformity* and CE Mark* are compulsory.

Machraq Group of countries (Egypt, Israel, Jordan, Lebanon and Syria) which has signed a cooperation agreement* with the EC*.

MADRAS (Modular Approach to Definition of RACE Subscriber Premises Network) Project in the RACE* Community programme* (Denmark, France, Italy). DG XIII of the Commission*.

Maghreb Group of North African countries, the Arab Maghreb Union: Algeria, Libya, Morocco, Mauritania and Tunisia.
Cooperation agreements* with the EC*. Proposal for a charter on immigration.

Mail Order Directive* 85/577, 1985.

Major Industrial Risks Community programme* for studying and preventing major chemical and petrochemical accidents.

Budget: 3m Ecus* (1986-1990). OJ* L 159, 14/6/1986. DG XII of the Commission*.
SEE CHEMISTRY.

Majority *The Commission** takes decisions by an *absolute majority* of it members (more than half of the number of votes cast).
Management committees act by a *qualified majority** (the same weighting as in the Council*).
*The European Parliament** may (with a minimum number of votes required in each case) amend at the first reading (and adopt these amendments* at a second reading) by a *three-fifths majority* that part of the budget* concerning non-compulsory expenditure*; reject the budget* proposed to it by the Council* or overthrow the Commission* with a motion of censure* by a *two-thirds majority*; adopt Council* joint positions* by a *simple majority*, or reject or amend them by an *absolute majority* (more than half of the votes cast).
The Council acts by *simple majority*, except where the treaties* or the Single European Act* require a qualified majority* or unanimity*.

Mandatory Requirements For products to protect consumers. Not to be confused with essential requirements*, they may be invoked by a Member State* of the Community* to exempt a product from the principle of freedom of movement of goods* for reasons of fiscal supervision, protection of public health*, in the interests of fair trade and to protect consumers*. (Cassis de Dijon* Judgement* 120/78, 20/2/1979.)
SEE LABEL, NEW APPROACH.

Marine Science and Technology Community programme* to promote the application of information and advanced technology to study, manage and protect the seas around the coasts of Europe: marine science, coastal engineering and marine technology. Budget: 104m Ecus* (1990-1994).

Marjolin (Robert) Former French Vice-president of the Commission* of the European Communities*, author of a report* on Economic and Monetary Union*.

Market Conversion Rate
SEE GREEN EXCHANGE RATE.

Market Rate Real exchange rate of one national currency with another, as it is represented on the currency markets.

MAST (MArine Science and Technology) Community research* programme*. Budget: 50m Ecus* (1989-1992). Decision* 89/ 413/EEC, 20/6/1989 (OJ* L 200, 13/7/1989). DG XII/E of the Commission*.

Materials
SEE EURAM, HTM–DB.

Matthaeus Community programme* concerning exchanges between customs officials. Objectives: preparation for the effects of the single market*; supplementary training*; staff mobility; cooperation between customs administrations. Adopted on 20/4/1989. DG XXI of the Commission*.

MCA (Monetary Compensatory Amounts) System set up in 1969 to compensate for the effects in changes in monetary parity between Member States*, where the latter have no desire to allow the consequential effects on agricultural prices*. In effect the single market* presupposes stable monetary parity. MCA are amounts applied in trade between Member States* or between Member States* and non-member countries* in order to compensate for Applied Monetary Gaps*.
A country whose currency has been revalued pays MCA on exports* and is paid them on imports* (*positive MCA*) and the opposite is the case for countries which devalue their currency, where agricultural prices* in the national currency are lower than common prices (in the national currency); these are *negative MCA*.
MCA allow distortions between official parities and green parities (SEE GREEN EXCHANGE RATE) to be avoided. *Fixed MCA* are those calculated by Member States* in respect of the 2.5% EMS* fluctuation margin.
Common prices (single internal prices) are fixed in Ecus*. *13/2/1988*: the European Council* recommends the abolition of current and future MCA.
SEE AGRICULTURAL PRICES, COMMON AGRICULTURAL POLICY, GATT.

MCAC Management and Coordination Advisory Committees.

MCN (Multilateral Commercial Negotiations) Occasional negotiations under GATT*.

Means of Redress Procedure by which an undertaking which considers itself to have been unjustly excluded from the process for awarding public works* or public supply contracts* (except for excluded sectors*) may appeal to a national court to state its rights. Directive* applicable on 1/1/1992. Member States* must have established adequate legal procedures to deal with this by then (including a facility for requesting the opinion of the Commission* on individual cases).

Measure Having Equivalent Effect Measure equivalent to quantitative restrictions* on imports* or exports*: administrative practice (DIR.* 70/50, 22/12/1969), technical standard*, health or plant health check, certain other forms of frontier control*, origin marking* of products, incentives for buying nationally produced products, payment and credit restrictions, exclusive rights relating to industrial and commercial property, dependent or exchange operation*, parallel import*, disproportionate penalties, insufficient or excessive periods of time for customs procedures, reciprocity* conditions, import timetables*, provisions concerning advertising*, etc., and any commercial or technical regulation by Member States* which hinders, directly or indirectly, actually or potentially, intra-community trade (Judgement* 11/7/1974, 8/74).
The EEC* treaty* laid down abolition of measures having equivalent effect for products from Member States* and from non-member countries* which are in free circulation* in Member States* (art. 9, 30 and 34).
The Commission* has the power to penalize infringements. Harmonization* of national provisions. Possibility of exemptions* (art. 36 of the EEC* treaty*).
SEE SINGLE MARKET.

Measurement and Testing Community programme* to improve measurement, technical tests and chemical analyses: supports Regulations* and Directives* in this area and sectoral testing; calibration methods and development of new methods for measurement. Budget: 140m Ecus* (1990-1994).
SEE CHEMISTRY.

Mechanisms for Stabilizing Budgetary Expenditure All such mechanisms used as interventions in the Common Agricultural Policy* (CAP). Budgetary constraints limit the rate of growth of EAGGF* guarantee section expenditure, which has an effect on a certain number of products: above given production

thresholds (maximum guaranteed quantities) the guarantees given to producers decrease in proportion to the amount of surplus.
SEE CORESPONSIBILITY, SET ASIDE, STRUCTURAL POLICY.

MEDIA (Mesures pour Encourager le Développement de l'Industrie Audiovisuelle) *(Measures to encourage the development of the broadcasting industry)*: Community programme* (1986) to encourage development in the production, distribution and financing of television programmes. COM (86) 255F. Replaced by the 1991-1995 Commission* programme (SEE BROADCASTING). DG X/B of the Commission*.
SEE BABEL, HDTV.

Medical Implants Directive* of 20/6/1990 on harmonizing legislation requiring pacemakers etc., which are put on the market, to conform to minimum provisions. See also OJ* L 189, 1990.

Medicinal Products A monopoly on their sale is justified on grounds of health protection (art. 36 of the EEC* treaty, Decisions of the CJEC*). Pharmaceutical Directives* have been extended to cover certain medicinal products (EG. 3/5/1989, OJ* L 142, L 181, 1989).
SEE HEALTH, MEDREP, PHARMACY, VETERINARY MEDICINAL PRODUCTS.

Medicine and Public Health Community research* programme*: coordination of the research* potential available at Community* level; increase of the scientific efficiency of national programmes. Budget: 65m Ecus* (1987-1991). OJ* L 334, 24/11/1987. DG XII of the Commission*.
SEE BIOMEDICAL RESEARCH AND HEALTH, HEALTH, HUMAN GENOME, PREVENTIVE MEDICINE.

Mediterranean Non-Member Countries Five year cooperation agreements* with the Maghreb* countries (Algeria, Libya, Mauritania, Morocco and Tunisia) and the Machraq* countries (Egypt, Israel, Jordan, Lebanon and Syria). 615m Ecus* (1987-1991); 1,425m Ecus* (1992-1996). EIB* loans. Development projects to produce economic reform and actions to promote investment.
SEE LESS DEVELOPED COUNTRIES, NON-MEMBER COUNTRIES.

Medium-Term Financial Aid Mechanism introduced by the Council* in 1984 for the medium-term financial support of Member States'* balances of payments. Replaced in June 1988 by medium-term financial support.
SEE MOVEMENTS OF CAPITAL.

MEDREP Data base* of biomedical and health* research* projects.

MEDSPA (MEDiterranean Special Programme of Action) Community programme* to protect the environment* in Mediterranean countries. 1988-1992. COM (88) 392F. DG XI of the Commission*.
SEE REGIONAL POLICY.

Member State of the Community One of the Twelve* states which have signed the ECSC*, EEC* and EURATOM* treaties* and the Single European Act*.

Memorandum Written communication to the Council* and the European Parliament* expressing the Commission's* point of view, intended to promote discussion or to announce future measures.

Merchant Navy Community* shipowners may submit a complaint to the Commission* if they consider themselves to be injured by abnormally low freight prices set by competitors from non-member countries* (REG.* 4057/86/EEC, 22/12/1986, OJ* L 378, 31/12/1986). It is possible for the Council* to authorize charging countervailing duty.
SEE DUMPING.

Merger Concentration* where two or more undertakings of equal size become one legal entity (concentration of a larger with a smaller undertaking is called an acquisition).
Transfrontier merger: the 10th Directive* on company law* (COM (84) 727, OJ* C 23, 1985) and the Directive* of 23/7/1990 reforming the common tax system are applicable to mergers between companies of different Member States* (OJ* L 225, 1990).
SEE COMPANY LAW, COMPETITION, GROUP TAXATION.

Messina (Italy) *1-2/6/1955*: negotiations between the foreign ministers of the Six*; P-H Spaak* was asked to prepare a report

on the possibility of general economic union and on union in the nuclear field.
SEE EEC, EURATOM, REPORT (SPAAK).

Metalworking
SEE BRITE, EURAM, HTM-DB, IRON AND STEEL POLICY, LIAISON GROUP FOR THE EUROPEAN ENGINEERING INDUSTRIES, VAMAS.

METRE (Mesure, Étalons et Techniques de Référence) *(Measurements, Standards and Reference Techniques)* Joint Research Centre* Community research* programme*.

MFA
SEE MUTLTIFIBRE ARRANGEMENT.

Milan (Italy) *30/6/1985*: European Council* (adoption of the White Paper*; decision to hold an intergovernmental conference. SEE SINGLE EUROPEAN ACT).

Minimum Requirements Directives* adopted by the Council* (qualified majority*) are applicable progressively, take account of technical regulations* already existing in each Member State* and are intended to contribute to promoting improvement in working conditions* with regard to health* and safety* (art. 118a of the EEC* treaty*). They must not impose administrative, financial or legal constraints on SME*.

Mining Council* Resolution* of 28/7/1989 on the development of the European mining industry. Framework programme (1990): dissemination of geological data; taxation and social security schemes; regulatory framework; foreign aspect; use of structural funds*.
SEE CONVENTION, ECSC, SYSMIN.

Mining policy
SEE MINING.

Minitel Telematic terminal linked to the Vidiotex* system for presenting information accessible via the French Teletel network.
Community* information services accessible via 3615: EEC* codes (general information on the EC* and the European Parliament*), EUROBASE* (EUREKA*), CIC INFO (public information: EEC* headings);

via 3616: CEDEC (Centre for Enterprise Development in the EEC), CEL (EURODEFI: data base* on business opportunities; translation), EUROGUIDE* (European Construction), EURONALP (for businesses), FIC (Fichier Industriel et Commercial – Industrial and commercial file: businesses and business opportunities; European economy), CCRE (Collectivités Locales et Régionales face à l'Europe – Local and regional authorities and Europe), MEET (Business Cooperation Centre; seminars, training etc.); via 3617: CCIPLUS (Review of the press by the Paris Chamber of Commerce), INFO 92* (Commission* progress of the 282 Directives* of the White Paper*), EURO 92* (French Industry ministry).
Via the SINORG host computer (French Chamber of Commerce and Industry): DELPHES (European markets); FIRMEXPORT, FIRMIMPORT (French export and import businesses); via 36290078: NORIANE PLUS (AFNOR* data base*); via 36282001: EXPORT (business opportunities – French Chamber of Commerce and Industry).
SEE DATA BASE, INFORMATICS.

MISEP Community data bank*: information on employment*. Administered by the Commission*. Access via ECHO*.

MITHRA Project in the EUREKA* programme ('EU 10'): development and industrialization of robots for remote surveillance and intervention in crisis situations.

Mixed Origin Relaxation of the normal rules within a preferential agreement, by which products are considered as originating in a country even if they use other products in their manufacture which are imported from countries which have not signed the preferential agreement (EFTA*, GSP*, Andean Pact, etc.). The product must have been processed to an extent justifying the designation of origin.
Bilateral cumulation (mixing of origins) is limited to preferential trade between two given countries (EEC* and non-member country*): products originating in one of the two parties (EEC* or non-member country*) which are processed (more than just simple working) in the other party (non-member country* or EEC*) are treated in the same way as products originating in this second party.
Diagonal cumulation (mixing of origins) covers trade between the EEC* and a number of countries subject to the same

preferential agreement; this may be total (ACP*, Maghreb*) or partial (EFTA*, Andean Pact).
SEE CUSTOMS, RULES OF ORIGIN.

Mobile Communications *28/6/1990*: Council* agreement on a draft Directive* (SEE ALSO COUNCIL* RECOMMENDATION* (87/371/EEC), 25/6/1987, OJ* L 196, 17/7/1987) on the coordinated introduction of mobile communications (radio telephones, wireless telephones, paging, etc., excluding internal communications networks in businesses).
Directive* (87/372/EEC, 25/6/1987) on reserving certain wavebands for the proposed paneuropean digital system.
SEE ISDN, TELECOMMUNICATIONS POLICY.

Monetary Committee Committee consisting of representatives of the Member States* of the Community*, responsible for preparing the work of the Council* on monetary policy and for carrying out the tasks assigned to it by the Council*.
SEE COREPER.

Monetary Compensatory Amounts
SEE MCA.

Monetary, Financial and Balance of Payments Statistics Committee Committee set up by the Council* on 25/2/1991, made up of the most senior representatives of the Commission* and observers from the Committee of Governors of central banks of the EC* and from the Monetary Committee*. ECU* working group.

Monetary Policy
SEE ECU, EMS, EMCF, MONETARY UNION, MOVEMENTS OF CAPITAL.

Monetary Realignment Changes to the central exchange rates of the Member States* in the EMS* exchange rate mechanism.

Monetary Union Area made up, via a written agreement, by several states, within which a *single* currency or a *common* currency is used.
On 1/7/1990 monetary union was established between the Federal Republic of Germany and the German Democratic Republic, using the German Mark, issued by the Bundesbank, as a single currency (agreement of 18/5/1990).

EEC: The objective of economic and monetary union is contained in the Single European Act*. This presupposes total and irreversible convertibility of currencies, the abolition of margins of fluctuation (with irrevocably fixed parities), complete liberalization of movements of capital* and of freedom to provide services* in banking and financial services and multilateral supervision*.
10/9/1968: Werner* Plan submitted to the Council*.
12/2/1969: 1st Barre Plan.
1-2/12/1969: the Summit in The Hague makes monetary union an objective in the construction of the Community*.
4/3/1970: 2nd Barre Plan.
13/10/1970: Werner* report* to the Council*.
28/6/1988: the European Council* of Hannover gives a committee presided over by Jacques Delors* the task of elaborating a report*, which was submitted to the Council* in April 1989: it proposed a three stage programme: 1. Increased economic and monetary cooperation. 2. The establishment of a European System of Central Banks* with a federal institution independent of the governments of Member States*. 3. Fixed parities and a common currency. An amendment* to the treaty* of Rome* would be required for the second stage.
26-27/6/1989: the European Council* of Madrid decides that the first stage of the Delors Plan should start on 1/7/1990 and asks the competent authorities to prepare an intergovernmental conference to introduce the final stages.
8-9/12/1989: the European Council* of Strasbourg proposes convening an intergovernmental conference before the end of 1990.
28/4/1990: confirmation of this proposal by the extraordinary European Council* of Dublin*.
25-26/6/1990: the European Council* of Dublin* decides to convene an intergovernmental conference and fixes the working plan, to be completed before the end of 1992 (confirmation by the extraordinary Council* meeting of 27-28/10/1990).
14/12/1990: intergovernmental conference in Rome*: 2nd phase of economic and monetary union to begin on 1/1/1994.
10–11/12/1992: European summit meeting at Maastricht* agreed a treaty creating Economic and Monetary Union to be signed *2/1992* and to come into effect in *1993*.

SEE CONVERGENCE, ECU, EUROPEAN ECONOMIC COMMUNITY, EUROPEAN FINANCIAL AREA, EUROPEAN MONETARY SYSTEM, EUROPEAN SYSTEM OF CENTRAL BANKS, REPORT, SINGLE EUROPEAN ACT.

MONITOR Community programme*: strategic analysis, forecasting and evaluation in the fields of research* and technology*. Budget: 22m Ecus* (1988-1992). Decision* 89/414/EEC (OJ* L 200, 13/7/1989). Sub-programmes: SAST* (scientific and technical development), FAST* (forecasting), SPEAR* (improvement of methods and efficiency of research* evaluation). DG XII of the Commission*.

Monnet (Jean) Senior French official (1888-1973), creative force behind the Treaty* of Paris*, first President of the ECSC* High Authority* (1952-1955), created the Action Committee for a United States of Europe (1955).

Mortgage The 2nd Directive* on banking lists it among the everyday banking services which will benefit from mutual recognition*. Specific draft Directive* (COM (87) 255, OJ* C 161, 1987).
SEE BANK, EUROPEAN FINANCIAL AREA.

Most-Favoured Nation Clause Clause inserted in a trade treaty which guarantees one of the parties no less favourable tariff treatment than the other party applies to other states. This clause applies multilaterally under GATT*.
SEE GENERALIZED SYSTEM OF PREFERENCES, LDCs.

Motion of Censure Motion which, if it is adopted by the European Parliament*, leads to the resignation of the Commission* (two-thirds majority* required in a quorate sitting). This motion has never been invoked. Roll-call vote.
SEE COOPERATION PROCEDURE.

Motor Vehicles Harmonization* Directives*.
SEE NEW APPROACH, SAFETY.
Proposed regulations on third-party insurance* (COM (89) 625, OJ* C 11, 1990).

Movable Property Any property which can be moved, or which is deemed as such by law, as opposed to immovable property.

Movement
SEE COMMON MARKET, INTRACOMMUNITY MOVEMENT OF GOODS, FREEDOM OF MOVEMENT, SINGLE MARKET.

Movement Certificate (EUR 1*) Certificate adopted in 1973 by the EEC* and EFTA* for trade between Member States*. Another more simplified form (EUR 2*) has been used for originating products of limited value. They may now be replaced by a simple declaration of origin*.
SEE CUSTOMS (ALL ENTRIES).

Movements of Capital A Directive* of 24/6/1988 (88/361/EEC, OJ* L 178, 8/7/1988) decided that movements of capital would be totally liberalized (with exemptions*) on 1/7/1990: abolition, for individuals and businesses, of exchange controls* and rules which could be applied to hold assets expressed in the currency of another Member State*. Any person may also open a bank account and make loans and investments in another Member State*.
SEE FREEDOM OF ESTABLISHMENT, FREEDOM TO PROVIDE SERVICES, NIMEXE, SAFEGUARD CLAUSE.

Movements of Capital Nomenclature 13 categories of movements of capital are listed in a nomenclature included in Directive* 88/361/EEC of 24/6/1988 (OJ* L 178, 8/7/1988).

MTFA
SEE MEDIUM TERM FINANCIAL AID.

Multifibre Arrangement (MFA) Agreements signed by the Member States of GATT* for the periods 1974-1977, 1978-1981, 1982-1986, 1986-1991 (international trade in textiles* and clothing). Imports into the Community*: EEC* agreements and bilateral agreements fixing import quotas*.

Multilateral Commercial Negotiations
SEE MCN.

Multilateral Supervision Biannual examination by the Council* of Economic and Financial Ministers (restricted sessions) with the president of the Committee of Governors of the Central Banks of each Member State's* economic difficulties in a world context.
SEE EUROPEAN FINANCIAL AREA, MONETARY UNION.

Mutual Information Procedure Information procedure established by Directive* 83/189 (24/3/1983) for standards* and technical regulations*.

SEE BARRIERS, NEW APPROACH. Procedure employed by the Commission* under art. 169 and 170 of the EEC* treaty* (failure to fulfil an obligation under the treaty*).
SEE APPEAL, BARRIERS, COMPETITION, COURT OF JUSTICE.

Mutual Recognition Recognition by a state of the validity on its own territory of rules made by one or more other states in well-defined areas. This principle is valid in the Community* for national technical standards* and regulations* ('Cassis de Dijon*' Judgement*). The Single European Act* laid down that application of mutual recognition in all areas not harmonized* by 1992 should be considered. The principle also covers higher education diplomas (specific Directives* and Directive* 12/1988).
SEE ARCHITECTS, BANK, DOCTORS, FREEDOM OF ESTABLISHMENT, FREEDOM TO PROVIDE SERVICES, INSURANCE, NEW APPROACH, NURSES, REGISTERED DESIGNATION OF ORIGIN, SINGLE EUROPEAN ACT, SINGLE LICENCE.

N

NACE (Nomenclature générale (ou statistique) des Activités économiques dans les Communautés Européennes) *(General (or statistical) nomenclature of economic activities within the European Communities)* Project proposed by the Commission* for 1/1/1993.

National Certification Mark Mark certifying that a product conforms to national standards*.
SEE BARRIERS, MUTUAL RECOGNITION, NEW APPROACH.

National Divergence Amendment or exception which puts obstacles in the path of the harmonization* of national standards*. May sometimes be maintained for a fixed transition period (B-divergence).
SEE BARRIERS, NEW APPROACH.

Nationalization Nationalization of businesses is not prohibited by the EEC* and ECSC* treaties* 'in so far as they in no way prejudice the rules governing the system of property ownership in Member States*'.
SEE AID, COMPETITION, PUBLIC UNDERTAKING.

NATO (North Atlantic Treaty Organization) Intergovernmental organization: defence and cooperation within the Atlantic Alliance (treaty of Washington 4/4/1949). 16 member countries: USA, Canada, the Twelve* (minus Ireland), Iceland, Norway and Turkey. International secretariat in Brussels, Belgium.
SEE NORTH ATLANTIC ASSEMBLY.

NCI
SEE NEW COMMUNITY INSTRUMENT.

NCPI (New Commercial Policy Instrument) Measures adopted by the Twelve* to guard against illicit commercial practices by non-member countries* either within or outside the Community* (REG.* 2641/84/EEC, OJ* 252, 1984). To be used only if other instruments of policy for commercial defence cannot be used (DIR.* 82/288/EEC).
SEE DUMPING, GATT, OECD, UNITED NATIONS CONFERENCE ON TRADE AND DEVELOPMENT.

Negative Clearance Declaration whereby the Commission* states that there is no cause for it to intervene concerning an agreement* between undertakings or a decision or practice which is covered by Community* competition law*.
SEE NOTIFICATION.

Negotiated Procedure National procedure whereby a contracting authority* consults the suppliers of its choice and negotiates the conditions for a public contract* with one or more of them.

NEPTUNE (New European Programme for Technology UtilizatioN in Education) Proposed Community programme*. DG V of the Commission*.

NET (Next European Torus) Sub-programme of the Controlled Thermonuclear Fusion* Community programme*. Also: Normes Européennes de Télécommunications* – European Telecommunications* Standards*.

NETT (Network for Environmental Technology Transfer) Project to promote pollution cleaning or non-polluting technology. DG XI of the Commission*.

New Approach Strategy laid out by the Council* (Resolution* of 7/5/1985) to harmonize* technical specifications*: harmonization* of national legislation limited to the essential requirements* which products must fulfil to enable them to enter free circulation* within the Community*; referral to European or national standards*; acceptance of certificates of conformity* issued by approved laboratories or private bodies.
SEE CE, MUTUAL RECOGNITION.

New Community Instrument (NCI) Financial instrument (called the 'Ortoli facility') which the Community* used in 1978 to encourage investment and increase the competitiveness of the Community* economy via the distribution of new technology* (to achieve greater economic alignment*).
Loans are granted by the European Investment Bank* (EIB) and are available to SME*. Interest rates are calculated according to current borrowing rates.
More specific areas covered: the rational use of energy*, regional or Community* infrastructures*, protection of the environment* in rural areas, new technology*, integrated Mediterranean

programmes* (IMP) and job creation. There have been five stages since 1978. NCI V (1989): priority to countering the depopulation of rural areas and destruction of the environment* and to use of new technology* in SME*. Under review in the light of increased EURATOM* borrowing.

New Industrial Countries Used for countries which have reached a certain level of economic development with an increased level of debt: Hong Kong, South Korea, Singapore, Taiwan, Thailand, India, Yugoslavia, Brazil, Mexico, Argentina ... Most of them belong to regional groups of countries which have signed agreements* with the EC*.
SEE GATT, NON-MEMBER COUNTRIES.

NGOs (Non-Governmental Organizations) Associations of private or public persons which are represented in international bodies.
SEE UNITED NATIONS ORGANIZATION.

NIMEXE Nomenclature of goods for the external trade* statistics* of the Community* and for statistics* of trade* between Member States* (Council* Regulation* of 24/4/1972).
SEE CCCN, COMMON CUSTOMS TARIFF, OJ (SERIES C).

Nine Name given to the nine states which were signatories to the treaties* as of 1/1/1973: the Six* plus Denmark, the Republic of Ireland and the United Kingdom.
SEE COMMUNITY, TEN, TWELVE.

Non-Community Goods Any goods other than Community goods*, or, irrespective of agreements* concluded with non-member countries* for the application of the Community transit* system, any Community goods* reintroduced onto the customs territory* of the Community* after having been exported outside this territory. See also Reg.* 222/77/EEC, 13/12/1976 (OJ* L 38, 9/2/1977).
SEE CUSTOMS (ALL ENTRIES).

Non-Discrimination One of the three rules relating to freedom of movement* of persons and the right of establishment*.

Non Europe Negative evaluation of the anticipated advantages of a single market*. The cost of not having a single market* has been estimated at between 4.3% and 6.5% of European GDP

(175,000m to 255,000m Ecus*). The Community institutions* used this study ('Cecchini* Report*') to work harder towards setting up the single market*.
SEE SINGLE EUROPEAN ACT, WHITE PAPER.

Non-Member Countries (Third Countries) Countries which do not belong to the Community*. Some have preferential relations with the Community*: member states of EFTA* (with whom customs duties* and quantitative restrictions* have been abolished) and states associated with or with links to the Community* via specific agreements. *Customs union**, set up by art. 9 of the treaty* of Rome*, lays down the adoption of a *common customs tariff** and free circulation* throughout the Community* of goods which are imported from non-member countries. Common Commercial Policy* has led to the Community* holding bilateral or multilateral negotiations, particularly under GATT*, on the existence of and time limits for quotas* and on reciprocity* clauses in relations with these countries. The Commission* introduces measures and implements Regulations* to ensure protection of trade* in the Community*.
*Liberalization of movements of capital** entails Member States* making an effort to attain the same degree of liberalization in their relations with non-member countries as with each other, with the possibility of concerted protective measures if short-term large-scale movements from or to non-member countries would cause serious financial strain.
The Ecu* is used for trade with certain non-member countries; some of the latter have also issued international bonds in Ecus*.
There are various measures connected to setting up the single market* which bear relation to non-member countries (especially reciprocity* clauses);
SEE PUBLIC CONTRACT.
Some *Community programmes** (EURAM*) may involve agreements with non-member countries.
Some *data bases** are also open to them.
The *ECSC* treaty** lays down the possibility of voluntary restraint arrangements with non-member countries which export steel and reciprocity* agreements with the EFTA* countries. Inter-parliamentary delegations with the European Parliament*.
SEE EUROPEAN ECONOMIC AREA, LESS DEVELOPED COUNTRIES, MEDITERRANEAN NON-MEMBER COUNTRIES, OWN RESOURCES, QUANTITATIVE RESTRICTION, RECIPROCITY, SAFEGUARD CLAUSE.

Non-Nuclear Energy Community programme* on various

sources of energy* which are more economical and less harmful to the environment* (solar energy, wind energy, geothermic energy, biomass energy; liquefaction of coal*; methods for saving energy*; analyses of energy systems; models). Budget: 155.4m Ecus* (1990-1994). DG XII of the Commission*. New programme in preparation (COM (90) 164).
SEE NUCLEAR ENERGY.

Non-Tariff Barriers Quantitative restrictions* and regulations intended to limit the import* of foreign made products into a territory.
SEE FRONTIER CONTROL, MEASURE HAVING EQUIVALENT EFFECT, QUOTA, STANDARDS, TAXATION, TECHNICAL REGULATION.

NORCAR-TRAMET Project in the EUREKA* programme ('EU 43'): development of soil preparation machines for the reforestation of dry land and escarpments.

NOREX (NOrmes et Règles techniques a l'EXport) *(Technical standards and rules for exports)* French network set up in 1977 by AFNOR*, the French Centre for Foreign Trade (CFCE), the French Scientific and Technical Centre for Construction (CSTB), the French Central Laboratory of the Electrical Industries (LCIE) and French National Testing Laboratory (LNE) to provide French businesses with information, training and technical advice necessary for exporting their products. Tour Europe, Cedex 7, 92049 Paris-La Defense.
SEE STANDARDS, TECHNICAL REGULATION.

NORIANE PLUS AFNOR* data base*.

North Atlantic Assembly Interparliamentary assembly of the Member States of the North Atlantic Treaty Organization (NATO*). One representative of the European Parliament* attends its annual meeting.

North Atlantic Treaty Organization
SEE NATO.

Notice *Public contracts*: indication by a contracting authority* that it intends to award a public supply contract* by means of open, restricted or negotiated procedure*. Published in the OJ* and the TED* database.

Letter addressed by the Commission* to the government of a Member State* summoning it to put an end to an infringement of a Community* Regulation* (treaties* or secondary Community law*). Precedes a reasoned opinion.

Notification Communication to the Commission* by an undertaking with a view to obtaining a Decision* declaring that any agreements* or associations* it intends entering into do not infringe art. 85.1 of the EEC* treaty* or that they fulfil the necessary conditions for an individual exemption*. Eg compulsory notification for concentrations*.
SEE COMPETITION, AGREEMENTS BETWEEN UNDERTAKINGS.
Notification of a Directive* or Decision* gives it legal status (see art. 191 of the EEC* treaty*).

NOW Commission* initiative to guarantee equal treatment of men and women. Budget: 120m Ecus* 1990.

Nuclear Energy
Directives*: 80/836/EEC; 89/618/EURATOM
Regulations*: 87/9716/EEC; 220/901/EURATOM
SEE CERN, CONTROLLED THERMONUCLEAR FUSION, DECOMMISSIONING NUCLEAR INSTALLATIONS, EURATOM, NUCLEAR ENERGY PROGRAMME, RADIATION PROTECTION, RADIOACTIVE WASTE, REPORT (SPAAK), TELEMAN.

Nuclear Energy Programme Community programme* on research* and development in the nuclear field (safety of reactors, radioactive waste* management, nuclear fuels and actinides, safety of fissile materials, decommissioning nuclear installations*). OJ* L 36, 5/1/1984; L 83, 25/3/1985. DG XII of the Commission*.
SEE EURATOM, JOINT RESEARCH CENTRE.

Nurses Nurses in general care benefit from the freedom to provide services* (DIR.* 77/452 AND 77/453 OF 17/6/1977).

O

Objective 1992 Time limit fixed by the Single European Act* (without being automatically legally binding for the Member States*) for establishing a unified European internal market. Following the European Council* in Dublin of 25-26/6/1990, this objective has been coupled with those of European Union* and Economic and Monetary Union*.
SEE HARMONIZATION, SPINELLI, WHITE PAPER.

ODETTE (Organization for Data Exchange by Tele Transmission in Europe) Community programme*. DG XIII of the Commission*.

OECD
SEE ORGANIZATION FOR ECONOMIC COOPERATION AND DEVELOPMENT.

Office for Official Publications of the European Communities (OOPEC) Office, attached to the Commission*, responsible for editing and distributing the official publications of the Community*. 2, rue Mercier, 2985 Luxembourg.
SEE OJ, STATISTICS.*

Official Authority A Member State* of the Community* may refuse a national of another Member State* eligibility to work, even on a part-time basis, in a position of official authority (art. 55 of the EEC* treaty).
SEE FREEDOM OF MOVEMENT, MUTUAL RECOGNITION, RIGHT OF ESTABLISHMENT.

Official Journal of the European Communities
SEE OJ.

Officials
SEE OFFICIAL AUTHORITY.

OJ (Official Journal of the European Communities) Publishes the acts of the Council* and the Commission* – SEE REGULATION, DECISION, DIRECTIVE – (L series), and communications* – information, memorandums*, proposals by the Commission*, written questions to the European Parliament* – (C series). Some acts are published in the S series. Published by the Office for Official Publications of the European Parliament* (OOPEC). 2, rue Mercier, 2985 Luxembourg.

ONP
SEE OPEN NETWORK PROVISION.

OOPEC
SEE OFFICE FOR OFFICIAL PUBLICATIONS OF THE EUROPEAN COMMUNITIES.

Open Network Provision (ONP) Open telecommunications* network. Commission* framework Directive* of 28/6/1990 on open access to monopoly telecommunications* networks and services (OJ* L 192, 1990) and harmonization* of technical standards*. DG XIII of the Commission*.
SEE MAC.

Open Procedure National procedure for awarding public contracts* in which any supplier may submit a tender.

Operator *Customs*: any person who carries out all or part of a processing* operation.
SEE INWARD PROCESSING, OUTWARD PROCESSING.

Opinion The opinion of a Community* institution* when consulted on a specific point.
SEE COMMISSION, COUNCIL, COURT OF JUSTICE, ECONOMIC AND SOCIAL COMMITTEE.
Single opinions expressed by Community institutions, eg by the European Parliament* or by the Economic and Social Committee*, are not binding.
Assent: required for a decision to be taken. For example: assent of the European Parliament* approving the accession of new Member States* and the conclusion of association agreements*; assent of the Council* for the Commission* to take important decisions or for adapting the rules of the treaties*.
SEE SINGLE ACT.
Common opinion: opinion expressed by a Community* institution* in agreement with another body (for example: the Commission* with the two sides of industry).
Own-initiative opinion: opinion expressed by the Economic and Social Committee* on its own initiative on subjects which it considers to merit specific comment. The Court of Auditors* submits own-initiative comments. *Opinions (contributions) from*

experts and from international institutions are expressed to a committee of the European Parliament* or of a section of the Economic and Social Committee* or to a committee of the Commission*.

Opt Out Dissent from a treaty or part of a treaty with the agreement of the other Member States.
SEE DEROGATION.

ORA Opportunities for Application of ITT in Rural Areas.

Order Act* of the Court of Justice* of the European Communities*: summons for witnesses to appear; amendments to judgements*; on recoverable costs; by the President of the Court – to suspend the application of certain acts* of other Community institutions*.

ORGALIME
SEE LIAISON GROUP FOR THE EUROPEAN ENGINEERING INDUSTRIES.

Organization for Economic Cooperation and Development (OECD) Intergovernmental organization. 24 member countries (the Twelve*, the members of the EFTA*, Turkey, Australia, Canada, the United States, Japan and New Zealand). Replaced (30/9/1961) the Organization for European Economic Cooperation which had been set up under the Marshall Plan of 16/4/1948.
Objectives: to coordinate economic policy, studies, expansion of international trade*. Permanent delegation at the EC*. EFTA* represented at some conferences. Development Assistance Committee* (DAC).
2, rue André Pascal, 75116 Paris.
SEE FREE TRADE, LDCs.

Organization for European Economic Cooperation (OEEC)
SEE ORGANIZATION FOR ECONOMIC COOPERATION AND DEVELOPMENT.

Origin Criterion used to describe imported goods. The EEC* considers goods to have originated in a country if they were completely produced there.
Goods which are produced by several countries are deemed to have originated in the country where they were last processed or subject to substantial working which was economically justified and carried out by an undertaking equipped for this purpose

and which led to the manufacture of a new product or which represented an important stage of the manufacturing process. Accessories, spare parts and tools delivered at the same time as a piece of equipment, a machine, or a vehicle and being part of its normal equipment are said to have the same origin (REG.* 802/68, 27/6/1968, OJ* L 148, 28/6/1968).
The *Committee on Origin** and the Court of Justice* are entitled to decide more precisely what constitutes 'substantial working'. *Preferential agreements* signed by the EFTA* and EEC* countries recognize that a product originates in a contracting country (and allow it more favourable tariff measures) if it is either completely produced within EFTA* or the EEC* or is produced by processing products imported from countries outside the agreement.
'Diagonal cumulation' is possible for the latter products if they undergo a series of processes in several EFTA* countries. Origin is proved by preauthenticated certificates, long-term EUR 1* certificates or by a declaration on the invoice. This is valid for all agreements concluded by the EEC*. *Documentary proofs of origin*: certificate of origin*, certified declaration of origin*, declaration of origin*.
SEE ASSOCIATION AGREEMENT, CUSTOMS (ALL ENTRIES), GENERALIZED SYSTEM OF PREFERENCES, INTERNAL MARKET, NON-MEMBER COUNTRIES, PRODUCT ORIGINATING IN THE EEC, RULES OF ORIGIN.

Origin Marking National regulation or practice which makes the marketing of certain products dependent on the condition that the country where they are manufactured must be marked on the packaging or on the product itself. May be considered to be a measure having equivalent effect*, in contravention of art. 30 of the EEC* treaty*.
SEE CONSUMPTION, LABEL.

Orion Community programme* to provide grants enabling education officers to make short visits to another Member State*.

Ortoli (François-Xavier) French statesman, former President (1973-1977) and Vice-president (1977-1984) of the Commission* of the European Communities. Creator of the New Community Instrument* and author of reports* on European Union*.

OSI (Open System Interconnection) International standard* for organizing data so that they can be used by different types of computer. Breaks down into seven layers, or levels for transmission, each one of these having its own standards*.

Outward processing Customs procedure which totally or partially suspends import duty* on goods exported from the Community* which are reintroduced after processing (partial suspension refers to the value added by the processing). Authorization is only granted if the operation does not seriously conflict with the interests of Community* businesses. Reg.* 636/82/EEC, 16/3/1982 (OJ* L 76, 20/3/1982); 2473/86/EEC, 24/7/1986 (OJ* L 212, 2/7/1986).
SEE CUSTOMS (ALL ENTRIES), EXPORT, IMPORT, INWARD PROCESSING, PROCESSING.

Overall Approach Complements the 'new approach'* for harmonizing the means by which evaluation of conformity* is carried out and to improve cooperation between national bodies. It is based on criteria (EN 45000 standards*) which make the competence and objectivity of the bodies which carry out the evaluation procedures objectively verifiable (the procedures are also harmonized: standard modules for the various phases of evaluation of conformity*). Council* Resolution* 21/12/1989. Joint position* of 30/6/1990.
SEE EOTC.

Overbooking Agreement at the Council* in June 1991 on compensation for passengers refused embarkation. Association of European Airlines (AEA) plan in application from 8 April 1991.

Own Resources Following the Decisions* of 21/4/1970, the part of the Community* income which is subject to control by the European Parliament* a) levies*, premiums, additional or compensatory amounts, duties laid down by the Community institutions* within the Common Agricultural Policy* for trade* with non-member countries* and other contributions provided for by the Common Market Organizations* (sugar); b) duties under the Common Customs Tariff*, duties on trade with non-member countries*, customs duty on products which come under the ECSC* treaty*; c) 1.4% of VAT* collected by Member States* (may be as much as 1.6% on a Council* Decision* taken by unanimity* and ratified by the Member States*).
6/1988: 'fourth resource*' established, calculated on the GDP of

Member States* (Decision* came into effect 1/1/1989), to finance the Common Agricultural Policy*.
SEE BUDGET.

Oxidipine Project in the EUREKA* programme ('EU 59'): to place a new hypertension drug on the market, the result of a new approach in pharmaceutical research*.

P

PABLI Data base* of development aid projects: ACP*, Mediterranean countries, LDCs* in Asia and Latin America. Access via ECHO*. DG VIII of the Commission*.
SEE EDF.

PACA (Pompes À Chaleur à Absorption) (*Absorption heat pump*): Project in the EUREKA* programme ('EU 109'): the industrial use of absorption heat pumps. Phase 3: 1990.

Package Deal A number of connected proposals which presuppose mutual concessions, for universal adoption, drawn up by a Community institution* in order to break a deadlock on a matter which has arisen due to a difference of opinion on policy.

Packaging A Member State* may not prohibit the sale of a foodstuff* imported from another Member State* in the packaging in which it is usually marketed except where that could confuse the consumer* with regard to the origin* or nature of the food and if labelling would not suffice to clarify this problem and except with regard to measures to protect the environment* (returnable deposit on empty containers). Prohibition could constitute a measure having equivalent effect*, contrary to art. 30 of the EEC* treaty*.
Draft Directives* on food packaging (recycling). Directive* on packaging of dangerous preparations (7/6/1988, OJ* L 187, 1988).
SEE ENVIRONMENT.

PAIA
SEE PROGRAMME OF AGRICULTURAL INCOME AIDS.

Paper
SEE EUROPEAN CONFEDERATION OF PULP, PAPER AND BOARD INDUSTRIES.

Parallel Import Imports other than on sole distribution circuits. If, in order to authorize this, a Member State* demands a certificate of authenticity which is more difficult for importers of an authentic product which is regularly in free circulation* in another Member State* to obtain than for importers of the same product from the country of origin, this constitutes a measure having equivalent effect* (Judgements* 8/74, 104/75, 20/5/1976).

Paris Capital of the Republic of France.
18/4/1951: ECSC* treaty*;
19-21/10/1972: a summit relaunches unification of the Community* (regional policy*, environment*, energy*, Economic and Monetary Union* by 1980);
9-10/12/1974: summit (ERDF* appropriations; idea of the European Council*, election to the European Parliament* by direct universal suffrage; Tindemans* report*);
9-10/3/1979: European Council* (EMS*);
13/7/1989: summit of the seven most industrialized nations (Community* aid to Poland and Hungary).
SEE EUROPEAN BANK FOR RECONSTRUCTION AND DEVELOPMENT, PHARE.
19/11/1990: Summit (CSCE*).

Parliamentary Assembly of the Council of Europe Debating body of the Council of Europe* (formerly Consultative Assembly until 1974); 170 members. Determines the members of the European Court of Human Rights*. Reports are submitted to it by the Commission* and the European Parliament*. Three plenary sessions per year (resolutions or recommendations). Palais de l'Europe, Strasbourg, France.

Parliamentary Committee Study groups in the European Parliament*. 18 standing committees: political affairs; agriculture*, fisheries* and food*; budgets*; economic and monetary affairs and industrial policy; energy*, research* and technology*; external economic relations; legal affairs and citizens' rights; social affairs and employment*; regional policy and town and county planning; transport* and the environment*; public health* and consumer* protection; youth, culture, education, information and sport; development and cooperation*; budgetary control; institutions; regulation, verification of credentials and immunities; womens' rights; petitions*. Members and alternates, elected on proposals from the groups, prepare Parliamentary Decisions* (SEE CONSULTATION PROCEDURE, COOPERATION PROCEDURE, OPINION). Commissions of inquiry (following the request of at least a quarter of the members of Parliament present): on infringements of Community* legislation or bad administration in the areas subject to Community* responsibility. Maximum of 15 members. Temporary committees (one year, may be extended).

Sub-committees and working parties: established by standing committees following the agreement of the enlarged Bureau*.

Partnership Cooperation agreement* between undertakings.
SEE EUROPARTENARIAT.

Partnerships between Undertakings If the decision to become partners or the collective will of a number of undertakings produces a detrimental effect on competition*, the Commission may prohibit such partnership, where the partners exert an appreciable influence on the effects of competition* on the market in question.

Patent for Invention Title granted by a government permitting exclusive rights to exploit a discovery or industrial invention for a fixed period of time to any person claiming to be its author or to their assignee, having applied in the correct manner. The abolition of quantitative restrictions* within the Community* does not apply to patents regarding the right of intellectual property. Exclusive patent rights end with the marketing of the product concerned (See art. 36 of the EEC treaty*). Harmonization* of national patents procedures is in progress.
SEE COMMUNITY PATENT, COPYRIGHT, EUROPEAN PATENT, RESEARCH POLICY.

Paul VI Pope from 1963 to 1978. Speeches to members of the European Parliament* (14/10/1964); to the ECSC* (8/10/1965), to the EEC* and to EURATOM* (29/5/1965), to the Committee of the Council of Europe* (2/9/1968), to the agriculture ministers of the EEC* (16/9/1971), to the European Parliament* (25/11/1971; 9/11/1973); to the members of the Court of Auditors* of the EC* (9/6/1973), to the Commission* of the EC* (6/5/1975) and to the Court of Justice* of the EC* (5/6/1975).

Payment Card Recommendation* by the Commission* for a 'European code of conduct on electronic payment' (8/12/1987, OJ* L 365, 24/12/1987). The Commission* ratified the agreement of 9/10/1987 between the main European banks on the inter-operability of payment cards within the Community*. See also the 'New impetus for consumer protection policy', a communication* from the Commission* to the Council*, OOPEC*, 1985, nos. 33 and 34.
SEE BANK.

Payments Union Name of an institution proposed by a commissioner* to ease the integration of the former COMECON* countries into international trade by compensating imbalances in bilateral trade with convertible currency.
SEE ECU.

PCTE (Portable Common Tools Environment) Common system for software* development.
SEE ESPRIT, INFORMATION TECHNOLOGY.

PEDIP (Programma Especifico para o Desenvolvimento da Industria Portuguese) (*Programme for the development of Portuguese industry*): Reg.* 88/53/EEC, OJ* L 185, 15/7/1988. DG XXII of the Commission*.

Penalty Payment A fine* accompanied by the obligation to pay a sum per day for each day of delay in implementing a Decision*. The Commission* may impose a penalty payment on undertakings* or on partnerships of undertakings where they have infringed competition law*. For example: penalty payments of 25,000 Ecus* per day of delay in supplying information on mergers* (REG.* 4064/89/EEC, 21/12/1989.) Possible appeal* to the CJEC*.

PERCALE (Programme Européen de Revitalisation des Campagnes et de l'Agriculture Lié à l'Environnement) (*European programme for the revitalization of the countryside and of agriculture with reference to the environment*): Project proposed by the European Parliament*. Budget: 495m Ecus*.

Perfume
SEE LIAISON COMMITTEE OF THE EUROPEAN FEDERATIONS OF THE PERFUME, COSMETICS AND TOILETRIES INDUSTRY (COLIPA).

Permanent Conference of Chambers of Commerce and Industry of the EEC (CPCCI) European body representing groups of chambers of commerce from Belgium, France, Italy, Netherlands, Luxembourg, Germany, United Kingdom (1958). Brussels, Belgium. Relations with the Community*.

Personal Effects *Customs*: effects for personal use of the person(s) concerned or for use in their household (movable effects and objects: bicycles, motorcycles, motor vehicles for private use and their trailers; caravans; pleasure boats and private aeroplanes; household provisions; household pets, horses and ponies; portable instruments which the person(s) concerned require to exercise their profession). Duty-free* import* at intra-community borders, within certain limits. Reg.* 919/83/EEC (OJ* L 105, 23/4/1983).

PESC (Politique Étrangère et de Sécurité Commune)
SEE COMMON FOREIGN AND SECURITY POLICY.

Petition Every citizen of the Community* has the right, individually or in association with other citizens, to submit written requests or complaints to the European Parliament*. They are examined by the petitions committee which may bring the matter before the European Parliament*, the Commission* or the Council* via the intermediary of the President of the Parliament.

PETRA Community* action programme for the vocational training* of young people and their preparation for adult and working life. The objective is to encourage young people to enter vocational training after leaving school. European network of training* initiatives; initiative projects for young people; the impact of training* provisions. Decision* 87/569/EEC, 1/12/1987 (OJ* 10/12/1987). DG V of the Commission*.
SEE EUROPEAN CENTRE FOR THE DEVELOPMENT OF VOCATIONAL TRAINING.

PHARE (Pologne, Hongrie, Assistance à la Restructuration Économique) *(Poland, Hungary, assistance for economic restructuring)*: Aid operation (food, training*, design and implementation of an agricultural development programme, protection of the environment* and economic restructuring) for Poland and Hungary, then Bulgaria, the former GDR, Czechoslovakia and Yugoslavia, adopted by the representatives of the seven most industrialized nations in Paris* on 15/7/1989 and entrusted to the Commission* to implement from June 1990. 24 countries involved, including the Twelve*. Budget: 2,350m Ecus* (1990-1992).
SEE EUROPEAN BANK FOR RECONSTRUCTION AND DEVELOPMENT, EUROPEAN FOUNDATION FOR VOCATIONAL TRAINING, EUROPEAN INVESTMENT BANK, TEMPUS.

Pharmaceutical association of the EEC Pharmacists' defence organization at Community* level (1959). Brussels.

Pharmacists Freedom of establishment* (DIR.* 85/432, 85/433 of 16/9/1985). Member States* retain their responsibility with regard to the geographical spread of pharmacists and monopolies for the dispensation of drugs. Mutual recognition* of diplomas*.
SEE MEDICINAL PRODUCTS, PHARMACY.

Pharmacy
SEE HEALTH, MEDICINAL PRODUCTS, PHARMACEUTICAL ASSOCIATION OF THE EEC, PHARMACISTS.

Physical Barriers
SEE BARRIERS.

PIIC (Politique de l'Information, de l'Informatique et des Communications) *(Information, informatics and communications policy)*: Committee of the OECD*: the contribution of information technology* to economic development; telecommunications* policy; the improvement of international rules.

PINC (Programme Indicatif Nucléaire pour la Communauté)
SEE ILLUSTRATIVE NUCLEAR POWER STATION DESIGN AND CONSTRUCTION IN THE EC.

Pious XII Pope from 1939 to 1958. Several broadcasts and speeches on Europe, in particular on 11/11/1948 at the congress of the European Union; on 15/3/1953 to members of the College of Europe in Bruges, Belgium; and on 4/11/1957 to the members of the ECSC* European Parliamentary Assembly.

Plant, Animal and Other Health Controls The Member States* of the Community* may impose these controls on agricultural products for import* or export*; they may also charge fees to cover the costs of these controls (charge having equivalent effect*, except where art. 36 of the EEC* treaty* is invoked: effects on the health* and life of persons and animals). A Community* control may be carried out pursuant to a Directive* based on art. 100 of the EEC* treaty*. In this case it does not constitute a measure having equivalent effect*. Controls carried out by Member States* may only be sporadic. Such a measure must be proportional to the result expected and must not be a means of arbitrary discrimination.
12/12/1989: Directive* on the abolition as of 1/1/1992 of controls of meat and products based on meat and milk, rabbits, game,

fish, shellfish, honey, snails and frogs' legs (examination to be carried out at place of departure or control at place of destination).

Plastics industry
SEE EUROPEAN PLASTIC CONVERTEUR.

Police
SEE FRONTIER CONTROL, RIGHT OF ASYLUM, SCHENGEN, TREVI GROUP, VISAS.

Population of the European Economic Community 325,472,000 inhabitants on 1/1/1989 (third in the world after China (1,100,000,000) and India (800,000,000)). 608,000 immigrants from non-member countries*. 2.1 children born per mother. Birth rate: 5.9 per 1000. Death rate: 9.9 per 1000.

POSEIDOM (Programmes d'Options Spécifiques a l'Eloignement et a l'Insularité des Départements d'Outre-Mer) *(Programme of options specific to the remote and insular nature of the overseas departments)*: Community aid programme for the French overseas departments (FOD*), the Azores and Madeira (Portugal) and the Canaries (Spain) to compensate them for their specific disadvantages (exemption from Community levies* on imports* from non-member countries* and those for animal feed). Budget: 250m Ecus* (1989-1992). COM (88) 730 F (OJ* C 53, 2/3/1989). General Secretariat of the Commission*.
SEE DOCK DUES, ERDF, EAGGF, EUROPEAN SOCIAL FUND.

Positive Discrimination Member States* cannot protect local banks* from the consequences of mutual recognition* of the conditions in which banks* offer their financial services without positively discriminating towards them; this is not yet prohibited by Community law*.

Powers of Investigation
SEE COMMISSION, COMPETITION.

Precedence Principle whereby primary Community law* has precedence over national law.

Precursors Substances which may be used for manufacturing chemical weapons. 20/2/1989: Council* Regulation* prohibiting the sale of 8 substances to countries on a war footing or to areas where there is a serious threat of war.
SEE CHEMISTRY.

Preference Favourable treatment granted to one or more countries in international trade relations.
SEE COMMUNITY PREFERENCE, GENERALIZED SYSTEM OF PREFERENCES, REGIONAL PREFERENCE.

Preferential agreement Trade agreement concluded by the EC* containing more favourable tariff provisions than those resulting from application of the standard GATT* rules: free trade*, association* and cooperation agreements*. Art. 113 of the EEC* treaty.
SEE MIXED ORIGIN.

Preliminary referral Referral procedure by a national judge to a Community* judge for assessment of validity or interpretation, provided for by the treaties* or by a Community* act*.

Prénorme Européenne
SEE DRAFT EUROPEAN STANDARD.

Preparation Second part of proceedings brought before the Court of Justice* of the European Communities*. Once the application* has been submitted to the Registrar of the Court, the defendant is notified and has one month to produce a statement of defence. The applicant has the right to reply, then the defendant, each within one month. The Court* decides if the matter requires special examination by a judge acting as Rapporteur* and by an Advocate-General. After the parties involved have made an appearance in person, or documents have been found, or witnesses or experts have been heard, or inspections have been carried out, or letters of request sent, etc., the written phase of the proceedings is closed with the judge's report.

Pressurized Containers
SEE PRESSURIZED VESSELS.

Pressurized Vessels (Containers) Directive* on safety* (87/104/EEC, OJ* L 220, 8/7/1987), currently being simplified (COM (89) 636); transition period of two years for its implementation (both European standards* and national legislation valid).

Presumption of Conformity Products which bear the CE* mark or which are accompanied by a declaration of conformity* issued by the manufacturer or his/her authorized representative*

in the Community* are presumed to be in conformity with the essential requirements* laid down by the relevant Directives* (according to AFNOR*).
SEE BARRIERS, NEW APPROACH.

Preventive Medicine Community research* programme* on human genetic material: risk prevention, treatment of disease, hereditary diseases. Budget: 30m Ecus* (1989-1991).

Price Guarantee National provision whereby export* prices are guaranteed against price rises and other risks if the products to be exported consist totally or partially of nationally produced products. May be considered to be a measure having equivalent effect*, in contravention of art. 30 of the EEC* treaty*.

Primary Community Law Part of Community law* based in international acts (treaties* establishing the Communities*, treaties or agreements amending or adapting the former), as opposed to Secondary Community Law*.

Primary Product In Community law* a primary product is any product which is to be exported after processing as a processed product or as goods.
SEE CUSTOMS (ALL ENTRIES), INWARD PROCESSING, ORIGIN, OUTWARD PROCESSING.

Principle of Proportionality
SEE PROPORTIONALITY.

Principle of Territoriality Principle whereby heavy goods vehicles pay taxes depending on which road networks they use as as opposed to the nationality of the haulier.
SEE TRANSPORT POLICY.

PRISMA (Preparing Regional Industry for the Single MArket) Community programme* to improve infrastructures and services in under-developed regions.

Proceedings Action brought before the Court of Justice* or the Commission* and, on the other hand, an action brought by the Commission* against the government of a Member State* (for example to put an end to an infringement of Community law* or to allow a Member State* to explain how an action conforms to Community law*).
SEE COMPETITION, PUBLIC CONTRACT.

Proceedings for Interpretation of a Judgement Exceptional appeal* before the Court of Justice* of the EC*, where the party bringing the appeal* is not only affected by, but also has difficulty in interpreting the meaning and the implications of, the judgement* in question.

Processing Working of goods (including mounting, assembly, adaptation to other goods). Repairs to goods. SEE CUSTOMS (ALL ENTRIES), INWARD PROCESSING, OUTWARD PROCESSING. See also Council* Regulation* 2473/86/EEC.

Processing of Goods for Entry for Consumption Customs procedure whereby imported* goods may, under customs control* and before entry for consumption*, undergo processing or working with the result that the amount of import duty*, and charges payable on the processed products, are lower than that which would have been paid on the imported* goods. See also Council* Decision* 86/103/EEC (Kyoto Convention).

Processing under Customs Control Customs procedure whereby import duties* are waived on goods imported* into the Community* for the purpose of undergoing operations which will change their character or state. The goods are then put into free circulation* and duty must be paid on them. Reg.* 2763/83/EEC, 26/9/1983, applicable on 1/7/1985 (OJ* L 272, 5/10/1983).
SEE CUSTOMS (ALL ENTRIES).

PRODCOM European nomenclature project handled by the Statistical Office of the European Communities*.

Product For the purposes of standards* and technical regulations*: the product of industrial manufacture, not including agricultural products as in art. 38 of the EEC* treaty*, all food products destined for human or animal consumption, medicinal products* and cosmetics.
SEE BARRIERS, COMPENSATING PRODUCT, NEW APPROACH, PRODUCT ORIGINATING IN THE EC, SECONDARY COMPENSATING PRODUCT.

Product Originating in The EC Product produced entirely in the Community* or produced in the Community* and containing materials which were not produced in the Community* (working or a sufficient degree of processing).
SEE CERTIFICATE OF ORIGIN, CUSTOMS (ALL ENTRIES), INWARD PROCESSING, ORIGIN, OUTWARD PROCESSING.

Profit Sharing Share of the profits of an undertaking by its workers, in the form of premiums or shares.
SEE WORKER PARTICIPATION.

Programme of Agricultural Income Aids (PAIA) Community* aid programme (graduated over a maximum of 5 years) for the farmers most affected by the reform of the Common Agricultural Policy*. Proposal for a Regulation* (COM (89) 61 F, OJ* C 97, 18/4/1989). DG VI of the Commission*.

PROMETHEUS Project in the EUREKA* programme ('EU 45'): to use modern information technology* to improve the road traffic system (in-car computers). Sub-projects include PRO-NET, PRO-ROAD and PRO-GENERAL (230 in total).

Proportionality Principle in Community law* which demands that appropriate means be used to achieve the end in question. For example it condemns disproportionate use of health* and safety* requirements to refuse a product entry onto the territory of a Member State* or of certain administrative formalities to refuse equality of treatment to nationals of another Member State* of the Community*.

Prospectus Information document upon whose publication admission of securities to quotation on a stock exchange* (DIR.* of 23/4/1990, OJ* L 112, 1990) or any public purchase offer* of securities (DIR.* 89/298/EEC, OJ* L 124/8, 5/5/1989) is conditional in a Member State*. In the latter case it must include the following details: those responsible for the operation; the public purchase offer* and the securities concerned; the issuer and its main business, its assets and its financial results, its administrative, management and supervisory bodies, its recent development and its prospects; the same information on guarantors where convertible or exchangeable bonds or bonds subject to warrants* are concerned (nature of the shares or bonds to which they pertain, the conditions and methods of conversion, exchange or subscription). Some of these details may be omitted if they are of minimal significance or if their publication would be contrary to the public interest. Mutual recognition* (DIR.* 87/345/EEC, OJ* L 185/81, 4/7/1987; 89/298/EEC, OJ* L 124/14, 5/5/1989).
SEE EUROPEAN FINANCIAL AREA, PUBLIC PURCHASE OFFER.

Protection of the Environment Community programme* to provide a scientific basis to the implementation of environmental

policy (pollution, chemical products, air, water and soil quality, noise, waste*; legislation). Budget: 55m Ecus* (1986-1990). OJ* L 101, 11/4/1981, L 159, 14/6/1986. DG XII of the Commission*.
SEE CHEMISTRY, NUCLEAR ENERGY.

Provision of Services Activity whereby labour is made available for remuneration without an employment contract being concluded with the user (as in the case of temporary employment agencies).
SEE EUROPEAN FINANCIAL AREA, FREEDOM TO PROVIDE SERVICES, SERVICE.

Prudential Supervision Harmonization* of measures designed to maintain the solvency of banks* by means of Directives* on supervision: the authorities in a bank's* state of origin are responsible for supervising the activities of the parent company and its subsidiaries in other Member States* (83/150/EEC, 13/6/1983, OJ* L 193, 18/7/1983); there is a common instrument for assessing the equity capital* of credit institutions* (89/229/EEC, 17/4/1989, OJ* L 124, 5/5/1989); publication of annual and consolidated accounts in all Member States* where there is a banking network (86/635/EEC, 8/12/1986, OJ* L 372, 31/12/1986); publication of accounting documents (89/117/EEC, 13/2/1989, OJ* L 44, 16/2/1989). Recommendations* by the Commission* on large credit risks, where the supervisory authorities must be notified when the liability is 15% of equity capital* (87/63/EEC, 27/12/1986, OJ* L 33, 4/2/1987), and on deposit guarantees (87/63/EEC, 27/12/1986, OJ* L 33, 4/2/1987); these recommendations are currently in practice in Belgium, Spain, France, Germany, the Netherlands and the United Kingdom.

PTOM (Pays et Territoires d'Outre-Mer) *(Overseas countries and territories)*: SEE FOD, POSEIDOM.

Publication of Information
SEE COMPANY LAW, PROSPECTUS.

Public Contract Contract concluded between an official administration and a business person.
The EEC* treaty* implied that public contracts would be reciprocally opened up under the free movement of goods and services. Reciprocity with the EFTA* countries. Since 1980 the GATT* code has applied (80/767/EEC, OJ* L 215, 18/8/1980). *1971, 1977*: harmonization* Directives* for national procedures for awarding public works* contracts (71/305/EEC, OJ* L 185, 25/8/1971; 78/669/EEC, OJ* L 225, 16/8/1978) and public supply contracts* (77/62/EEC, OJ* L 13, 20/11/72).

1987: Advisory committee on opening up public contracts (OJ* L 152, 12/6/1987); Vademecum* on public contracts (OJ* C 358, 31/12/1987).
22/3/1988: coordination of procedures for awarding public contracts (OJ* L 127, 1988).
1978, 1980, 1989 (DIR.* 88/295/EEC, OJ* L 127, 12/6/1988): liberalization of public supply contracts* (200,000 Ecus* for central administrations, 130,000 for others); objectives: to ensure real transparency in the awards and equality of treatment of the tenderers; to ensure economies of scale and greater competition*, etc. *Sectors* currently *excluded* from these measures: production and distribution of water and energy*, telecommunications* and transport*.
19/7/1989: coordination of procedures for awarding public works* contracts (OJ* L 210, 1989).
22/12/1989: 'appeal' Directive* (application of Community* rules to procedures for awarding public supply contracts* and public works* contracts); arbitration, in case of litigation, by the European Parliament*; appeal* to the Advisory committee and to the Commission* (DG III); adoption of the principle of reciprocity* with non-member countries*.
1990: liberalization of public works* contracts (10m Ecus*).
17/9/1990: Directive* on the opening up of excluded sectors*. Proposals for opening up public service contracts.
Public contract *notices must be published* in the supplement to the OJ*, where the contract is covered by a Directive*.
Information: TED* data bank*, Euro info centres*.
A Member State* may not give preferential treatment to its less-favoured regions* (Judgement* of 20/3/1990).
SEE ACP, AUTOMATIC PUBLIC TENDERING, COMPETITION, EDF, EEIG, EUROPEAN TECHNICAL APPROVAL, NON-MEMBER COUNTRIES, NOTICE, PROCEDURE, PUBLIC SUPPLY CONTRACTS, REGIONAL PREFERENCE, STANDARDS, SUBCONTRACT, WHITE PAPER, WORKS.

Public Exchange Offer
SEE PUBLIC PURCHASE OFFER.

Public Limited Liability Company Directive* of 21/12/1989 (OJ* L 395, 1989) on public limited liability companies with a single member.
SEE COMPANY LAW.

Public Limited Liability Company in European Law A proposed optional legal entity whose articles of association and rules would be the same in all the countries of the Community*, with

tax benefits and various options for the representation of the interests of the workers (draft Regulations* of 1970 and 1989 Commission*). See COM (89) 268 FINAL SYN 218.
SEE WORKER PARTICIPATION.

Public Purchase Offer Offer made to holders of stocks which give the right to vote in a company (shares, convertible bonds*, subscription rights, options and warrants*) to acquire them in exchange for cash or other stocks. The intention is usually to obtain more controlling power in a company or to strengthen such power.
Public purchase offers may be subject to prohibition under art. 85 and 86 of the EEC* treaty*. Draft Regulation* (COM (88) 823 FINAL-SYN 186, 16/2/1989).
The *13th Council* Directive* on Company Law** sets rules concerning information for shareholders, control of operations, guarantees for those to whom the offer is made, etc.

Public Supply Contracts Written contracts concluded for a pecuniary consideration for the purchase, leasing, rental or leasing purchase (with or without a purchase option) of products between a *supplier* (natural or legal person) and a *contracting authority* (state, local authority or public agency). Delivery of products may also involve laying or installation (DIR.* 77/62/EEC).
Sectors excluded from the Directives* until 1993 (1996 for Spain; 6/1998 for Portugal and Greece): inland transport; production, transport and distribution of water and energy* (over 400,000 Ecus* for electrical equipment); telecommunications* (over 600,000 Ecus*).
Air and sea transport are provisionally excluded. Exemptions are provided for water concessions and gas, coal and oil prospecting. Community preference*. Dir.* 77/62/EEC, 80/67/EEC, 88/295/EEC.
Contracts granted in respect of international agreements with non-member countries*, or by international bodies, or concerning arms, munitions or military equipment are excluded.

Public Undertaking Undertaking which may be subject to direct or indirect influence from public authorities due to ownership, financial participation or the rules which govern it. The EEC* treaty* and the Commission* have adopted a neutral attitude to nationalization*. Public undertakings are subject to the same rules governing competition* as other undertakings; exemptions are possible, within certain limits, for undertakings

which are responsible for administering services in the general economic interest or which have the character of a revenue-producing monopoly (Judgement of 3/4/1974, 155/73).
Prohibition of official aid (art. 92 of the EEC* treaty*). A Directive* (25/6/1980, OJ* 198P 195), amended on 24/7/1985, lays down that the Commission* may ask for details of accounts (with regard to art. 90 of the EEC* treaty* on the equality of treatment of undertakings; financial transparency).
*Prohibition of discrimination** (art. 7 of the EEC* treaty*). DG IV of the Commission*.
SEE AID, COMPETITION, EUROPEAN CENTRE OF PUBLIC ENTERPRISES, NATIONALIZATION.

Q

Quaestor Member of the European Parliament* elected by it to supervise administrative and financial matters affecting members and their working conditions. 5 quaestors are elected for two and a half years; they are present in the Bureau* in an advisory capacity.

Qualified Majority Method of calculating the result of a vote based on the votes having to be at a statutorily fixed threshold above an absolute majority (more than half of the votes). *Council*: the qualified majority is 54 votes out of 76. The votes are also weighted to take into account the population sizes of the Member States* (10 for France, Germany, Italy and the United Kingdom, 8 for Spain, 5 for Belgium, Greece, the Netherlands and Portugal, 3 for Denmark and Ireland, 2 for Luxembourg).
A qualified majority was required in the Council* by the EEC* treaty* for the right of establishment* and the freedom to provide services*, competition* law, the Common Agricultural Policy*, liberalization of capital, transport policy*, the Common Commercial Policy*, policy regarding the way the institutions work, economic and protective measures, prohibition of discrimination on grounds of nationality and origin or regarding the destination of exported products, and the European Social Fund*.
*The Single European Act** extended qualified majority voting in the Council* to cover measures for introducing the single market* at the end of 1992, with the exception of fiscal provisions, freedom of movement* of persons and the rights and interests of paid workers*, as well as other areas: Directives* on movements of capital* involving non-member countries*, implementing decisions* concerning air and sea transport (SEE TRANSPORT POLICY), on modifications or unilateral suspensions of duties under the Common Customs Tariff*, on freedom to provide services*, on improving working environments to protect the health* and safety* of workers* (minimum provisions*) (SEE EUROPEAN SOCIAL AREA) and in relation to the ERDF*, etc.
The Council* defines which decisions* concerning improvement of the quality of the *environment** are taken by qualified majority (art. 130s).

*The Council** may amend by qualified majority amendments* to draft budgets* made by the European Parliament* where compulsory expenditure* is concerned.
*The European Parliament** adopts its internal regulations by *absolute majority**, as well as motions of censure* on the Commission*, decisions on amendments* made by the Council* to its amendments* to the draft budget*, rejection of the draft budget*, amendments* to the ECSC* treaty*, requests to convene an extraordinary sitting and assent.
SEE SINGLE EUROPEAN ACT.

Quality
SEE CERTIFICATION OF QUALITY CONTROL SYSTEMS.

Quantitative Restriction Limit imposed on the import* of certain products. Quantitative restrictions have been abolished between Member States* of the EEC* (art. 30 of the treaty*) and between the EEC* and EFTA*. The Community* enjoys full power to negotiate with non-member countries*, to liberalize or distribute import quotas*.
SEE QUOTA.

Question Requests for information in plenary sittings of the European Parliament*: written, oral, debated and not debated. Replies by the Council*, the Commission* and European Political Cooperation*.
Question time: time set aside in each parliamentary sitting for questions by the members of the European Parliament* to the Council*, the Commission* and the foreign ministers of the governments of the Community*. The member who poses the question may pose an additional question following the reply, after which other members may intervene.

Question Time
SEE QUESTION.

Quorum Number of members of an institution whose presence is required to enable it to debate a matter. In the European Parliament*, the quorum is one third of its members.

Quota Quantity of goods authorized for import*, fixed by a state or a group of states for a certain period of time (= import* quota).

The White Paper* lays down that national import* quotas are to be replaced by Community* quotas.
SEE QUANTITATIVE RESTRICTION.

Quota Scale *Customs*: method for breaking down goods for temporary export* into the various compensating products* depending on the quantity of the goods. See also Reg.* 2473/86/EEC (Implementing provisions).

R

RACE (Research and development programme in Advanced Communications technologies in Europe) Community research* programme. Objective: to have established by 1995 a standardized integrated broadband communications network (ISDN* and IBC (Integrated Broadband Communications)). Budget: 550m Ecus* (1987-1991). Decisions* 85/372/EEC, OJ* L 210, 7/8/1985; 88/28/EEC, 14/2/1987, OJ* L 16, 21/1/1988. DG XIII of the Commission*. DG XIII F of the Commission*.
SEE EUROPEAN CONFERENCE OF POSTAL AND TELECOMMUNICATIONS ADMINISTRATIONS, MADRAS, RESEARCH AND TECHNOLOGICAL DEVELOPMENT FRAMEWORK PROGRAMME, STANDARDS, TELECOMMUNICATIONS POLICY.

Radiation Protection Community research* programme* on protection against atomic radiation.
SEE ENVIRONMENT, EURATOM.

Radioactive Waste Community research programme* on the management of nuclear waste and on protecting the environment*. Budget: 79.6m Ecus* (1990-1994). OJ* C 144, 10/6/1989. DG XII of the Commission*.
SEE DECOMMISSIONING NUCLEAR INSTALLATIONS, RADIATION PROTECTION.

Railways The rules concerning railway companies' financial relations with their states have been harmonized* (COUNCIL* DECISION* of 20/5/1975, OJ* L 152, 12/6/1975). Prices for the international transport of goods (DECISION* OF 19/7/1982, OJ* L 234, 9/8/1982) and of passengers (DECISION* OF 25/7/1983, OJ* L 237, 26/8/1983) are fixed freely by the companies concerned. Directive* of July 1991 allowing autonomous management of railway companies and the right to access to networks. Regulation* of 21/6/1991 allowing the notion of public service to be replaced by that of *public service contracts*.
SEE INTERNATIONAL UNION OF RAILWAYS, TRANSPORT POLICY.

RAPID Community* data base* served by EUROBASES*: unabridged texts of press releases (notes, speeches, memos) from the Spokesman's Service of the Commission* of the EC*.

Rapporteur Spokesperson for European Parliament Committees for discussion on relevant proposals.

RARE (Réseaux Associés pour la Recherche Européenne) *(Associated networks for European research)*: European organization supported by the EEC* and promoted by the Twelve* (except Italy), Austria, Finland, Iceland, Norway and Sweden to further communication between scientists and to facilitate the use of information and information services.
SEE OSI.

Rate of Growth of Agricultural Expenditure
SEE GUIDELINES.

Rate of Yield Quantity or percentage of compensating products* produced from the processing of a fixed quantity of imported goods. See also Reg.* 1999/85/EEC; 2473/86/EEC.
SEE CUSTOMS (ALL ENTRIES), INWARD PROCESSING.

Raw Materials and Recycling Community research* programme* to improve competitiveness of businesses in the field of exploitation of raw materials, mining technology and metal extraction. Budget: 45m Ecus* (1989-1991). OJ* L 359, 8/12/1989.
SEE FOREST, REWARD.

Real Estate Investments Purchases of property and land; construction of buildings by private persons for financial or personal ends.
SEE EUROPEAN FINANCIAL AREA, FREEDOM TO PROVIDE SERVICES, MOVEMENTS OF CAPITAL.

Real Monetary Gap (RMG) Difference between the green exchange rate* and the central rate*, expressed as a percentage. Under the Switchover* mechanism, the real monetary gap for Member States* with weak currencies (negative RMG) consists of two parts: *the artificial RMG* (part of a positive RMG which would arise from a change in the central rate* of the strongest currency and would become a negative RMG by using the corrective factor) and the *natural RMG* (or part of the negative RMG arising from a change in the central rate* of Member States'* currencies).

RECHAR (REconversion des bassins CHARbonniers) *(Conversion of coal-mining areas)*: Five-year Community programme* to give aid to the restructuring of declining coal-mining areas in the EEC*. DG XVI of the Commission*.
SEE COAL, ENERGY.

Recipient of Authorization *Customs*: person to whom authorization for inward processing* has been issued. See also Reg.* 1999/85/EEC.

Reciprocity The Community* reserves the right to make the advantages of the single market* conditional, for business-persons in non-member countries*, upon the guarantee of similar or at least non-discriminatory measures in their own countries. This does not mean that all the countries with which the Community* has signed cooperation agreements* should make the same concessions, nor does it mean that the Community* requires them to pass the same legislation, nor does it mean that the Community* wants sectoral reciprocity based on a comparison of levels of trade (Commission* information memo, 10/1989). SEE BANK, COMPETITION, DUMPING, GATT, NEW APPROACH, PUBLIC CONTRACT, RECIPROCITY CLAUSE, TELECOMMUNICATIONS, TRANSPORT POLICY. For the free movement of goods SEE ALSO CONDITION OF RECIPROCITY.

Reciprocity Clause Advantage granted by one state to another in return for a similar advantage.
SEE BANK, FREEDOM OF ESTABLISHMENT, FREEDOM TO PROVIDE SERVICES, INSURANCE, NON-MEMBER COUNTRIES.

Recommendation Community* act* made under the EEC* (art. 189) and EURATOM* (art. 161) treaties* which is not binding on the addressee. Act* made by the Commission* under art. 14 and 15 of the ECSC* treaty*, binding as to the aims to be pursued, with a statement of reasons for the act* and which takes effect upon publication in the OJ* (L series) if it is of a general character or upon being notified to the party concerned if it is of an individual character.

Recovery of Undue Payments Request for the refund of an undue payment incurred by a business-person as a result of the application of a provision under the national law of a Member State*. The fee* incurred must have been deemed by the Court of Justice* to be a charge having equivalent effect*. The request is submitted to national courts.

Referral Right of a legal institution to refer a matter to a Community institution*.

Refund Payment to exporters of agricultural products to non-member countries* of sums of money equivalent to the difference between the Community* market price (including the cost of transportation to the port for export) and selling price which may be obtained on the world market.
Objective: to ensure that the revenue of Community* producers does not decrease because their prices are higher than those on the world market. Financed by the Community* budget*.
SEE AGRICULTURAL PRICES, AUTOMATIC PUBLIC TENDERING, COMMON AGRICULTURAL POLICY, REFUND SYSTEM.

Refund System Inward processing* system for goods put into free circulation*, whereby the import duties* payable on these goods are refunded or remitted if they are re-exported out of the customs territory* of the Community* as compensating products*.
SEE CUSTOMS (ALL ENTRIES).

Reg. Abbreviation of Regulation*.

REGIO EEC* data base* of regional statistics (EUROSTAT*).

Regional Policy Adaptation and development of the regions of the EC*, mentioned in the EEC* treaty*, is described in the Single European Act* as a priority for Community* action, to be implemented by the common policies and their financial instruments. Regional policy programme; regional policy committee; coordination and supervision (SEE AID, COMPETITION) of Member States'* regional policies, integrated regional development operations, a European map of priority regions; specialized regional facets of Community* policy. 1988: priority to aid for restructuring* and conversion. DG IV, XVI, XXII of the Commission*. Section of the Economic and Social Committee*; European Parliament committee.
SEE COMETT, COMMUNITY SUPPORT FRAMEWORK, DRIVE, EAGGF, ECSC FUNDS, EURATOM, EUROPEAN COAL AND STEEL COMMUNITY, EUROPEAN INVESTMENT BANK, EUROPEAN REGIONAL DEVELOPMENT FUND, EUROPEAN SOCIAL FUND, FOD, INTEGRATED MEDITERRANEAN PROGRAMMES, INTERREG, NEW COMMUNITY INSTRUMENT, REGIS, RENAVAL, RESIDER, RURAL-NET, STRIDE, STRUCTURAL FUNDS, TELEMATICS.

Regional preference Exemption, laid down in the Directive* on public works contracts*, to the rule whereby public contracts* in a Member State* are open to any undertaking in the Community*: the rule may not apply to local authorities, or its application may be deferred for serious economic or social reasons.

REGIS Community programme* to develop outlying regions (FOD*, Canaries, Azores, Madeira) with the participation of the Structural Funds*. Budget: 200m Ecus* (1990-1993). OJ* 196, 1990.
SEE INTERREG, LEADER.

Registered Designation of Origin National regulatory measure to preserve the identity of certain foodstuffs*. A Member State* may only use it to prevent the import* of products from other Member States* if it contains false or improper information or deters competition* or innovation. Planned mutual recognition*, under certain conditions.

Regulation *Community* act**, adopted by the Council* or, in some cases, the Commission* (following debate in the European Parliament*), for general application, binding in all its parts and directly applicable in every Member State* (art. 189-191 of the EEC* treaty*, art. 161-163 of the EURATOM* treaty*). Comes into effect on the date specified or twenty days after publication in the Official Journal of the European Communities* (OJ*, L SERIES).
Internal regulations of Community institutions*.
SEE COURT OF JUSTICE, EUROPEAN PARLIAMENT.

Reimporting Member State The Member State* where compensating products* are put into free circulation*, exempted partially or wholly from import duties*, under outward processing* arrangements.

Relevant Community Patrimony All of the acts* already adopted by the Community* in the industrial field (or possibly all the proposals in the White Paper*), proposed by EFTA* as the basis for discussions on an overall agreement with the EEC* for establishing a 'European economic area'*, with exceptions provided for according to basic requirements in the fields of fisheries*, the environment*, health*, safety* etc.
SEE EUROPEAN ECONOMIC AREA.

REM (Radioactive Environmental Monitoring) Data base* of radioactivity measurements made in Member States* of the EEC*. Joint Research Centre.

RENAVAL (REconversion des zones de chantiers NAVALs) *(Conversion of shipbuilding areas)*: Community programme* to give aid to the conversion of shipbuilding areas. Regulation* 2506/88/EEC, OJ* L 225, 2/8/1988. DG XVI and XXII of the Commission*.

Report Document drawn up occasionally by a Community institution*, body or working party on the request of another institution.
Own-initiative report: report drawn up on the initiative of a Community institution* or body (SEE COURT OF AUDITORS, ECONOMIC AND SOCIAL COMMITTEE, EUROPEAN PARLIAMENT).
Study requested by one institution of another (eg: the Council* of the Commission*) or of a working party chaired by a prominent personality.
Publication of certain reports has contributed to the progress of Community* dossiers or to accelerating institutional procedures. Some important reports: *Albert-Ball* (1983): on the cost of 'Non Europe*'; *Bertrand* (1974-1975): on European Union*; *Bocklet* (1985): to the European Parliament* on the method for electing its members (supplemented the *Seitlinger* report); *Cecchini** (1988): on the cost of 'Non Europe*'; *Davignon** (1970): on 'achievable progress in the field of the political unification of Europe'; *Delors** (1989): on Economic and Monetary Union*; *Marjolin** (1975): on Economic and Monetary Union*; *Neumark* (1962): on VAT*; *Ortoli* (1975): on European Union*; *Spaak** (1956): on general economic union in the nuclear* field; *Seitlinger* (1982): to the European Parliament* on the introduction of a mixed system (proportional representation and representation by district) for electing its members; *Spinelli** (1984): on European Union*; *Spierenburg* (1974, 1979): on Economic and Monetary Union* and on the development of the institutions after expansion of the Community*; *Tindemans* (1975): on European Union*; *Vedel* (1972): on increased powers for the European Parliament*; *Werner** (1970): on Economic and Monetary Union*.
SEE EUROPEAN POLITICAL COOPERATION.

Research and Development Agreement Agreement whose

object is the research* and development of products or processes, and the exploitation of the results.
SEE COMPETITION, EXEMPTION.

Research and Technological Development Framework Programme (RTD Framework) Programme to set the main scientific objectives, the level of financing, and how this money is to be spent over the periods 1984-1987 and 1987-1990, of the various Community* actions in this field (health*, environment*, climatology*, major technological risks, preventive medicine*; information technology*, industrial technology; biological and marine resources; energy*; development, scientific and technical cooperation).
3rd framework programme: Budget: 5,700m Ecus* (1990-1994): information and communications* technology*; industrial technology and materials; human science and technology; environment*; energy*; human capital and mobility*. To be reviewed in 1992. OJ* L 117, 1990.
DG XII (Science, research* and development) and DG XIII (Telecommunications*, information industries and innovation) of the Commission*.
SEE COMMUNITY PROGRAMME, RESEARCH POLICY.

Research Policy One of the tasks assigned to the Community* by the ECSC* treaty* (art. 55) and the EURATOM* treaty* (art. 4) was to carry out research. The Single European Act* made this official (art. 130f to 130t of the EEC* treaty*), in particular by establishing a multiannual research framework programme and by promoting cooperation between businesses, research centres and universities, as well as with non-member countries* and international organizations, and distribution of the results of research and by promoting training* and mobility for researchers.
In agriculture* the Community* has centred its efforts around the conservation and use of natural resources (energy*, water), structural problems (regional, agri-foodstuffs), and improving animal and plant productivity (art. 41 of the EEC* treaty*). DG VI and DG XII of the Commission*.
SEE ACE, AERONAUTICS, AGREEMENTS BETWEEN UNDERTAKINGS, AGRICULTURAL AND AGRO-INDUSTRIAL RESEARCH, AGRICULTURAL RESEARCH, AGRICULTURE, AIM, AQUARIUS, BAP, BCR, BIOMEDICAL RESEARCH AND HEALTH, BIOTECHNOLOGY, BRAIN, BRIDGE, BRITE, CADDIA, CARMAT 2000, CERISE, CERN, COAL, COMETT, COMMUNITY PATENT, COMMUNITY PROGRAMME, COMPETITION, CONTROLLED THERMONUCLEAR FUSION, CORDIS, COSINE, COST, DELTA, DOSES, DRIVE, ECLAIR,

ECSC RESEARCH, EEIG, EFICS, EHLASS, ENVIRONMENT, ENVIREG, EPOCH, ERMES, ES2, ESPRIT, ETP, EURAM, EUREKA, EUROPEAN PATENT, EUROPEAN RESEARCH AND DEVELOPMENT COMMITTEE, EUROPEAN SPACE AGENCY, EUROTECNET, EUROTRA, FAMOS, FAST, FISHERIES, FLAIR, FORCE, GALILEO, HALIOS, HANDYNET, HERMES, IES-DCI-3, IMP, IMPACT, INFORMATION TECHNOLOGY, IRIS, ISIS, ITER, JESSI, JET, JOINT RESEARCH CENTRE, JOULE, LARGE-SCALE INSTALLATIONS, LEDA, MADRAS, MAST, MEASUREMENT AND TESTING, MEDSPA, MITHRA, MONITOR, NEPTUNE, NET, NON-NUCLEAR ENERGY, NORCAR-TRAMET, ODETTE, ORION, OXIDIPINE, PACA, PAIA, PATENT FOR INVENTION, PEDIP, PERCALE, PETRA, PINC, PROMETHEUS, RACE, RADIATION PROTECTION, RADIOACTIVE WASTE, RAW MATERIALS AND RECYCLING, RECHAR, RENAVAL, RESEARCH AND DEVELOPMENT AGREEMENT, RESIDER, REWARD, SAST, SAVE, SCIENCE, SCIENCE AND HUMAN TECHNOLOGY FOR LDC, SCIENCE AND MARINE TECHNOLOGY, SINGLE EUROPEAN ACT, SME, SPEAR, SPES, SPRINT, STAR, STD, STEP-EPOCH, STRIDE, STRUCTURAL FUNDS, TEDIS, TELEMAN, THERMIE, UPAC, VALOREN, VALUE, VAMAS.

RESIDER (REconversion de zones SIDÉRurgiques) *(Conversion of iron and steel producing areas):* Community programme* to give aid to the conversion of iron and steel producing areas. Budget: 300m Ecus* (1988-1992). Reg.* 88/328/EEC, OJ* L 33, 5/2/1988. DG III and XVI of the Commission*.
SEE EUROPEAN COAL AND STEEL COMMUNITY, IRON AND STEEL POLICY.

Resolution Act* of the European Parliament* sanctioning the result of a vote, following a committee report. Equivalent to an Opinion* or a Recommendation* addressed to the Council* or the Commission*.
Council* Decision* for policy application.

Restricted Procedure National procedure where only those suppliers invited to do so by the contracting authority* may submit a tender for a public contract*.

Restructuring Measures to encourage farmers to amalgamate their holdings.
SEE COMMON AGRICULTURAL POLICY, EAGGF, STRUCTURAL POLICY.

Returned Goods Goods which, having been exported temporarily or completely out of the customs territory* of the Community*, are reintroduced to be placed into free circulation* if, at the moment of export*, they fulfilled the conditions laid down in art. 9 and 10 of the EEC* treaty* or consisted of compensating products* resulting from an inward processing* operation (REG.* 754/76/EEC, 25/3/1976, OJ* L 89, 2/4/1976). Also used

to describe certain goods which have given rise to customs export formalities with a view to granting refunds* or other sums provided for by the Common Agricultural Policy* (REG.* 2945/76/EEC, 26/11/1976, OJ* L 335, 4/12/1976).
SEE CUSTOMS (ALL ENTRIES).

Revenue-Producing Monopoly
SEE PUBLIC UNDERTAKING.

Review
SEE APPEAL.

Review Committee Committee established within EFTA* to consider complaints relating to disputes arising between member states.

Revision of the Treaties Normal procedure provided for by the ECSC* treaty* (art. 96), the EEC* treaty* (art. 236) and the EURATOM* treaty* (art. 204). Member States* or the Commission* may submit proposals for amendments to the treaties* to the Council* at any time. The initiative may also come from another Community institution*.
SEE SINGLE EUROPEAN ACT.

REWARD (REcycling of WAste R and D) Community programme* on sampling, analysis and classification of waste*; recycling technology; fuel and energy* production from waste*. Cooperation between Member States*, for example with the EEIG*. 1990-1992. DG XII of the Commission*.
SEE ENERGY, ENVIRONMENT.

Right of Asylum
SEE FREEDOM OF MOVEMENT, SCHENGEN, VISAS.

Right of Establishment
SEE FREEDOM OF MOVEMENT, FREEDOM OF ESTABLISHMENT.

Right of Initiative Right of a Community institution* or body to deliver opinions on its own intiative.
SEE ECONOMIC AND SOCIAL COMMITTEE.

Right of Residence Nationals of one Member State* may take up residence in another Member State*.
28/6/1990: adoption of three Directives to be applied before

30/6/1992, covering: unemployed nationals of Member States* and their families who have health insurance (for the host Member State*) and sufficient resources; paid workers and retired workers with sufficient pension and health insurance; students, their spouses and children, with sufficient resources and health insurance and who are enrolled in an approved educational institution, for the period of their training*.
SEE FREEDOM OF MOVEMENT, SCHENGEN.

Risk Insurance Funds Financial aid to research* and development projects by newly-created specialist companies: operating advances or capital endowments.

Rolling Programme Working plan adopted by the Council* since 1985, in joint agreement between the current presidency and the two subsequent presidencies, to allow for more cohesive policy which is indispensable for realizing the single market*.
SEE TROIKA.

Rome Capital of the Republic of Italy. Headquarters of the Food and Agriculture Organization of the United Nations*.
25/3/1957: treaties* establishing the EEC* and EURATOM*, which came into effect on 1/1/1958; a convention establishes the European Parliamentary Assembly, the Court of Justice* of the European Communities* and the Economic and Social Committee*.
30/5/1967: Summit of the Six*.
1/12/1975: European Council* (confirms the election of the European Parliament* by universal suffrage).
13/12/1990: intergovernmental conference (Economic and Monetary Union*).
14/12/1990: intergovernmental conference (European Union*).
14-15/12/1990: European Council* (European Social Charter*; environment*; Mediterranean countries).

Round Table of European Industrialists Association of presidents of large European undertakings. 1983. 15, rue Guinard, 1040 Bruxelles, Belgium.

RTD Framework
SEE RESEARCH AND TECHNOLOGICAL DEVELOPMENT FRAMEWORK PROGRAMME.

Rules All the rules decreed by the Community* (Decisions*,

Recommendations*, Regulations*) in application of the treaties* or in order to establish the single market*.
SEE AGRICULTURAL REGULATIONS, COMMISSION, COMMUNITY LAW, COUNCIL, COURT OF JUSTICE, CUSTOMS REGULATIONS, SECONDARY COMMUNITY LAW.

Rules of Origin In free trade* agreements*: the conditions which goods must fulfil to benefit from exemption from duties when they are traded between the countries or areas concerned. The agreements between the Community* and EFTA* established joint committees which study the application of the rules of origin.
SEE ORIGIN.

RURAL-NET Community* data base* of rural development projects. Access via ECHO*.

SABINE (Système d'Accès à la Banque Informatique des Nomenclatures Européennes) *(Access system to the data bank of European nomenclatures)*: Nomenclature or classification scheme by country and by product (EUROSTAT* data base*).

SAD

SEE SINGLE ADMINISTRATIVE DOCUMENT.

Safeguard Clause Clause provided for in the treaties* or a measure allowing for exemptions to the principles in one of their articles. Eg: where there is disturbance in the *capital market* or balance of payments difficulties (PRINCIPLE OF FREEDOM OF MOVEMENT* OF CAPITAL, ART. 73, 108, 109 OF THE EEC* TREATY*; DIR.* OF 26/6/1988); *national safeguards* to prevent deflections of trade or economic difficulties (art. 115 of the EEC* treaty*) relating to the principle of free circulation* (art. 9.1 and 113: freedom of movement* of goods* and Common Commercial Policy*; Reg.* 288/82/EEC: imports* from non-member countries* which are harmful to Community* producers of similar products or competing products). The Commission* has the power to control safeguard clauses and assesses the expediency of safeguard measures in cases of serious injury or threat of serious injury.

Safety The measures taken by the Community* under art. 118a of the EEC* treaty* concern improving working conditions* for workers*: minimum requirements for work-places and for the use of equipment at work. Directives* on visual display units (VDUs*) (OJ* L 156, 1990), handling heavy loads, provision of signs, individual protection (FRAMEWORK DIRECTIVE* OF 1989, 30/11/1989, OJ* C 393, 1989), exposure to carcinogenic agents (OJ* L 196, 1990), etc. Draft Directive* on safety* for pregnant women.
There are other Regulations* to protect consumers* (monitoring of chemical products used in foods, of hazardous substances, of inflammable textiles, of toys* and of motor vehicles*). See also the Directive* on the manufacturer's liability for products (85/37444/EEC, OJ* L 210, 1985); the draft Directive* on the liability of the person providing services (protection of the person, the health and property of the consumer*).

SEE ATYPICAL WORK, CHEMISTRY, CONSUMPTION, EUROPEAN SOCIAL AREA, EUROPEAN SOCIAL CHARTER, GAS APPLIANCES, HEALTH, MACHINES, PRESSURIZED VESSELS, TOYS, VDU, WORKER PARTICIPATION, WORKING CONDITIONS.

Sales Monopoly A monopoly of sales of medicinal products* is justified on grounds of health* protection (art. 36 of the EEC* treaty*, decisions of the CJEC*).

Salt
SEE EUROPEAN COMMITTEE FOR THE STUDY OF SALT, ENVIRONMENT, FOODSTUFFS, STANDARDS, TECHNICAL REGULATION.

SAST (Strategic Analysis in Science and Technology) Subprogramme in the MONITOR* Community programme: analysis of research* and development policy (strategic impact analyses). DG XII of the Commission*.
SEE FAST, SPEAR.

SAVE (Special Action programme for Vigorous energy Efficiency) Community programme* to stimulate vigorous pursuit of a number of actions to increase energy* efficiency (not electricity*). Cf. art. 235 of the EEC* treaty* 1990-1994. DG XVII of the Commission*.

Savings
SEE CIUTS, EUROPEAN FINANCIAL AREA, TAXATION.

SCA
SEE SPECIAL COMMITTEE ON AGRICULTURE.

SCAD (Système Communitaire d'Accès à la Documentation or **Service Central Automatisé de Documentation)** *(Community system for accessing documentation* or *Computerized central documentation system)*: Community* data base*: documentation published by the EEC* (Community* acts*, official publications, positions, and opinions by the two sides of industry) and articles on the EEC*. 1983. Updated daily. DG IX/E/3-SCAD of the Commission*. JECL 1/107-200, rue de la Loi, 1049 Bruxelles, Belgium.

SCAR
SEE STANDING COMMITTEE ON AGRICULTURAL RESEARCH.

Schengen (Luxembourg) Accord originally between the Benelux* countries, France and Germany (14/6/1985 – Italy, Spain and Portugal joined in 1991. Ratified by France in June 1991; adopted 19/6/1990) on the progressive abolition of controls at common frontiers, to be applicable also at the external frontiers of these countries: preliminary harmonization* of legislative and regulatory provisions and additional measures to safeguard security (increased cooperation against drug trafficking, organized crime and the illegal immigration of nationals of non-member countries* of the EC*, with the right of prosecution, and exchanges of information – SIS*). List of and harmonization of the conditions for issuing visas*. Right of asylum*. Liability of carriers. Exchanges of computer data.
SEE FREEDOM OF MOVEMENT, NON-MEMBER COUNTRIES, TREVI.

Schengen Accord
SEE SCHENGEN

Schuman (Robert) French statesman (1886-1963). Creative force behind (declaration of 9/5/1950) and signatory of the treaty* of Paris* establishing the European Coal and Steel Community*.

SCIENCE (Stimulation des Coopérations Internationales et des Échanges Nécessaires aux Chercheurs en Europe) *(Stimulation of international cooperation and exchanges necessary for researchers in Europe)*: Community programmes* to stimulate scientific, economic and social cooperation, to promote training*, via research, and the mobility of researchers in Europe. Research* allowances. Linking-up of research* projects. Scientific networks. Contracts (100%). Budget: 167m Ecus* (1988-1992). Decision* 419/88/EEC, 29/6/1988 (OJ* L 206, 30/7/1988). DG XII of the Commission*.
SEE CODEST, COMETT, DELTA, ERASMUS, RESEARCH AND TECHNOLOGY DEVELOPMENT FRAMEWORK PROGRAMME.

Scientific and Technical Committee (of EURATOM*) 33 member advisory committee established by the EURATOM* treaty* (art. 134), to be consulted compulsorily in certain cases. Members nominated for 5 years by the Council*.

Scientific and Technical Information and Documentation Tool used in a Community* three-year plan.

Scientific and Technical Research Committee (CREST) Committee answerable to both Council* and Commission* (set up 14/1/1974). Coordinates national and Community* policy. Community* actions. Senior national officials.

Sea
SEE DOCK DUES, EROS, FISHERIES POLICY, INTERNATIONAL MARITIME ORGANIZATION, NEPTUNE, POSEIDOM, SHIPOWNERS.

SEA
SEE SINGLE EUROPEAN ACT

Secondary Community Law Part of Community law* based on acts passed to ensure the application of the treaties* establishing the Communities*. The Council* has given the Commission* extended powers to ensure the application of Secondary Community Law: to draw up texts for the application of acts adopted by the Council*, in particular for the implementation of common policy (art. 43 and 75 of the EEC* treaty*) and for the harmonization* of national legislation. See art. 100, 100(a) (Single European Act*), 145, 235 of the EEC* treaty*.
SEE COMITOLOGY, COURT OF JUSTICE, DECISION, DELEGATION, DIRECTIVE, EURATOM, EUROPEAN COAL AND STEEL COMMUNITY, OPINION, RECOMMENDATION, REGULATION, SINGLE EUROPEAN ACT.

Secondary Compensating Product Compensating product* other than that for which the procedure was authorized and which of necessity results in an outward processing* operation.

SEDOC European System for the International Clearing of Vacancies and Applications for Employment.

Seed Capital Financial assistance given by the Community* to young graduates who wish to set up a business.
SEE EUROPEAN INVESTMENT BANK.

Self-Drive Vehicle Hire Directive* of 24/7/1990 (OJ* L 202, 1990) on the use of self-drive hired vehicles (under 6 tonnes) to transport goods by road.

Service Any service provided in a professional capacity or any independent public service: may be for payment, not being solely and directly for the manufacture of movable property, or

for the transfer of right in rem or intellectual right (proposal for a Directive* on the liability of the person providing the services, art. 2, par. 1).
SEE EUROPEAN FINANCIAL AREA, FREEDOM TO PROVIDE SERVICES, INVESTMENT SERVICES.

SESAME Data base* of EEC* projects in the fields of technology* and energy*. Access via ECHO*. DG XVII of the Commission*.

Session Period during which the European Parliament* holds its sittings. One session per year. Plenary sittings are fixed by the enlarged Bureau* (one week per month, in principle) and take place in Strasbourg. The Parliament meets automatically on the first Tuesday following a period of one month after the fixed period for elections to the Parliament.
Extraordinary sessions are convened on request by a majority of the members, by the Council* or the Commission* or by the President following a request by a third of the members. The agenda is drawn up by the enlarged Bureau* and put to a vote in the Parliament. The President proposes how the speaking time is to be divided up and establishes the quorum*.

Set Aside Optional measure decided upon at the European Council* of Fontainebleau whereby producers are ensured a minimum revenue per hectare of land which they consent not to cultivate for a certain period of time while continuing to maintain it. The reformed Common Agricultural Policy* intends to set aside a million hectares of arable land in 5 years.
SEE EAGGF.

Setting up a Business
SEE EUROCREATION, RISK INSURANCE FUNDS, SEED CAPITAL.

SIGLE (System for Information on Grey Literature in Europe) Community data bank*: Access via INKA, BLAISE.

Single Administrative Document (SAD) Customs document which replaced (1/1/1988) previous administrative forms in internal and external trade by the Twelve* and the EFTA* countries. (OJ* 1985 L 79).

Single Council, Single Commission On the 1/7/1967 the High Authority* of the ECSC* and the Commissions* of the EEC*

and EURATOM* were replaced by a single Commission* and the three Councils by a single Council*; they continued to act in accordance with the rules of each of the Communities* (SEE TREATIES).
This was the result of the treaty of 8/4/1965, signed by the Six*, which made the existence of the Committee of Permanent Representatives* official; the merger was intended as the first stage towards setting up a European Community* ruled by a single treaty. The process is still continuing.
SEE SINGLE EUROPEAN ACT.

Single Currency
SEE MONETARY UNION.

Single European Act (SEA) A document amending and supplementing the EEC* treaty (and, with regard to the Court of Justice*, the ECSC* and EURATOM* treaties), drawn up by an intergovernmental conference (European Council* of Milan*), adopted by the European Council* of Luxembourg* on 2/12/1985, signed by the governments of the Member States* of the Community* on 17/2/1986; came into force on 1/7/1987 after being ratified by the Twelve* Member States* of the EC*.
Objectives to supply the institutions* of the Community* with a legal instrument with which to implement the Commission's* White Paper* on establishing the internal market*; to extend the Community's* sphere of competence; to strengthen the institutions* of the Community*.
Contents: four titles: II amends both the ECSC* and the EURATOM* treaties and IV the EEC* treaty (general and final provisions):
the objectives of an *area without frontiers* and 'European Union'* to be official on 31/12/1992; extension of *qualified majority* voting in the Council* (art. 100A) to achieve this objective (except with regard to freedom of movement* of persons, taxation* and the rights and interests of workers*), with the possibility of national exemptions*; to strengthen the institutions*; *cooperation procedure** between the Commission*, the Council* and the European Parliament*; extension of the powers of implementation of the Commission* (SEE COMITOLOGY, SECONDARY COMMUNITY LAW); existence of the European Council* and the name of the European Parliament* made official; powers of opinion for the Council* corresponding to those of the European Parliament* for treaties of accession, and association* and cooperation* agreements; extension and/or

updating of *Community policy** in research* and development, the environment*, the social* field and monetary cooperation;

coordination of *Community funds** (ESF*, EAGGF*, ERDF*) and other financial instruments (EIB*);

introduction of the EMS in the treaty* and the objective of economic and monetary union*; establishment of a *court of the first instance* beside the Court of Justice* of the EC* (common provision for the ECSC* and EURATOM*);

legal status accorded to European political cooperation* (permanent secretariat, in association with the Commission*). Article 100B states that the Council* will decide in 1992 on the implementation of the principle of mutual recognition* for everything which will not have been harmonized by that time.

2/1987: proposals by the Commission* to 'make a success of the Single Act' (SEE BUDGET, COMMON AGRICULTURAL POLICY, COMMUNITY FUNDS, EUROPEAN MONETARY SYSTEM, QUALIFIED MAJORITY), adopted 2/1988 at the European Council* of Brussels*.

31/12/1988, 13/6/1989, 31/12/1990: progress reports by the Commission* to the Council* on the establishment of the internal market*.

SEE COMMISSION, COUNCIL, COURT OF AUDITORS, OBJECTIVE 92, WHITE PAPER.

Single Licence Licence granted by the Member State* of origin to a service undertaking (for example, a bank*, a credit institution* or an insurance* company) to carry out its business freely throughout the whole Community*, by way of establishment or freedom to provide services*, being under the jurisdiction only of the authorities of the country of origin. Mutual recognition* of licences and safeguard checking systems for banks* (single banking licence). This applies to EEC* undertakings and to those of non-member countries*, so long as they are subsidiaries* (DIR.* 89/646/EEC, OJ* L 386, 30/12/1989).

SEE EUROPEAN FINANCIAL AREA, HARMONIZATION, RECIPROCITY, RIGHT OF ESTABLISHMENT.

Single Market Term used to describe the establishment of an 'area without internal frontiers, in which the free movement of goods, persons, services and capital is ensured', as the Single European Act* and the Commission* White Paper* describe it.

SEE FRONTIER CONTROL.

Single-Member Company Public limited liability company which may be set up by one natural or legal person (under special national provisions in the case of a single shareholder of several companies). Protection of the business-person's private assets (liability for limited debts covered by the capital he/she has underwritten) and guarantees for third parties (12th Directive* on Company Law* of 21-22/12/1989).

SIS (Système d'Information Schengen) *(Schengen Information System)*: Computerized data exchange system on persons covered by the Schengen* Accord. Data protection is ensured by independent bodies appointed by each state.
SEE FREEDOM OF MOVEMENT, VISAS.

SITC
SEE STANDARD INTERNATIONAL TRADE CLASSIFICATION.

Sitting Meeting of the members of the European Parliament*. Plenary sittings in Strasbourg during the session*. Formal sittings (speeches by heads of government).

Six The six states which signed the treaty* of Paris* in 1951 (ECSC*), and the treaties* of Rome* in 1957 (EEC*, EURATOM*): Benelux* countries, France, Germany, Italy. 'The Europe of Six': the European Community* from 1952 to 1972.
SEE NINE, TEN, TWELVE.

Small and Medium-Sized Enterprises
SEE SME.

SME (Small and Medium-Sized Enterprises) Enterprises with less than 500 employees, whose capital is less than 75m ECU* and of which less than a third may belong to a larger company. An SME Task Force was set up in June 1986 within DG III of the Commission* (now DG XXIII). Council* Recommendation* of 28/5/1990 on simplifying administration.
SEE BCNET, BUSINESS INNOVATION CENTRES, COMMITTEE OF SMALL AND MEDIUM-SIZED COMMERCIAL ENTERPRISES OF THE EEC COUNTRIES, DRIVE, EURO INFO CENTRES, EUROPARTENARIAT, EUROPEAN INVESTMENT BANK, IMPACT REPORT, SEED CAPITAL.

SNA (System Network Architecture) Network (computerized architecture) belonging to IBM.
SEE OSI.

Social Charter
SEE EUROPEAN SOCIAL CHARTER.

Social Policy
SEE EUROPEAN SOCIAL AREA.

Social Rights
SEE EUROPEAN SOCIAL CHARTER, SOCIAL SECURITY BENEFITS.

Social Security Benefits The principle of equality of treatment* applies to migrant workers* within the Community* (REG.* 1612/68). See Regulations* 1408/71/EEC and 574/72/EEC (amended 30/10/1989) on the application of social security schemes to paid and unpaid workers* and to members of their families resident inside or outside the Community*.
SEE EUROPEAN SOCIAL AREA, FREEDOM OF MOVEMENT.

SOEC
SEE STATISTICAL OFFICE OF THE EUROPEAN COMMUNITIES.

Software Directive* 91/250 of 14/15/1991 on software copyright* protection, based on authorship, for 50 years. (OJ* L 122, 17/5/1991 AND BERNE CONVENTION ON COPYRIGHT PROTECTION FOR ARTISTIC AND LITERARY WORKS). 'Decompilation' authorized in certain cases for interoperability. A contracting authority* may use the negotiated procedure* to grant, without previous competitive tendering, public contracts* for software destined to be used solely for research*, experimentation, study or development (without any intention to be cost-effective or to be able to recover costs) or, under certain conditions, for supplementary deliveries by the initial supplier.
SEE INFORMATICS.

Sole Distribution Agreement* whereby a supplier commits to supply a sole distributor in a fixed area, for which the sole distributor may accept certain restrictions, ie that he/she will not act as distributor for the supplier's competitors.
SEE COMPETITION, EXEMPTION.

Solvency Ratio Ratio which expresses the ability of a bank* to cover risks, in particular losses on credits which could cause its customers to default. Directive* of 18/12/1989.
SEE CREDIT INSTITUTION, EQUITY CAPITAL.

Spaak (Paul-Henri) Belgian statesman. Creative force behind the EEC* and EURATOM* treaties* (Messina conference).
SEE REPORT.

Space
SEE AERONAUTICS, EUROPEAN SPACE AGENCY.

SPAG (Standards Promotion and Application Group)
SEE STANDARDIZATION.

SPEAR (Support Programme for a European Assessment of Research): Sub-programme in the MONITOR* Community programme*. DG XII of the Commission*.
SEE FAST, SAST.

Special Committee on Agriculture (SCA) Committee of representatives of the Member States* of the Community*, responsible for preparing the work of the Council* on agriculture* and for carrying out the tasks which are assigned to it by the Council*.
SEE COREPER.

Special Drawing Rights (SDR) The central bank of a state which is a member of the International Monetary Fund* has the right to buy a quantity of currencies given to another member state of the IMF under the SDR system with no obligation to sell them back within a fixed period of time. As a unit of account, the value of an SDR is determined against a 'basket of currencies'.

Specialization Agreement Agreement whereby undertakings agree not to manufacture a series of products in order to concentrate on one each, or to only manufacture certain products jointly in order to make more rational use of their capacity and to increase their productivity.
SEE COMPETITION, EXEMPTION.

Special National Condition A national characteristic or practice which may not be amended, even in the long term.
SEE BARRIERS, EUROPEAN STANDARD, HARMONIZATION DOCUMENT.

Specific Measures of Commercial Policy Non-tariff measures laid down within the Common Commercial Policy* by Community* provisions relating to customs procedures applicable on imports* and exports* of goods, such as protective and

supervisory measures, quantitative restrictions* or limits, and import* and export* prohibitions. Eg Reg.* 2473/86/EEC on outward processing* and the standard exchange* system.
SEE CUSTOMS (ALL ENTRIES).

SPES (Stimulation Programme for Economic Sciences) Community programme* of cooperation and exchanges between top level economists: internal market*, the economy of European integration, growth factors in western Europe, monetary policies, commercial policy, employment, health*, social policy, methodology, etc. Budget: 6m Ecus* (1989-1992). Decision* 88/118/EEC, 13/2/1989 (OJ*; L 44, 16/2/1989).

Spinelli Italian member of the European Parliament*, author of a project for European Union*.
SEE REPORT.

SPRINT (Strategic PRogramme for INnovation and Technology transfer) Community programme* to promote new technology and innovation by setting up national innovation networks, promoting specific projects of high demonstrative value, cooperating national policy for promoting innovation (invention, financing, marketing of new products and services; information exchange via the TII* network; cooperation by sector). Budget: 90m Ecus* (1989-1993). Decision* 89/285/EEC, 17/4/1989 (OJ* L 112, 25/4/1989). ICONE* data base*, EURO TECH ALERT*, SPRINT network (250 development agencies, chambers of commerce, private advisers). DG XIII/C of the Commission*.

SQUALPI (Service de la QUALité des Produits Industriels et de la normalisation) (*Quality of industrial products and standardization service*): Part of the French Ministry of Industry.
SEE CERTIFICATION, STANDARDS, TECHNICAL SPECIFICATIONS.

SSII (Sociétés de Service et d'Ingénierie Informatique) *(Computer services companies)*: Industrial companies specializing in software* and computer services.

STABEX (STABilization of EXport earnings of agricultural products under the Lomé Convention) System set up by the Lomé* Conventions* to guarantee the ACP* states over a number of years against a reduction in export* earnings

caused by fluctuations in the price of certain basic products or by a reduction in exports*.
SEE COMMON AGRICULTURAL POLICY, LDCs.

Stabilization
SEE MECHANISMS FOR STABILIZING BUDGETARY EXPENDITURE.

Standard Exchange System whereby a compensating product* can be replaced by an imported product ('replacement product'). This is allowed by the customs authority* where the processing* operation involves repairs to Community goods* other than those subject to the CAP* or specific procedures applicable to certain goods produced by processing agricultural products. Replacement products must come under the same CN* sub-heading, be of the same commercial quality and possess the same technical features as the Community* goods would have if they had undergone the processing operation. Reg.* 2473/86/EEC, 31/121/1986.
SEE OUTWARD PROCESSING.

Standard International Trade Classification (SITC) Nomenclature administered by the United Nations* and used in international trade. It inspired the Harmonized* Commodity Description and Coding System worked out by the Customs Cooperation Council*.

Standardization Elaboration of national, European or international standards*. A memorandum* from the Commission* (COM (89) 209, 15/6/1989, OJ* C 267, 19/10/1989) encourages states to promote the use of European standards* and to only accredit bodies and laboratories which use them. Proposal for a single Community trade mark*. Draft Green Paper* on European standardization policy OJ* C 20 28/1/1991).
SEE BARRIERS, MEASUREMENT AND TESTING, MUTUAL RECOGNITION, NEW APPROACH, STANDARDS.

Standardization Authorization Authorization granted by the Commission* at the start of work on a Directive* in order to accelerate the process of European standardization*. It includes financial support from the Community*.
SEE STANDARDS.

Standardization Programme Document listing the objects for which it is intended to elaborate a standard* or to modify one.
SEE BARRIERS, NEW APPROACH.

Standards Technical specifications* approved by a recognized standards body for repeated and continued use, whose use is however not compulsory unless the state decides otherwise. Since Directive* 83/189 came into effect national standards bodies must notify the Commission* of their programmes and their counterparts in other Member States* via the central secretariat of CEN*/CENELEC*. An institute may make comments, request that it take part in the work of another or request the elaboration of a European standard*.
SEE BARRIERS, BROADCASTING, CEN, CENELEC, CERTIFICATE OF CONFORMITY, CERTIFICATION OF CONFORMITY, CONSUMPTION, DRAFT EUROPEAN STANDARD, ETSI, EUROPEAN STANDARD, ISO/IEC STANDARD, ITSTC, MAC, MEASUREMENT AND TESTING, MUTUAL RECOGNITION, NEW APPROACH, OVERALL APPROACH, PUBLIC CONTRACT, STANDARDIZATION, TECHNICAL REGULATION, TECHNICAL SPECIFICATIONS.

Standing Committee on Agricultural Research (SCAR) Advisory committee (set up 27/6/1974): coordinates and promotes agricultural research*.
SEE CAP.

Standing Committee on Employment (SCE) Provides information and facilitates co-ordination of the labour market policies of Member States; also, a forum for representatives of workers, employers and of the Commission and Council to express views on employment issues and advise EC institutions.

STAR (Special Telecommunications Action for Regional development) Community programme* to give aid to the development of certain less-favoured regions of the Community* via better access for SME* to advanced telecommunications* services. Budget: 1500m Ecus*, of which 780m from the European Regional Development Fund* (1986-1991). Reg.* 86/3300/EEC, 1986 (OJ* L 305, 31/10/1986). DG XIII and DG XVI of the Commission*.

State Monopoly of a Commercial Character By which a Member State* controls, directs or significantly influences, de jure or de facto, directly or indirectly, imports*; or exports* between Member States*. Art. 35 of the EEC* treaty* lays down progressive abolition of all monopolies of this kind, including a monopoly delegated by the state to others (public institution, nationalized company, person in private law to whom the state has conferred the power to exercise certain exclusive rights) in Member States*. To be distinguished from a dominant position*.

Statistical Office of the European Communities (SOEC or EUROSTAT) Community* office which publishes series of statistics on European countries and a monthly review, 'Eurostatistics' (OOPEC*). Bâtiment Jean Monnet, Centre Européen, rue Alcide de Gasperi, 2920 Luxembourg.

Statistics Proposed regulations on trade statistics (COM (88) 810, OJ* C 84, 1989). Regulation* of 11/6/1990 on the transfer of secret information to the SOEC*.
SEE COMBINED TARIFF AND STATISTICAL NOMENCLATURE, DOSES, ECU, EUROSTAT, FRONTIER CONTROL, NACE, NIMEXE, OOPEC, STATISTICAL OFFICE OF THE EUROPEAN COMMUNITIES, TES.

STD (Science and Technology for Development) Community programme* to aid LDCs* (tropical and subtropical agriculture, medicine, health* and nutrition in subtropical areas). Budget: 80m Ecus* (1987-1991). Reg.* 3300/86/EEC, 27/10/1986 (OJ* L 305, 31/10/1986). See also OJ* L 355, 17/12/1987. DG XII of the Commission*.

Steel Aims for 1995: return to competition*, fight pollution, broaden the ECSC's* working methods in the fields of training and professional qualification; seek a multilateral agreement within the framework of GATT*.
SEE ENVIRONMENT.

Steel Research
SEE ECSC RESEARCH, STEEL TECHNOLOGY RESEARCH.

Steel Technology Research Community programme* on technological research* (separate from RTD Framework*): increased competitiveness of production costs and steel processing; promotion of consumption*. 1990-1995. OJ* L 359, 8/12/1989.
SEE REWARD.

STEP (Science and Technology for Environmental Protection) Community research* programme* on environmental protection. Budget: 75m Ecus* (1989-1992). COM (88) 632 F-SYN 168 (OJ* C 327, 20/12/1988). DG XII of the Commission*.
SEE STEP-EPOCH.

STEP-EPOCH Double Community programme*. Scientific and technical support for Community* environment* policy; improvement of the productivity of and the scientific and technical quality of environmental research*. Budget: 115m Ecus* (1989-1992). See also OJ* C 359, 8/12/1989.

STOA (Scientific and Technological Options Assessment) European Parliament* project.

Stockholm Capital of Sweden.
SEE EUREKA, EUROPEAN ECONOMIC AREA, FISHERIES POLICY.

Stock Exchanges Project for interconnecting stock exchange computers (IDIS*) to facilitate international transactions and to harmonize* national clearing systems.
SEE EUROPEAN FINANCIAL AREA.

STRIDE (Science and Technology for Regional Innovation and Development in Europe) European Regional Development Fund* Community programme*: to increase regional research* and technological development capacity by technological transfer to aid regional development and to promote business innovation: framework programmes in certain less-favoured regions (support infrastructures, investments in businesses linked to research* and development; common research* services between businesses; encouragement for research* and development). Programmes are implemented by the regional or national authorities concerned. Budget: 400m Ecus* (1990-1993). DG XVI of the Commission*.
SEE REGIONAL POLICY.

Structural Funds Community funds* (ERDF*, EAGGF*-guidance, ESF*) to enable Community* interventions (subsidies and loans) in matters relating to social, regional*, research* and development, energy* and environment* policy. They are different from guarantee funds (SEE EAGGF-guarantee).
SEE COMMUNITY PROGRAMME, COMMUNITY SUPPORT FRAMEWORK, ECSC FUNDS, EUROPEAN INVESTMENT BANK, INTEGRATED MEDITERRANEAN PROGRAMMES, NEW COMMUNITY INSTRUMENT.

Structural Policy *Agriculture**.
1962: coordination of national structural policies (Standing Committee on Agricultural Structures); SEE EAGGF.
1964: financing of individual projects and of certain specific measures.
1968: the Mansholt plan presents proposals for the modern-

ization of farms with concomitant social measures; applied from 1972 (DIR.* 72/159/EEC, 72/160/EEC, 72/161/EEC).
1975: this policy is supplemented by actions centred on specific problems: mountainous agricultural regions and less favoured agricultural regions (DIR.* 75/268/EEC), Mediterranean countries, Ireland.
1977: Community* financing of investments in the modernization and extension of marketing and processing facilities.
1979: 'integrated' operations, concentrating all available resources on sectors whose expansion might have a 'lever effect' on regional development.
1985: development plans replaced by plans to improve farms, revision of investment aid (structurally surplus production), equipment installation aid, services for farmers, increased and adjusted aid for vocational training, increased support for agriculture in less-favoured regions, reforestation (REG.* 797/85/EEC), large-scale integrated development programmes (IMP*), extensification, set aside* of land, temporary income aid.
SEE COMMON AGRICULTURAL POLICY, EAGGF, FORESTRY POLICY, REGIONAL POLICY, STRUCTURAL FUNDS.

Stuttgart (Germany) *19/6/1983*: European Council* (formal declaration on European Union*, role of the European Council*, role of the European Parliament*).
SEE EUROPEAN POLITICAL COOPERATION.

Subcontract Whereby an undertaking, the 'subcontractor', supplies goods, works or services to another undertaking, the 'contractor', to the requirements of the latter.
SEE COMPETITION, PUBLIC CONTRACT.

Subsidiarity Principle of appropriate responsibility at appropriate levels. This states that anything which can be done by those at lower levels of responsibility must not be done by those at higher levels. This principle is often used in relation to establishing the single market*, ie businesses, local authorities, national states do whatever can be done at their respective levels before referring the matter to a higher level and, in the last resort, to Community* level.

Subsidiary In Community law*: company set up by another company in another Member State* in conformity with the legislation of that State. A parent company must be already

established in the Community* to be able to do business in another Member State* by means of a subsidiary or branch*. Agreements between a parent company and its subsidiaries, or between subsidiaries, are not prohibited if the subsidiary is not free to determine its own behaviour on the market (Judgement* of 12/7/1984, 170/83).
SEE COMPANY LAW, FREEDOM OF ESTABLISHMENT, GROUP TAXATION.

Subsidi ed Imports Practice prohibited by art. VI of the GATT*, art. 17 of the EFTA* convention and art. 92-94 of the EEC* treaty*.

Suitable Community Patrimony
SEE EUROPEAN ECONOMIC AREA, RELEVANT COMMUNITY PATRIMONY.

Surplus If a structural agricultural surplus is produced in an important sector, the Community* may restrict the production guarantee granted to producers.
SEE AGRICULTURAL PRICES, COMMON AGRICULTURAL POLICY, CORESPONSIBILITY.

Suspension of Application Protective measure whereby the application of a Community* or national measure is partially or temporarily suspended to prevent serious problems of application.
SEE APPEAL, COMMISSION, COMMUNITY LAW, COURT OF JUSTICE.

Suspension System Inward processing* system for non-Community goods* which are to be reexported out of the customs territory* of the Community* as compensating products*. See also Reg.* 1999/85/EEC, art. 2/A.
SEE CUSTOMS (ALL ENTRIES).

SWIFT Computerized information transfer system linking 2000 banks* in 56 countries.

Switchover Method of calculating MCA*, adopted in April 1984, whereby the central rate* of each state in the EMS* exchange rate mechanism is multiplied by a corrective factor. The objective is to dismantle existing positive MCA* while preventing new positive MCA* by permanently aligning the agricultural conversion rates (green exchange rates*) with the actual currency exchange rates.
The real monetary gap* between the green exchange rate*

and green central rate* is reduced for countries with strong currencies (with a corresponding reduction in positive MCA*) and increased for countries with weak currencies (with a corresponding increase in negative MCA*).
SEE COMMON AGRICULTURAL POLICY.

SYSMIN (SYStem of aid for MINeral products) System set up by the second Lomé* Convention* to guarantee over a number of years the production capacity of certain ACP* countries of mineral products which are exported to the EEC* – by compensating reductions in earnings – and to guarantee the EEC* a supply of strategic products. Equivalent to STABEX* for other basic products but without guaranteed earnings: special loans for the exploitation of deposits and the export of minerals.
SEE LDCs.

SYSTRAN Community* automated translation system invented in the USA and adopted by the Commission* for use in its departments. 13 pairings of European languages: 7 from English, 4 French, 2 from German. Patent* translation project.
SEE EUROTRA.

TARIC (Tarif integré des Communautés Européennes *(Integrated customs tariff of the European Communities)*: *Customs*: tariff including the Community* subdivisions (TARIC 'subheadings') needed to describe goods which are subject to specific Community* measures, rates of customs duty* and other applicable taxes, code numbers and anything else required to implement or manage Community* measures in this field. See also Reg.* 2658/87/EEC, 23/7/1987 (OJ* L 256, 7/9/1987).

Tariff Nomenclature Nomenclature established according to the legislation of the Contracting Party for the collection of import duties*. Council* Decision* 87/369/EEC.

Tariff Quota Import* quota* for goods from non-member countries* admitted to the territory of a Member State* exempt of or suspended from duties under the common customs tariff*. *Transport*: authorization for international transport. The authorization is of a bilateral or Community* nature depending on whether it is issued under the quotas* fixed by bilateral agreements or as a result of Regulation* 76/3164/EEC of 16/12/1976.
Common policy provides for the reduction of bilateral quotas* at the same time as Community* quotas* become more widespread until trade is completely liberalized from 1/1/1993.

Tariff Union

SEE FREE-TRADE AREA.

Taxation

SEE COMPANY LAW, EXCISE, FISCAL BARRIERS, GROUP TAXATION, HARMONIZATION, SINGLE EUROPEAN ACT, SINGLE MARKET, VAT, WHITE PAPER.

Tax-Free Shop Practice where businesses sell via the intermediary of a common body. An agreement of this type, which prevents individual businesses from setting their own prices and from selling as they wish, is illegal in Community* competition* law* if the businesses are competitors.

Technical Barriers
SEE BARRIERS, STANDARDS, TECHNICAL REGULATION.

Technical Barriers to Trade Barriers to trade caused by varying national technical specifications* for a product: technical features, testing, control and certification* methods (certifying the safety* of products). May be considered to be measures having equivalent effect*, in contravention of art. 30 of the EEC* treaty* and of EFTA* and GATT* rules.
SEE BARRIERS.

Technical Committee (TC) Committee established by the technical bureau of CEN*/CENELEC* to prepare standards*.

Technical Regulation Compulsory technical specification* laid down by an official authority. A Member State* may only adopt a new technical regulation three months after having notified the Commission* about it (DIR.* 83/189). The Council* adopts European technical regulations by a qualified majority* (art. 100a of the EEC* treaty*).

Technical Rules All technical specifications*, including the relevant applicable administrative provisions, which are compulsory, de jure or de facto, for the marketing or use of a product* in a Member State* or in a significant part of this State.
SEE BARRIERS, NEW APPROACH, STANDARDIZATION, STANDARDS.

Technical Specifications Compulsory specifications for a given product.
SEE CERTIFICATION, STANDARDIZATION, STANDARDS, TECHNICAL REGULATION.

Technology
SEE AERONAUTICS, BRITE, COMETT, DELTA, DISSEMINATION AND USE, ESPRIT, IES-DC1, MAST, MONITOR, RACE, RESEARCH AND TECHNOLOGICAL DEVELOPMENT FRAMEWORK PROGRAMME, SESAME, SPRINT, STOA, THERMIE.

TED (Tenders Electronic Daily) Community* data base*: invitations to tender for public works* and public supply contracts* in Member States* (over the minimum thresholds) or connected to the EC* (services contracts, or contracts financed under the Lomé convention* (ACP*) in LDCs*) published in the OJ* Supplement. Access via ECHO*; terminals in Euro Info Centres*.

TEDIS (Trade Electronic Data Interchange System) Community programme* to coordinate the development of electronic data transfer systems (EDI) for trade*, industry and administration, with the emphasis on SME*. Coordination with the CADDIA* system. Budget: 31.5m Ecus* (1991–1994. Decisions* 87/499/EEC (OJ* L 285, 8/10/1987); 89/241/EEC (OJ* L 97, 11/4/1989). DG I and XIII/C of the Commission*.
SEE TELECOMMUNICATIONS POLICY.

Telecommunications Policy European harmonization* in this field operates on the following levels:
1) by passing responsibility for operation and regulation to the Member States* (proposals in the Green Paper* on telecommunications);
2) by liberalization (May 1988 Directive* on Member States'* freedom to import*, market and install telecommunications equipment; Commission* Directive* of 17/7/1990 on the liberalization of telecommunications services, with the exception of vocal telephone communications, to come into effect on 1/1/1993, with the exception of some countries);
3) by technical harmonization* (framework Directive* from the Commission* (28/6/1990) on Open Network Provisions*; Directive* of 29/4/1991 on mutual recognition* of approval for telecommunications equipment: *EC Label**).
6/9/1991: Communication* from the Commission* (OJ* C 233) on guidelines concerning the application of competition* rules in the telecommunications sector.
Telecommunications is provisionally an excluded sector* from the opening up of public contracts*. See also COM (89) 671. DG XIII of the Commission*.
SEE EUREKA, DECT, ERMES, EUROPEAN INVESTMENT BANK, EUROPEAN REGIONAL DEVELOPMENT FUND, EUROPEAN TELECOMMUNICATIONS STANDARDS INSTITUTE, FREEDOM TO PROVIDE SERVICES, HDTV, IES-DC1, INTEGRATED MEDITERRANEAN PROGRAMMES, ISDN, JOINT RESEARCH CENTRE, NEW COMMUNITY INSTRUMENT, OPEN NETWORK PROVISION, PIIC, RACE, RESEARCH AND TECHNOLOGICAL DEVELOPMENT FRAMEWORK PROGRAMME, STAR, TELECOMMUNICATIONS TERMINALS.

Telecommunications Terminals Proposed regulations on opening them up to competition*. (COM (88) 301, OJ* L 131, 1988).

TELEMAN (TÉLÉ-MANipulation dans les environnements nucléaires dangereux et perturbés) *(Remote-controlled handling in nuclear hazardous and disordered environments)*: Community research* and training* programme* in all sectors of nuclear energy*. Improvement of the safety* of persons and installations. Accident management. Decision* 89/464/ EURATOM (OJ* L 226, 3/8/1989). Budget: 19m Ecus* (1989-1993). DG XII of the Commission*.

Telematics Community programme*: the use of advanced telecommunications services in less-developed regions.

Television without Frontiers A Directive* (3/10/1989) fixed the rules for the free provision of television services. December 1989: Council* Decision* (OJ* L 363, 13/12/1989): commitment to common action within the International Radio Consultative Committee* to get the European standard* accepted HD–MAC*, via the intermediary D2–MAC (EUREKA* project 95).
SEE BROADCASTING, HDTV.

Temporary Admission Customs procedure which allows certain goods which have been imported to a specific end and which are intended for reexport to be received in a customs territory* under suspension (total or partial) of import duties* and taxes for a fixed period of time, during which they are not modified in any way except for normal depreciation of the goods caused by the use which is made of them. This does not cover the means of transportation. Total exemption is made for professional equipment, that which is intended for use at fairs*, exhibitions and congresses, for educational, scientific, medical/surgical and laboratory equipment or equipment to be used to counter the effects of catastrophes, packaging etc. Partial exemption is made for other items or for those which do not completely fulfil the conditions for total exemption. See Reg.* 3599/82/EEC, 21/12/1982 (OJ* L 376, 31/12/1982); Reg.* 1751/84/EEC, 13/6/1984 (OJ* L 171, 29/6/1984); Reg.* 2096/87, 13/7/1987 (OJ* L 196, 17/7/1987); Reg.* 4027/88, 21/12/1988 (OJ* L 3555, 23/12/1988); Council* Decision* 87/593/EEC, etc.

Temporary Export Administrative procedure whereby goods are reimported duty-free* and without import licence* for temporary use (repairs or working, exhibition, etc.).
27/2/1989: amendment to the Regulation* on the intra-community movement of goods, allowing simplified customs procedures to apply to virtually all goods.

Temporary Storage Status of goods submitted to customs and awaiting customs destination (release for free circulation*, free zone, destruction, abandonment to the public revenue department).
SEE INTERIM STORAGE.

Temporary Use *Customs*: system applying to certain goods which are sent or transported from one Member State* to one or more other Member States* for temporary use there and which are not subject to any prohibitions or restrictions on the territory of the Member State* of departure. The system operates under the conditions laid down in art. 9 and 10 of the EEC* treaty*, unless the goods are in free circulation* (ECSC* products). They must have fulfilled the fiscal provisions of the Member States* concerned. Reg.* 3/84/EEC, 19/3/1983 (OJ* L 151, 7/6/1984); 1277/88/EEC, 3/5/1988 (OJ* L 118, 6/5/1988).

TEMPUS (Trans-European Mobility Scheme for University Studies) Community programme* aimed at students from Eastern Europe (courses in universities and social institutions for 1000 Polish and Hungarian students in 1990-1991). Budget: 2m Ecus*. Supplements the PHARE* programme. Decision* of 7/5/1990.
SEE EUROPEAN FOUNDATION FOR VOCATIONAL TRAINING.

Ten Name given to the Member States* of the Community* between 1981 and 1985: the Nine* plus Greece.

Territoriality
SEE PRINCIPLE OF TERRITORIALITY.

TES (Tableaux Entrées-Sorties) *(Input-output tables)* Statistical data base* on the national accounts of the Member States* (production and consumption*).
SEE STATISTICAL OFFICE OF THE EUROPEAN COMMUNITIES.

Testing and Certification Organization Proposed European testing and certification* organization which would allow those desiring to conclude mutual recognition* agreements to meet and come to agreement under the auspices of CEN*/CENELEC* (aid, advice, impetus given to groups at industry level).
SEE EFTA, EOTC, OVERALL APPROACH, STANDARDIZATION.

Textiles
SEE COMITEXTIL, EUROPEAN TRADE UNION COMMITTEE OF THE TEXTILE, CLOTHING AND LEATHER INDUSTRIES.

TFTR (Tokamak Fusion Test Reactor)
SEE CONTROLLED THERMONUCLEAR FUSION.

The Hague (Netherlands). *1-2/12/1989* Summit (revival of Economic and Monetary Union*, strengthening of the institutions and political cooperation* (SEE REPORT (Davignon)); financing of the Common Agricultural Policy*, increased budgetary powers for the European Parliament*).
SEE BENELUX, EUROPEAN COUNCIL, EUROPEAN POLITICAL COOPERATION.

THERMIE (TecHnologies EuRopéennes pour la MaÎtrise de l'Énergie) *(European technologies for energy management)*: Community programme* to promote energy-related technology for the rational use of energy*, renewable sources of energy* and solid fuels, oil and natural gas, and their commercial use. Budget: 700m Ecus* (1990-1995). (REG.* OF 29/6/1990). DG XVII of the Commission*.

Thesauri
SEE THESAURUS GUIDE.

Thesaurus Guide Data base* of thesauri in at least one of the official languages of the Community*, Canada and the USA. Access via ECHO*. DG XIII of the Commission*.

Third Countries
SEE NON-MEMBER COUNTRIES.

Third-Party Proceedings Appeal* procedure before the Court of Justice of the European Communities* open to Member States*, Community institutions* and any natural or legal person to contest any Judgement* which is injurious to their rights and which was passed without them being summoned.

Three-Way Traffic *Customs*: procedure whereby compensating products* are put into free circulation*, with total or partial relief from import duties*, in a Member State* other than the one where the temporary export* procedure took place. See also Reg.* 2473/86/EEC on outward processing*.

TII (European association for the transfer of Technology, Innovation and Information) Association grouping together more than 500 advisers on innovation and on technology* management, universities and technical colleges, contracted research* companies, scientific centres, innovation centres, venture capital companies, financial bodies, patent* advisers and brokers, Chambers of Commerce, local and regional authorities, engineering companies and organizers of technological and industrial exhibitions. 1984, Luxembourg.
Objectives: to exchange technological information and experience, to provide concrete services with the financial support of the SPRINT* programme. Supported by DG XIII of the Commission*. 3, rue des Capucins, 1313 Luxembourg.

Tindemans (Leo) Belgian statesman.
SEE EUROPEAN UNION, REPORT.

TIR (Transport International de marchandises par Route) *(International transport of goods by road)* Transport of goods from a customs office* of departure to a customs office* of destination under the rules laid down by the Geneva Convention of 14/11/1975 on the international transport of goods (CAME INTO EFFECT VIA REG.* 2112/78/EEC, 25/7/1978). See also Reg.* 3680/86/EEC. 1/12/1986 (OJ* L 341, 4/12/1986; 1544/87/EEC, 3/6/1987 (OJ* L 141, 4/6/1987). Abolished on 1/1/1992.

Tobacco Draft Directives* on consumer taxes and advertising restrictions on tobacco and cigarettes (COM (87) 325 AND 326, OJ* C 251, 1978).

Tokyo Capital of Japan. September 1973: GATT* negotiations (Tokyo round).

TOM (Territoires d'Outre-Mer) *(Overseas departments)*
SEE FOD, POSEIDOM, REGIS.

Tools
SEE ORIGIN.

Total Turnover Sum of the gross turnover for all products and services sold by businesses wanting to operate in combination* (excluding the internal transactions of a group). For banking institutions: one tenth of total results. For insurance* companies: the value of premiums received.
SEE COMPETITION.

Tourism Policy *9-11/3/1990*: the Council* gives the Commission* a mandate to elaborate a Community* action programme for June of the same year. 1990 was declared 'European tourism year'.

Toys Harmonization* Directive* on safety*. (88/378/EEC, 3/5/1988, OJ* L 98, 11/4/1989). DG XII/E of the Commission*.

Trade A section of the Economic and Social Committee* is devoted to trade. There is an advisory committee on trade and distribution at the Commission* (DG III).
SEE EUROPEAN CENTRE OF RETAIL TRADE, FRENCH NATIONAL COUNCIL OF EMPLOYERS, INTERNATIONAL COUNCIL OF COMMERCIAL EMPLOYERS, INTERNATIONAL FEDERATION OF RETAIL DISTRIBUTORS, KANGAROO.

Trade Description Administrative measure taken by a state to guarantee to consumers the authenticity of the description of an agricultural product. A Member State* may not refuse the use of a description on a product imported from another Member State* where the product is legally marketed under this description (prohibition of rules reserving a trade description for products manufactured in the importing state or for products made from certain raw materials or containing a fixed content of a certain ingredient or for 'fresh' produce). The prohibition may be challenged where foodstuffs* are so different from products known under the same trade description in the Community* that they could be regarded as belonging in a completely different category altogether (CJEC* Judgements* 14/7/1988, 22/9/1988).
SEE FOODSTUFFS, LABEL, REGISTERED DESIGNATION OF ORIGIN.

Trade Mark Definition of the origin of a product in the terms chosen by a certain firm. 1st Harmonization* Directive*: 21/12/1988 (OJ* L 40, 1988).
SEE COMMUNITY TRADE MARK, CE MARK, NATIONAL CERTIFICATION MARK.

Training Policy Policy to improve professional qualifications and employment opportunities for workers*, supported in particular by the European Social Fund*. Training opportunities are equally available to migrant workers* and their children (Judgement* OF 3/7/1974, 9/74 AND of 21/1/1975, 68/74).
SEE ARION, ATYPICAL WORK, BABEL, BUSINESS INNOVATION CENTRES, CENTRE FOR INDUSTRIAL DEVELOPMENT, COMETT, COMMON AGRICULTURAL POLICY, DELTA, DIPLOMAS, EAGGF, ERASMUS, EUROFORM, EUROPEAN CENTRE FOR THE DEVELOPMENT OF VOCATIONAL TRAINING, EUROPEAN FOUNDATION FOR

VOCATIONAL TRAINING, EUROPEAN SOCIAL AREA, EUROPEAN SOCIAL CHARTER, EUROPEAN SOCIAL FUND, EURYDICE, FORCE, HORIZON, IRIS, JOINT RESEARCH CENTRE, LINGUA, NOW, PETRA, SCIENCE, TELEMAN, YES, YOUTH FOR EUROPE.

Transeuropean Networks (Large-Scale) *22/12/1990*: Council* Resolution* calling upon the Commission* to submit, before the end of 1990, a working plan and proposals for measures concerning the development and interconnection of trans-european networks, in particular in the fields of air traffic control, energy* distribution, transport infrastructures, the most efficient land-based methods of communication, telecommunications* and the implementation of existing Community training* programmes*. Broadly speaking these networks could also encompass services*.
SEE ISDN, TRANSPORT POLICY.

Transit *Energy**
SEE ELECTRICITY, GAS, TRANSEUROPEAN NETWORKS.

Transport Policy Freedom to provide services from 31/12/1992. Liberalization under art. 74 to 84 of the EEC* treaty* for rail, road, river, sea and air transport.
1. *Air transport*: December 1987: 1st phase of liberalization, 4-5/12/1989: the Council* launches the 2nd phase. 18-19/6/1990: Council* agreement on Regulations* concerning a three-tier pricing system (normal, reduced, very reduced), access of carriers to the market and the allocation of seating capacity.
2. *Road transport*: 21/6/1988: abolition of Community* quotas* from 1/1/1993 and an increase in the transition period. (REG.* 88/1841/EEC, OJ* L 163, 30/6/1988). 21/12/1989: cabotage* authorized from 1/7/1990 (REG.* 89/4059/EEC, OJ* L 190, 1989). 25/4/1990: 40% increase to Community* quota* for 1990 (REG.* 90/1053/EEC). 18-19/6/1990: Council* agreement on a new Directive* on self-drive car hire.
3. *Sea transport*: freedom to provide services*; free competition* rules – prohibition of unfair tariff practices and free access to trade – in international sea transport (COUNCIL* REG.* OF 1986: 4055, 4056, 4057, 4058).
4. *River transport*: free commercial negotiations everywhere but on the Rhine. Reg.* 89/1101/EEC and 89/1102/EEC.
5. *Rail transport*: project on the non-discriminatory availability of the European rail network and on clarifying relations between rail operators and official authorities (See also COM (89) 564).
DG VII of the Commission*.

6. *Combined transport*: European agreement on main combined international transport routes and their related installations, signed from 1/4/1991 under the aegis of the United Nations Economic Committee for Europe: legal centre, applying especially to road/rail transport.
7. *Railway companies*: road transport companies and water transport companies may opt for a system of public service contracts.
SEE CABOTAGE, COMMITTEE OF TRANSPORT WORKERS' UNIONS IN THE EUROPEAN COMMUNITY, CUSTOMS (ALL ENTRIES), EURENVIRON, EUROPEAN CONFERENCE OF MINISTERS OF TRANSPORT, EUROPEAN HIGH SPEED TRAIN, EUROPOLIS, HERMES, LIAISON COMMITTEE FOR PROFESSIONAL CARRIERS OF THE EUROPEAN COMMUNITIES, SELF-DRIVE VEHICLE HIRE, STRUCTURAL FUNDS.

Transposition Measures Measures for transposing Community* acts* into national law.

Treaties of Maastricht New treaties creating European Political Union and Economic and Monetary Union* were agreed 11/12/1991 and signed 2/1992. Special protocol on social policy agreed by all Member States* except the United Kingdom. On Economic and Monetary Union* the introduction of the common currency* is scheduled to take place at the latest by 1999 by those who qualify. There is a specific 'opt out'* protocol for the United Kingdom and a protocol for Denmark, which take account of their political circumstances. On European Political Union the treaty creates the European Union* covering the Community's* existing and increased responsibilities and has specific new features. These are: the creation of a common foreign and security policy covering the formulation in the longer term of a common defence policy, which may in time lead to a common defence; an increase in the role of the European Parliament* which includes specific measures such as a right of enquiry, a more formal right of petition, and the appointment of a ombudsman plus an improvement in the Parliament's legislative powers by the introduction of the co-decision procedure. The Commission* will in future be appointed by Member States* after investiture by the European Parliament*. From 1 January 1995 the term of office will be five years. A further conference will take place in 1996 in order to carry forward the process of European Union*.

Treaties of Rome Signed on 25/3/1957 by the six Member States* of the European Coal and Steel Community*: established the European Economic Community* (EEC), the European

Atomic Energy Community (EURATOM*), and the Common Assembly* (to be competent for all three Communities*).

Treaty of Brussels Signed by the Nine* on 22/7/1975, came into effect on 1 June 1977: amended the treaties* of Rome* by increasing the budgetary powers of the European Parliament* (own resources*) and by establishing the Court of Auditors*.

Treaty of Luxembourg Signed by the Six* on 22/4/1970, came into effect on 1/1/1971: amended the treaties* of Rome* by giving the Community* the own resources* system and increasing the budgetary powers of the European Parliament*.
SEE BUDGET.

Treaty of Paris Signed on 18/4/1951 by Belgium, France, Germany, Italy, Luxembourg and the Netherlands: established the European Coal and Steel Community* (ECSC).

TREVI Group (Terrorisme, Radicalisme Et Violence International) *(Terrorism, radicalism and international violence)*: Group of interior ministers and European experts in police cooperation, established in 1976 to fight terrorism in the Community*.
SEE FREEDOM OF MOVEMENT, FRONTIER CONTROL, SCHENGEN, SIS, VISAS.

Trialogue Conciliation procedure between the European Parliament*, the Council* and the Commission* which prevents adoption of the draft budget* being delayed when the Council* amends or rejects amendments* proposed by the Parliament.

Troika System whereby delegations of the countries holding the presidency of the Council* of the European Communities* before and after the present 6 month term assist the presidency currently in office; it ensures continuity in the Council's* activities.

Twelve (The) Name given to the Member States* of the Community*, following the accession of Spain and Portugal in 1985.

U

UIC (Union Internationale des Chemins de fer)
SEE INTERNATIONAL UNION OF RAILWAYS.

UN
SEE UNITED NATIONS ORGANIZATION.

Usable (Utilized) Agricultural Area (UAA)
SEE COMMON AGRICULTURAL POLICY.

Unanimity Where all votes or opinions are expressed in the same way.
*EC**: Required by several articles in the treaties* for Council* votes; confirmed and extended by the Luxembourg* Compromise (1966), then considerably limited by the Single European Act* (2/1986) which laid down qualified majority* voting for several areas. In all other areas the Council* may only amend a proposal from the Commission* by unanimity.
When the European Parliament* rejects a joint position* by the Council*, the Council* may only act by unanimity at the second reading. The same is true for amending a Council* position which has been reexamined by the Commission*.
Unanimity is also required in the Council* for admitting a state to the Community*, for association agreements*, measures which reverse liberalization of movements of capital* to any extent, actions taken to protect and improve the quality of the environment* (except areas defined by the Council*) and for pluriannual research* framework programmes.

UNCTAD
SEE UNITED NATIONS CONFERENCE ON TRADE AND DEVELOPMENT.

UNEP
SEE UNITED NATIONS ENVIRONMENT PROGRAMME

Unfair Practices Unfair competition* with the Community* and on the markets of non-member countries*.
SEE COMPETITION, GATT, OECD, UNITED NATIONS CONFERENCE ON TRADE AND DEVELOPMENT,

UNICE

SEE UNION OF INDUSTRIES OF THE EUROPEAN COMMUNITY.

UNIDO

SEE UNITED NATIONS INDUSTRIAL DEVELOPMENT ORGANIZATION.

Union of Industries of the European Community (UNICE) Organization created in 1958, representing 33 professional federations from 22 European countries. President: Carlos Ferrer. Secretariat: 40, rue Joseph II, 1040 Bruxelles, Belgium.

Unit of Account Monetary unit of account, used to gauge the value of products in international trade.
SEE AGRICULTURAL UNIT OF ACCOUNT, ECU, EUROPEAN MONETARY SYSTEM, EUROPEAN UNIT OF ACCOUNT.

United Nations (UN) Abbreviation for the United Nations Organisation* (UNO).

United Nations Conference on Trade and Development (UNCTAD) Institution established by the UN* on 30/12/1964. As a body of the General Assembly, its purpose is to further trade between industrialized countries and LDCs*. The Community* is involved in its work. Not respecting its multilateral principles may be considered to be commercial practice contrary to UN competition* policy. Palais des Nations, 1211 Genève, Switzerland.
SEE GSP, LDCs.

United Nations Environment Programme (UNEP) Multiannual programme on which the EC* collaborates (SEE ENVIRONMENT). Elaboration of conventions (on biological diversity, etc.).

United Nations Industrial Development Organization (UNIDO) Specialized agency of the United Nations Organization* (1985). 155 member countries, including the Twelve*. Based in Vienna, Austria.

United Nations Organization (UNO) Global intergovernmental organization (1945). 158 members, including the Twelve*. International secretariat in New York City, USA. Specialized agencies: Food and Agriculture Organization*, International Civil Aviation Organization*, International Fund for Agricultural Development, International Labour Organization*,

International Maritime Organization*, International Telecommunications Union, UNESCO, United Nations Industrial Development Organization*, Universal Postal Union, World Health Organization*, World Intellectual Property Organization*, World Meteorological Organization*,

UNO
SEE UNITED NATIONS ORGANIZATION

Unprocessed Goods Imported goods* which have not undergone any processing operation.
SEE CUSTOMS (ALL ENTRIES).

UPAC Project in the EUREKA* programme ('EU 4'): adaptable manufacturing unit for clothing (to increase productivity in the ready-to-wear clothing industry with new technology and new organizational principles). 1985-1990.

V

Vademecum Guidance document issued by the Commission*.
SEE PUBLIC CONTRACT.

VALOREN (VALORisation du potential ÉNergétique endogène) (*Valorization of indigenous energy potential*) Community programme* to develop certain less-favoured regions of the Community*. Reg.* 86/3/EEC, 27/10/1986 (OJ* L 305, 31/10/1986). DG XVI of the Commission*.
SEE ENERGY, EUROPEAN REGIONAL DEVELOPMENT FUND, SME.

VALUE (VALorization and Utilization for Europe) Community programme* to disseminate the results of scientific and technological research*. 38m Ecus* (1989-1992). Decision* 3/89/EEC, 20/6/1989 (OJ* L 200, 13/7/1989). DG XII/C of the Commission*.

Value Added Tax (VAT) Tax calculated at each stage of production according to the value added (difference between the value of a product when it leaves a business and its value or the value of its components on entering) to a product by a business.
Extended to all Member States* after 1962 (SEE REPORT (Neumark)). Unification or harmonization* of VAT rates has been proposed by the Commission* in accordance with the objective of harmonizing* indirect taxation* as laid down in the treaties* and in the White Paper*.
19/6/1989: abolition of certain exemptions from Dir.* 73/378.
18/12/1989: commitment by the Twelve* not to change their VAT rates below 14% or above 20% until 31/12/1992; an agreement to be reached before 31/12/1991 on the rate to be applied after 1/1/1993; limited reduced rates for goods and services of primary necessity; system of taxing goods in the country of consumption to be maintained for a transitional period; fiscal controls at frontiers to be abolished at the beginning of 1993. See also COM (87) 321 and 324 (OJ* C 250, 1987); (88) 846 (OJ* C 76, 1986).
SEE CONVERGENCE, DUTY-FREE, REPORT.

Value for Customs Purposes Value of goods estimated in order to collect customs duty on imported goods. See also GATT* agreement of 1/11/1979, which set up the Technical Committee on Customs Valuation under the auspices of the Customs Cooperation Council*. Since 1980 (REG.* 1224/80/EEC, 28/5/1980, OJ* L 134, 31/5/1980) value is evaluated on the goods' actual sale value (as opposed to their theoretical value), ie the price paid for the goods or the price the goods will command when they are sold at their destination on the customs territory* of the Community*.

Value Scale *Customs*: Breakdown of goods for temporary export* into the various compensating products* depending on the value of the compensating products*.

VAMAS (Versailles project on Advanced Materials And Standards) Community action and research* programme* project on raw materials and advanced materials, continued in the programme Industrial and Materials Technology*.

VAT
SEE VALUE ADDED TAX.

VDU (Visual Display Unit) Draft Directive* on minimum health and safety requirements for work on equipment with VDUs. (OJ* L 156, 1990).

Venice (Italy) 29/5/1956: Spaak* report* approved by the foreign ministers of the Six*; decision to start intergovernmental negotiations.
SEE EURATOM, EUROPEAN ECONOMIC COMMUNITY.

Veterinary Medicinal Products Draft Regulation* establishing a Community* procedure for fixing maximum residue limits for veterinary medicinal products.
SEE HEALTH.

Veterinary Surgeons
SEE VETERINARY MEDICINAL PRODUCTS.

Videotex Interactive telecommunications* service which allows those with Videotex terminals to communicate, using standardized access procedures, with data bases* and other computer-based installations.
SEE MINITEL, TELECOMMUNICATIONS.

Visas A list has been proposed to show those non-member countries* which require a visa of EC* nationals and those countries of which the EC* requires visas for specific reasons.
SEE FREEDOM OF MOVEMENT, FRONTIER CONTROL.

Warrant Promissory note guaranteed by a person's signature.

Waste Waste management committee, set up on 21/4/1976 (Decision* 76/431/EEC) Council* Resolution* (April 1990): to define a universal policy based on the principle of regional responsibility (integrated European network of regional waste disposal installations). Draft framework Directive* (COM (89) 560, OJ* C 326, 1989) and draft Directives*: COM (89) 560 (OJ* C 42, 1990) on dangerous waste; COM (89) 282 (OJ* C 251, 1989) on third-party liability for damage caused by waste; COM (90) 9 (OJ* C 55, 1990) on the disposal of dangerous waste in water.
SEE AQUARIUS, ENVIRONMENT, HEALTH, RADIOACTIVE WASTE, SAFETY.

Weapons Directive* of 19/6/1991 on the control of the acquisition and possession of weapons (OJ* L 256, 13/9/1991). Applicable on 1/1/1993.

Werner Luxembourg statesman.
SEE MONETARY UNION, REPORT.

Western European Union (WEU) Intergovernmental organization comprising the Six* and the United Kingdom (1948, 1954). Council, assembly. Cooperation on defence and foreign policy and armaments control. Political and economic cooperation. Working relations with the European Parliament* via the 'Security and disarmament' sub-committee. Secretariat: 9 Grosvenor Place, London, UK. Assembly in Paris: 43, avenue du Président Wilson, 75116 Paris, France.

White Paper Multiannual programme of the Commission*. Usually refers to the programme on completing the European internal market* (1985-1992) which was presented at the European Council* in Milan in June 1985 as 300 measures (later reduced to 286) to abolish physical, technical and fiscal barriers*. The Single European Act* which was signed in February 1986 by the governments of the Member States* and ratified on 1/6/1987, gives the Community* the necessary legal instruments to achieve this programme.
SEE EUROPEAN COUNCIL (especially Luxembourg and Brussels).

WIPO

SEE WORLD INTELLECTUAL PROPERTY ORGANIZATION.

WMO

SEE WORLD METEOROLOGICAL ORGANIZATION.

Women

SEE EUROPEAN SOCIAL CHARTER, EUROPEAN SOCIAL FUND, IRIS, LEI, NOW, SAFETY, SOCIAL SECURITY BENEFITS,

Wood Industries Executive Committee for the EEC Part of the European Confederation of Wood-working industries*; responsible for representing the industry in the Community* (1958). Paris, France

SEE CEI-BOIS

Wood-Working It is acknowledged that this sector would benefit from a certain amount of official aid*.

SEE CEI-Bois, WOOD INDUSTRIES EXECUTIVE COMMITTEE, EURAM, EUROPEAN CONFEDERATION OF WOOD-WORKING INDUSTRIES.

Worker Participation Consultation and cooperation of workers in the day-to-day running of businesses. A Directive* (Vredling) has been proposed by the Commission*. The idea has been taken up in a proposal for a Directive* from the Council* to supplement the articles of association of a European company*: agreement between the management and workers' representatives in accordance with the laws or practice of the Member State* concerned or, failing that, a choice between three models (election or co-opting of staff representatives to the supervisory committee; election or appointment of representatives to a separate body; or other models set up by means of an agreement, ensuring three-monthly reports on the company's progress and information or consultation of the workforce before the implementation of certain decisions). Capital participation by means of an agreement would be optional. See 89/C 263/08, OJ* C 263/89.

Also used to describe participation in the fruits of expansion, a form of profit sharing*.

SEE EUROPEAN SOCIAL CHARTER, PUBLIC LIMITED LIABILITY COMPANY IN EUROPEAN LAW, TRADE UNIONS.

*Company law**:

SEE ACQUISITION OF HOLDINGS, PROSPECTUS.

Workers
SEE ATYPICAL WORK, DOMICILE, EMPLOYMENT, EQUAL TREATMENT, EUROPEAN SOCIAL CHARTER, EUROPEAN SOCIAL FUND, FREEDOM OF MOVEMENT, HEALTH, RIGHT OF RESIDENCE, SAFETY, SOCIAL SECURITY BENEFITS, TRAINING POLICY, WORKER PARTICIPATION.

Working Conditions
SEE ATYPICAL WORK, EUROPEAN FOUNDATION FOR THE IMPROVEMENT OF LIVING AND WORKING CONDITIONS, EUROPEAN SOCIAL AREA, EUROPEAN SOCIAL CHARTER, HEALTH, SAFETY, TRANSPORT POLICY, WORKERS.

Work-Place Equipment Directive* of 30/11/1989 on new safety standards* to come into effect on 1/1/1993.

Works Public contracts*: written contracts between a businessman and a contracting authority* for building or civil engineering work (SEE ALSO Dir.* 71/305/EEC).
SEE NACE.

World Bank
SEE INTERNATIONAL BANK FOR RECONSTRUCTION AND DEVELOPMENT.

World Health Organization (WHO) Specialized agency of the United Nations Organization* set up in 1946 to improve levels of health throughout the world. Based in Geneva, Switzerland.
SEE FAO, INTERNATIONAL LABOUR ORGANIZATION.

World Intellectual Property Organization (WIPO) Specialized agency of the United Nations Organization* (1974): harmonization* of regulations. Participation by the EEC* and EFTA*. Based in Geneva, Switzerland.

World Meteorological Organization (WMO) Specialized agency of the United Nations Organization*: meteorological forecasting and exploitation of the results.

Y

Yaoundé Capital of Cameroon. *20/7/1963*: convention* between the EEC* and 17 African countries, Madagascar and Mauritius (commercial, technical and financial cooperation). Came into effect on 1/6/1964; *29/7/1970*: convention* (came into effect on 1/1/1971). SEE LDCs, LOMÉ.

YES (Young Exchange Scheme) Community programme* of short exchanges between young workers* between the ages of 15 and 25 (youth organizations, socio-educational officers, NGO*). Budget: 18.5m Ecus* (1989-1991). DG V of the Commission*. SEE COMETT, ERASMUS, EUROPEAN CENTRE FOR THE DEVELOPMENT OF VOCATIONAL TRAINING, EUROPEAN UNIVERSITY INSTITUTE, TRAINING POLICY.

Youth For Europe Community programme* to promote exchanges between young Europeans between the ages of 16 and 26. Priority for socially deprived young people or those living in countries where exchanges are less common. BCJE, rue de la Concorde 51, 1040 Bruxelles, Belgium. UK: Youth Exchange Centre, Seymour Mews House, Seymour Mews, London W1H 9FE.

Z

Zurich (Switzerland) *19/9/1946*: speech by Winston Churchill on the creation of the United States of Europe.

BIBLIOGRAPHY

Eurojargon A dictionary of EC acronyms, abbreviations and sobriquets. Anne Ramsay. CPI

European Communities Glossary. HMSO.

The European Community Fact Book Alex Roney. London Chamber of Commerce/Kogan Page Ltd.

Treaties Establishing The European Communities. 1987. HMSO.

QUICK CHECKLIST

INDEX

INDEX